THIS IS MADNESS TOO

Critical perspectives on mental health services

edited by
Craig Newnes, Guy Holmes
and Cailzie Dunn

First published in 2001

PCCS BOOKS LTD
Llangarron
Ross-on-Wye
Herefordshire
HR9 6PT
UK
Tel +44 (0)1989 77 07 07
email contact@pccs-books.co.uk
www.pccs-books.co.uk

This is Madness Too:
Critical Perspectives on Mental Health Services

British Library Cataloguing in Publication Data.
A catalogue record for this book is available from the British Library.

ISBN 1 898059 37 3

Cover design by Denis Postle.
Photograph on back cover taken by Vivien J. Lewis
Printed by Bookcraft, Midsomer Norton, Somerset, UK

DEDICATION

To our friend and colleague, Professor Steve Baldwin

This is Madness:
A Critical Look at Psychiatry and the Future of Mental Health
Services
Edited by **Craig Newnes**, **Guy Holmes** and **Cailzie Dunn**
ISBN 1 898059 25 X £16.00 1999

This is Madness Too:
Critical Perspectives on Mental Health Services
Edited by **Craig Newnes**, **Guy Holmes** and **Cailzie Dunn**
ISBN 1 898059 37 3 £14.00 2001

Personality as Art:
Artistic approaches in psychology
Peter Chadwick
ISBN 1898059 35 7 £18.00 2001

Spirituality and Psychotherapy
Edited by **Simon King-Spooner** and **Craig Newnes**
ISBN 1898059 39 X £15.00 2001

CONTENTS

1   Continuing madness   1
    Guy Holmes, Craig Newnes and Cailzie Dunn

Part One: The lunatics have taken over the asylum

2   Mental health policy: a suitable case for treatment   11
    Peter Beresford and Suzy Croft

3   Integrating critical psychiatry into psychiatric training   23
    Duncan Double

4   Policing happiness   35
    Mark Rapley

Part Two: Risk and dangerousness

5   What people need to know about the drug treatment of children 47
    Peter Breggin

6   The SSRI suicides   59
    David Healy

7   'I've never said "No" to anything in my life': helping people with
    learning disabilities who experience psychologcal problems   71
    Biza Stenfert Kroese and Guy Holmes

8   Coming off neuroleptics   81
    Peter Lehmann

Part Three: Rights . . . and wrongs

9   Surviving social inclusion   93
    Peter Campbell

10 When 'No' means 'Yes': informed consent themes with   103
    children and teenagers
    Steve Baldwin

11 Controlled bodies, controlled eating: the treatment of   115
    eating disorders
    Vivien J Lewis and Sara Cureton

12 Relatives and carers   127
    Olive Bucknall and Guy Holmes

Part Four: An end to madness

13 Survivor research   135
    Vivien Lindow

14 This is therapy: a person-centred critique of the   147
    contemporary psychiatric system
    Pete Sanders and Keith Tudor

15 The future approach for community mental health   161
    Fran Silvestri and Susan Hallwright

16 Developing a survivor discourse to replace the   177
    'psychopathology' of breakdown and crisis
    Jan Wallcraft and John Michaelson

    Contributors   191

    Name index   194

    Subject index   197

CHAPTER 1

Continuing madness

GUY HOLMES, CRAIG NEWNES AND CAILZIE DUNN

THIS BOOK FOLLOWS on from where *This is Madness* (Newnes, Holmes and Dunn, 1999) ended. In the concluding chapter of *This is Madness* we wrote about the future of mental health services: these ideas remain very much alive. The authors in *This is Madness Too* give even greater weight to the arguments for: a separation of the social policing and therapeutic roles of psychiatry; an abandonment of the medical model and a challenge to the power of the pharmaceutical industry; the need for informed consent and advocacy; the validation of the expertise of current and ex-users of services and the need for properly funded service user controlled services; and political effort and community work aimed at tackling the roots of experiences that subsequently become individualised and labelled mental illness (poverty, racism, abuse, sexism, lack of opportunity, and so on).

The energy around mental health that we referred to in *This is Madness* (see Newnes and Holmes, 1999) still sparkles. One of the strange things is that, perhaps more than at any other time in the history of psychiatry, it is not the clinicians that are fuelling or even guiding that energy. There appear to be two tracks, with ideas racing along on both. Although these ideas frequently conflict, they both appear to be gaining pace. For example, the concept of informed consent in medicine in general is almost constantly being aired in public debate. In the age of the Internet, people have access to information previously kept from them. Knowledge is power, and medical paternalism seems antiquated in the 21st century. But at the same time, the British Government's new Mental Health Act brings an even wider group of people under its remit — a remit which gives doctors and other professionals the power to take away basic human rights (to liberty, to refuse treatment, etc.) let alone the principle of informed consent. On the one hand the stigma of mental health seems to be reducing: people are more accepting that at times in their lives they might break down, have crises, and need help. People speak openly about being depressed, having counselling or psychotherapy and drugs such as Prozac have become de rigeur. On the other hand the stigma of a diagnosis of schizophrenia, with media and government propaganda about its links with violence, and the stigma of the psychiatric hospital have increased. Similarly, ideas that mental health problems are physical and genetic and need medical treatment seem, paradoxically, to be both challenged and accepted more in our society.

On the one track the government and mental health professionals are speaking a new language — of clinical governance, evidence-based practice and risk assessment — and are creating new ways of categorising people (through DSM and more general categories like 'severe and enduring mental illness', without defining what those categories mean). On the other track, the service user/survivor movement is returning to old language — breakdown, madness, crisis, recovery — language that brings fresh ways of thinking to the area of mental health, language that does not emphasise 'otherness', language which holds out hope (see Wallcraft and Michaelson, Chapter 16). Along with different language, there is a creativity and an openness to new ways of helping people. But while this flourishes and more and more mental health professionals adopt ideas from people in the user movement, the government is trying to stifle debate, through insisting mental health services follow a textbook, or recipe book — the National Service Framework — that defines what services must consist of. Similarly the pronouncements of NICE (the National Institute for Clinical Excellence) are meant to be an end to debate about the most effective ways of helping people. Mental health professionals are increasingly receiving training from psychiatric system survivors at the same time as training courses narrow down the debate about what helps people.

In a system that reifies evidence-based practice, who controls the evidence and what weight is given to different types of evidence are critical areas. Gourevitch (1998) stated that: 'Power largely consists in the ability to make others inhabit your story of their reality, even if you have to kill a lot of them to make that happen' (p. 181). The indoctrination that characterises compliance therapy and behavioural family therapy, the remits of assertive outreach teams, the emphasis on safety and dangerousness, the cabinet control not only of policy but of practice, the power being given to mental health professionals to decide who is a 'risk' and to be compulsorily treated, all point to a system where that power is being more brutally exercised. At the same time there has been an enormous growth in humanistic counselling, with over 26,000 members of the BACP (British Association for Counselling and Psychotherapy, formerly BAC), and counsellors are becoming commonplace in GP surgeries. Gourevitch's quote is applicable to all mental health professionals, to anyone who describes themselves as a therapist, not just those who work in the areas of the mental health system that exert social control (see Chapter 14 by Sanders and Tudor), but the gulf between those who try to help people find their own ways of understanding and coping with their difficulties and those who argue with people until they accept the professional's way of explaining things seems to be getting bigger. Britain is starting to resemble America, where the poor and socially deviant and devalued receive social control and biological psychiatry and the rich and conforming choose psychotherapy. We should applaud the National Service Framework for Mental Health in promoting the usefulness of humane psychological therapies for people with a diagnosis of psychosis, but it seems mad that the British Government proposes to employ a thousand graduates in primary care to 'treat people with anxiety and depression' at a time when it is obvious that individual therapy cannot possibly meet the needs of the people and in no way addresses the social causes of distress. As Hillman and Ventura (1992) said: 'We've had a hundred years of psychotherapy and things are getting worse'.

Why *This is Madness Too?*

The first volume was incomplete. We did not mention children, informed consent was only discussed in relation to adults being given ECT and medication, and the world of learning disabilities was nowhere to be seen. Issues about women and eating distress were only briefly touched upon. *This is Madness* also failed to include critical psychiatrists amongst the authors prepared to speak out. In this volume there are chapters on children (Chapter 5 by Peter Breggin and Chapter 10 by Steve Baldwin), people with learning disabilities (Chapter 4 by Mark Rapley and Chapter 7 by Biza Stenfert Kroese and Guy Holmes) and eating distress (Chapter 11 by Vivien Lewis and Sara Cureton). Several of the authors are psychiatrists — Duncan Double writes about psychiatric training (Chapter 3), Peter Breggin about the drug treatment of children (Chapter 5), David Healy about SSRIs (Chapter 6) and Susan Hallwright on community mental health. These authors join an array of people from the service user/survivor movement in an attempt to recreate the mix that made *This is Madness* so successful. But another reason for re-entering the fray is our continuing frustration with the psychiatric system and our confusion at the paradoxes to be found at every turn: the decent psychiatrist who sees little reason to stop using ECT; the general practitioners who wouldn't dream of taking drugs (any drugs) themselves but who willingly give out repeat prescriptions of major tranquillisers; the psychologists who claim publicly to work as evidence-based scientist practitioners, but in private admit that they have little evidence for anything; the people who espouse the benefits of multi-disciplinary teams but protect their clients from team members they do not trust; the government that consults with service users then ignores their human rights in its proposals for a new mental health act. We meet mental health workers who are far more mixed up and needy than their patients, and system survivors with more wisdom than a room full of NHS planners. We wanted to be involved in a project that published that wisdom, hence the contributors to this volume include Peter Beresford and Suzy Croft (Chapter 2), Peter Lehmann (Chapter 8), Peter Campbell (Chapter 9), Sara Cureton (Chapter 11), Olive Bucknall (Chapter 12), Vivien Lindow (Chapter 13) and Jan Wallcraft (Chapter 16) — people whose ideas come from a wide range of sources, but who share the experience of having been recipients of psychiatric services.

The evidence game

Evidence is all the rage in mental health services. It is as if professionals have never received any training, never read journals and spend their time randomly pulling treatments off their shelves. But it is more complicated than that. What one person calls evidence another calls prejudice. Earlier this year (2001) newspapers carried stories from the USA about how the eugenic practice of sterilisation was based on science and scientific evidence (see Stenfert Kroese and Holmes, Chapter 7, for more on this), and how the recent banning of Darwinian theories has been justified by educationalists on the basis that 'evolution is not good science' (*Independent*, 16.2.01). All interest groups are claiming that their policies are evidence based (see Beresford and Croft, Chapter 2, for a discussion of SANE's evidence base), and the field of ethics is not getting a look in. People who claim to be evidence-based practitioners need to ask major questions about the ways in which research is funded and the ways in which results are disseminated. The research reported is frequently only a fraction of that carried out, and it is invariably only the results which suit the vested interests of researchers or funders that appear (see Healy, Chapter 6).

So where might we find information about the human condition which appealed to people's sense of what it is to be human rather than the psychology and psychiatry of diagnosis, drug trials and involuntary treatment? How can we find out about the lived experience of service users, what they want and what they don't? Vivien Lindow (Chapter 13) suggests a move towards research controlled and directed by service users and survivors themselves. A further challenge for the pseudo-scientific community of psychiatry would be embrace the common place wisdom of philosophy, literature and poetry.

There are good text-books on the human condition (Judith Shklar's *Ordinary Vices* or Dorothy Rowe's *Wanting Everything* spring to mind) but if psychiatry is to take its subject-matter seriously then Dickens and Zola (in particular *Hard Times* and *Germinal*, respectively) cover class oppression pretty exhaustively and should be compulsory reading. Psychiatry treats the mind/body divide as if it is unproblematic, but how many mental health professionals have read Descartes or Ryle? The angst, desperation and anxieties of the middle classes are described throughout Balzac's *Comedie Humaine*. Catholicism and the power of faith is to be found in Burgess (*Earthly Powers*) and Greene (*The Power and the Glory*) while murderous hate is no better explained than in Mailer's *The Executioner's Song* and *The Collector* by John Fowles. Grief weeps off the final pages of Byatt's *Still Life* and madness permeates *Titus Alone* by Mervyn Peake. A brilliant exposition of hallucinatory paranoia is at the centre of Terry Gilliam's film *The Fisher King*, while the drug-induced variety saturates Waugh's *The Ordeal of Gilbert Pinfold* and *Fear and Loathing in Las Vegas* by Thompson. Hypocrisy is laid bare in Miller's *The Crucible* and love is no better explored than in *Birthday Letters* by Ted Hughes.

None of this counts for much in psychiatry or psychology. Nor is the criticism new. In the late nineteenth century the wholly subjective introspection of William James epitomized psychology. Jung broke from Freud, in part, because Freud saw his respect for spirituality, an essential human concern, as pandering to neurosis. Freud himself had considerable respect for the power of mythology. Duncan Double (Chapter 3) refers to the psychiatrist Meyer's project to bring a philosophical approach back into the domain of an overwhelmingly biological psychiatry, and Forsyth (1988) has argued:

> Psychologists do not study the mind, they do experiments. If psychologists were genuinely interested in the mind they would use every scrap of evidence they could lay their hands on; novels, poems, films, folklore, introspection, dreams. (p. 23)

It is, however, as if the eternal truths explored by philosophers, novelists and other artists are of no concern to mental health professionals who continue to absorb a diet of drug company propaganda and Government dictats. Indeed, Double (2001) has noted that many psychiatrists and junior medical staff actually receive their so-called training in psychopharmacology from drug company salespeople. A recent Government publication, *Effective Health Care*, in reviewing the newest so-called anti-psychotic medication concluded, 'Most relevant trials are undertaken by those with clear pecuniary interest in the results' (December, 1999). Strikingly, a review by Jorm (2000) remarks: 'The public's view of psychotropic medication is almost uniformly negative, contrary to the views of clinicians and to evidence from RCTs [Randomized Controlled Trials]'. The reading lists of counselling and psychology courses contain very little on pharmacology, let alone the iniquities of research funding, and don't even pay lip service to the world of literature. So much for evidence. All we can hope is that, as with a good novel, the reader of this volume will get a more colourful view of the area of mental health than the black and white orthodoxy that tends to characterise the field.

The impact of speaking out

Publishing *This is Madness*, this volume and numerous related articles can be seen as a form of speaking out. It can often feel that speaking out changes nothing. On a small scale, however, saying clearly what is seen as wrong with a system or process can change hearts, minds and conduct. In psychiatry, for example, concerted efforts by service users and their allies have resulted in the establishment of better information for recipients of psycho-active medication (although Chapter 8 by Peter Lehmann on withdrawal from neuroleptics is one of the first articles published in English that counters the argument that these drugs are not addictive and gives advice about how to come off these drugs). There has been a shift in the attitudes of mental health professionals to issues of race, gender and (to a lesser extent) poverty and deprivation. All these changes are, of course, part of a wider cultural change. Speaking out in advance of these cultural changes can be deemed premature, to be hailed as visionary or dismissed as unrealistic. When Survivors Speak Out first claimed, over ten years ago, a place for service users on mental health planning committees, the idea was seen to be preposterous, a classic case of the inmates taking over the asylum. At the beginning of the 21st century, the question is not whether to include services users, but how, and how much to pay them (see Chapter 9 by Peter Campbell). Changes of this type are seeded by those brave enough to speak out, seeds which will grow and bear fruit when the conditions are right. Equally major shifts can be made in clinical regimes. Peter Breggin's successful campaigning almost single-handedly prevented lobotomy being carried out in the USA in the 1970s (Isaac and Armat, 1990). Similarly, ECT has been banned in Holland, Italy and Germany through campaigning pressure groups (Arscott, 1999).

Speaking out can have detrimental effects on the critic including threats to personal safety, which result from an identification of the advocate with devalued and marginalised people. Bender and Wood (1994) discuss the likely impact on whistle-blowers' careers — leaving a current employer is likely. In one case, that of Moira Potier, Consultant Clinical Psychologist, her departure during the first Ashworth inquiry was followed by the award of an MBE in recognition of her services to the public good and a return to Ashworth Special Hospital as head of the clinical psychology service. As less high profile people speaking out, we have noticed other effects, both negative and positive. These include a recurring sense of self-doubt — perhaps madness really is only the result of faulty brain biochemistry, perhaps clinical psychology is not just another profession, perhaps management really is concerned, first and foremost, about patients. Being shot as the messenger is commonplace. Remarking, for the umpteenth time, that a management process is flawed or a clinical procedure dubious eventually pushes the speaker into a corner, to be marginalised as the (unheard) voice of reason, or marked as politically motivated and a trouble-maker. The process is tiring, not least due to the energy taken up in defending against feeling disliked and waking in the middle of the night overwhelmed with paranoid anxiety. The effects on colleagues, so often the only support to a person who speaks out, can be considerable. In our department clinical psychologists are routinely branded trouble makers because it is assumed they share our own critical stance. A certain amount of verbal abuse goes with the territory. We have been called mad and dangerous, people have simply walked out on us during what we considered conversations and, memorably, a consultant once threw a copy of Breggin's *Toxic Psychiatry* at the second author before storming off. We would not want to claim that these effects are comparable to the emotional consequences for system survivors, nor even with the utterly isolating and rejecting experience of some professionals (e.g. Johnstone, 1993). One outcome of speaking out is, however, exhaustion.

Other effects are more personally idiosyncratic — drinking more alcohol, driving faster, becoming arrogant, even getting bored with the same arguments. It is difficult to keep in mind that just as every new cohort of mental health trainees is exposed to the rhetoric of organic psychiatry and the unsurpassed excellence of psychiatry, clinical psychology and counselling, each cohort will need a dissenting, more critically reflexive voice. Keeping that voice from going hoarse is a strain. So why do it?

Speaking out in the world of mental health is part of a much larger resistance movement; to glibness, to oppression, to the sheer smugness of the psy-complex (Breggin's term for the vested interests of the pharmaceutical industry and the mental health professions). It protects the person from a position of bad faith: if some things considered bad are inevitable, then at least we can say they are bad, if others can be changed through voicing concern, then to do otherwise would be cowardly. This is not to say that the courage in speaking out should be taken for granted. For some people, such action is not realistically possible; for many others, speaking out is only possible with a considerable amount of support from friends, colleagues, unions or local and national networks. The response from people, often strangers across the other side of the world, is immensely heartening. To receive a postcard from someone thousands of miles away saying they have been inspired by your stance compensates for many of the voices speaking against you. In the psychiatric field, speaking out as a professional can be enormous fun; inevitably a patients' council meeting is more interesting and diverting than most management meetings. Sitting alongside a psychiatric service user at a rally or on the platform of a conference is at least as satisfying as offering that person psychotherapy. To speak out in psychiatry is ultimately to side with less powerful people against powerful industries and elites, even if one is considered to be part of that elite. We are grateful to all of the authors in this volume for speaking out, for taking a stand against the maddening orthodoxy of the psy-complex.

The future of mental health services

When we look to the future, we are again struck by the paradoxes. Whilst NICE has approved the use of Ritalin in children with a diagnosis of Attention Deficit Hyperactivity Disorder (ADHD), it acknowledges that the condition itself is 'controversial'. This is something of an understatement. All psychiatric diagnoses are hopelessly flawed (Boyle, 1999; Kutchins and Kirk, 1999). Further, the diagnosis of ADHD is frequently made at the request of, or even by, teachers and relatives in order to get hold of Ritalin, even when all of the child's behaviour is normal and understandable (see Breggin, Chapter 5). The fact that Ritalin is an amphetamine-like stimulant which would be illegal if taken under other circumstances and is dangerous to the brain of the child receiving it seems not to feature when considering the issue of informed consent (see Baldwin, Chapter 10), yet another paradox for a government committed to informed consent of patients and their carers. If the future treatment of children is to embrace informed consent then NICE may need to think again.

The information revolution holds out some promise for mental health service users and survivors. Imagine sitting with a therapist who says that your difficulties will respond to a cognitive-behavioural approach. Via your voice-activated Internet ear-piece you ask, 'Cognitive-behaviourism; please advise'. Information is power. Unfortunately, your ear-piece informs you there are 17,500 sites listed under this heading. Where do you start? Most clients are likely to fall back on the expertise of the therapist. Although people who access information through the Internet are not likely to be very different from the people who have traditionally accessed information from books, the speed with which it is possible to get a wide range of information that challenges psychiatric orthodoxy does hold out promise. Having terminals in GP practices and mental health service premises should help service users and mental health workers alike.

Change in the aged bureaucracies of health and social services is inevitably slow; there remain entrenched policies and attitudes and an addiction to form-filling both for its own sake and because of a constant fear of litigation (a still remarkably rare event in real life, though not in the imaginations of mental health professionals and their managers). Organisational change is a disruptive inevitability in mental health services. The government's plan for the English mental health system to be largely subsumed into GP led primary care seems strange; not only will it further medicalise mental health care but it places the power of decision-making in the hands of the same GPs that the government has at times branded arrogant and unaccountable.

It is tempting to suggest that mental health services should be scrapped altogether and that we should start again with a user-led agenda (see Pembroke, quoted in Lewis and Cureton, Chapter 11). Survivor groups would be instrumental in starting fresh initiatives and not paralysed by managerialism and the fear of things going wrong and being sued. People offering help would come from a position of feeling they have a responsibility *to* distressed people seeking help, rather than act like (and be made to feel that) they are responsible *for* the other person. It may be naïve to think that this could possibly happen in a social world which requires the controlling features of psychiatry just as much as it craves the healing promise of mental health services. It is unlikely that any professionals, including ourselves, could be so radical as to support their own ultimate unemployment, but at the very least professionals could speak out more about the inadequacies of services. Mental health nurses have a particular role here: it is nurses who spend most time with patients, do most of the form-filling, have to restrain violent people on wards and are tasked with the unrewarding job of tracking and engaging unwilling service recipients via assertive outreach teams. It is nurses who inject patients and nurses who find themselves on the receiving end of criticism when things go wrong. They should be well placed to empathise with those abused by services and, of course, are the closest professional group to patients in socio-economic terms. Survivors and radical professionals seem to have little power to change things from the inside. The vast numbers of mental health nurses in the system could make all the difference.

There remains a difficulty recruiting psychiatrists and all the psychiatrists we know are planning early retirement. So who is going to make all the judgements about whether paedophiles and violent sadistic men who haven't been convicted of a crime should be free? There is a myth that behaviour is easily predictable and mental health professionals are better at this than anyone else, a myth some are happy to exploit in a culture demanding certainty from experts and the control of frightening conduct. In the absence of psychiatrists taking on the mantle of being able to treat the untreatable (those diagnosed with personality disorders) clinical psychology shows every sign of stepping into the breech, a paradox indeed and hardly commensurate with a stance of either true science or clinical humility.

So, what do we suggest? Well, *This is Madness* and *This is Madness Too* are full of terrific ideas. To pick up on a few, we would like to see people with learning disabilities defined and honoured for their abilities as much as their disabilities. We would like a coherent model of mental health care for children that does not involve giving them damaging — and in other contexts illegal — drugs. The language of recovery and health ought to be incorporated into all government plans for mental health services (see Sylvestri and Hallwright, Chapter 15). The national lottery as well as the Mental Health Foundation could allocate more funds to more radical projects, for example service-survivor-run crisis houses. We would like mental health professionals to simply ask people what they need in order to recover and then help them get it. When researching the effectiveness of treatments, we could start by asking people where they want to be and later asking them if they got there (Booth, Goodwin, Newnes and Dawson, 1997). This research would be user-led. Advocacy would be freely available and mental health professionals would support advocacy schemes while respecting their independence (Newnes, 2001).

Psychiatric, psychological and other mental health training ought to honour the wisdom of philosophy, literature and the experience of those in the service user movement: such wisdom would be respected as the real evidence base. People in training should not just be exposed to a myriad of ideas about mental health, they should come away with a degree of humility and an open-minded curiosity about how much they have yet to learn, rather than an arrogance based on the fear of being found out about how little they know. Drug company sponsorship of journals, conferences and other media should be banned. The vested interests of funding bodies ought to be more explicitly stated in the published papers of psychiatric researchers. Counselling should be explicit about the value base of the practitioner and the best kinds of counselling and psychotherapy would be recognised as those placing the individual in a cultural context rather than those implying a quick-fix of the internal worlds of deranged individuals (see Sanders and Tudor, Chapter 14). We would like to see a government that really did consult. Service users would be respected and properly paid for their expertise on planning committees and in case conferences, and for the work that they do in helping others. If this sounds familiar it is because much of it can be traced to the first manifesto of Survivors Speak Out, published in 1987. It is time to enact that manifesto.

References

Arscott, K. (1999) ECT: The facts psychiatry forgot to mention. In: C. Newnes, G. Holmes and C. Dunn (eds) *This is madness: a critical look at psychiatry and the future of mental health services.* Ross-on-Wye: PCCS Books

Bender, M., and Wood, R. (1994) When the nightmares come home: maintaining one's integrity in unacceptable places. *Clinical Psychology Forum, 63,* 5–9

Booth, H., Goodwin, I., Newnes, C., and Dawson, O. (1997) Process and outcome of counselling in general practice. *Clinical Psychology Forum, 99,* 32–40

Boyle, M. (1999) Diagnosis. In: C. Newnes, G. Holmes and C. Dunn (eds) *This is madness: a critical look at psychiatry and the future of mental health services.* Ross-on-Wye: PCCS Books

Double, D.B. (2001) Can psychiatry be retrieved from a biological approach? *The Journal of Critical Psychology, Counselling and Psychotherapy, 1,* 1, 27–30

Forsyth, R. (1988) *From here to humanity: a manifesto for survival.* Nottingham: Pathway Publishers

Gourevitch, P. (1998) *We wish to inform you that tomorrow we will be killed with our families: stories from Rwanda.* London: Picador

Hillman, J. and Ventura, M. (1992) *We've had a hundred years of psychotherapy and the world's getting worse.* San Francisco: Harper

Isaac, R.J. and Armat, V. (1990) *Madness in the streets.* New York: Free Press

Johnstone, L. (1993) Psychiatry: are we allowed to disagree? *Clinical Psychology Forum, 56,* 30–34

Jorm, A.F. (2000) Mental health literacy: Public knowledge and beliefs about mental disorders. *The British Journal of Psychiatry, 177,* 396–401

Kutchins, H. and Kirk, S.A. (1999) *Making us crazy, DSM — the psychiatric bible and the creation of mental disorders.* London: Constable and Company

Newnes, C. (2001) The commitments? Advocacy and clinical psychology. *Openmind, 107,* 14–15

Newnes, C. and Holmes, G. (1999) The future of mental health services. In: C. Newnes, G. Holmes and C. Dunn (eds) *This is madness: a critical look at psychiatry and the future of mental health services.* Ross-on-Wye: PCCS Books

Newnes, C., Holmes, G., and Dunn, C. (1999) *This is madness: a critical look at psychiatry and the future of mental health services.* Ross-on-Wye: PCCS Books

CHAPTER 2

Mental health policy: a suitable case for treatment?

PETER BERESFORD AND SUZY CROFT

EARLY LAST YEAR, I (PB) was invited back to the psychiatric hospital where I was an in-patient when Mrs Thatcher was Prime Minister, to speak at a conference on participation in clinical audit, research and governance. It was a strange feeling to be back, more disconcerting than I had expected. The hospital is a large forbidding Victorian institution, set in lush grounds, with tennis courts and some fine stone faced buildings. It still has the same long echoing corridors and institutional signs for the ECT Room and Dispensary for Major Tranquillisers. I couldn't get my bearings and quickly got lost. When I found it, I discovered the ward that I had been in had become a mother and babies unit. There is now a large, attractive and reasonably priced restaurant for patients and visitors; a new conference centre in a converted chapel where we met and a strongly expressed commitment to user involvement in all areas. The conference included a large number of service users and service users were also involved in organising it.

Mental health policy: an enigma

A friend of ours has been an in-patient in this hospital much more recently and can offer an update on the situation under a Labour administration. He spoke of some positive support from nursing staff, as well as, of course, from other patients. But it still didn't feel safe. He didn't want to take his radio in, in case it was stolen. The food was poor. The nurses were:

> Not too bad, this time, some were ok, they'd talk, but it's five minutes and then they've got to be doing something else, seeing someone else. It's the way it always is. Not enough of them.

This time he noticed more cuts; even less time seeing the psychiatrists, fewer nurses, less activities and resources.

During the discussion at the hospital conference, one service user raised an issue which is being expressed with increasing frequency in many other places:

I'm exhausted. I feel used and bruised (from being involved). If it was anyone I was concerned with, I'd think twice before saying they should get involved. It's not necessarily empowering. I've been knocking my head against a brick wall for 10 years.

There is an interest in the mental health trust which runs the hospital in employing more service users and in involving service users more in training. These are activities and aspirations which could not have been imagined when I was a patient there. But 40 years on from Enoch Powell's water towers speech, how could we ever have dreamed that hospitals like this would still be there at all?

Policy and complexity
This scenario sums up the contradictions and complexities which dominate mental health policy and provision at the start of the new millennium. The meanings of any local situation (like our local psychiatric hospital; whether, for example, plans for more participatory management, training and employment policies will mean a lot or are merely marginal and rhetorical) are difficult to determine. What we probably can say is that the outcomes will be decided by the thrust of central government policy. While we can expect there to be differences over mental health policy between Labour and any other future governments, for example over priorities and resource allocation, commitments to a mixed economy of welfare, public safety and a medical model are likely to continue. How these are interpreted and operationalised is likely to vary, but the principles will be similar. There has essentially been cross-party agreement about mental health policy since the late 1990s. Labour merely offers a case study of one approach which, paradoxically, is likely to mean it is of more enduring significance. Government mental health policy is poised for change. Reform, 'thinking the unthinkable' have been the watchwords of New Labour social policy, including mental health policy. Radical health and welfare reform are also at the heart of the agendas of all the main political parties.

This brings us to the first and crucial problem in examining government social policy under Labour. It is difficult, if not impossible to decode. This isn't simply for the usual reason that policy is in process of change and it is just too early to comment on it definitively. Government social policy has been *characterised by* ambiguity and conflict. Perhaps, because of this, there is little agreement about it, so while some academics conclude that Labour social policy is based on pragmatism and populism (Powell, 2000), others come to more positive conclusions. Government policies can arguably be all things to all people. Perhaps that is why ideas of 'spin' have come to be seen as so central to them. The presentation becomes the policy. Meanings and realities are in the interpretation — unless of course you are on the receiving end.

This has major ramifications for us here trying to make sense of current mental health policy. We cannot assume that this can be done by the usual route of setting out its provisions and proposals, examining their theoretical and value bases and developing conclusions on that basis. Current approaches to policy are more complex and opaque than this allows. A traditional social administrative approach to policymaking is unlikely to be helpful here (although it persists). More subtle and sensitive approaches are likely to be necessary.

The social politics of New Labour: a case study

New Labour developed its own new vocabulary for politics and policies which has since included retreating from the 'new' in its title. Many of its terms are new, or at least new to the UK. Many have come in for considerable criticism for being vague, value-laden, ill-defined or even meaningless. Whatever we may think of them, however, they are important. New Labour has tended to judge all its policies and professional practice by them. Policies and practitioners are expected to fit into the frameworks they provide. Key ideas include the 'third way', 'communitarianism', 'social exclusion', 'partnership' (between state, citizen and market), 'joined up thinking' and 'modernisation'. There is no consensus of meaning about any of these. Each in its way has become a battlefield for ideological and policy dispute. Proposals and policies for mental health cannot be considered in isolation from these terms and the ideas behind them. Labour's 'modernising agenda' has been one of its overarching concerns. Modernisation may be code for the divorce which it has sought to bring about from its socialist and trade union-based past. But it also has broader implications.

In its rush to embrace the 'modern' and disassociate itself from its past, the government appears to have placed a low value on history and been reluctant to learn lessons from the past. As a result, old often seems to be confused with new. So far the irony of a government committed to 'modernisation' in a determinedly *post-modern* age seems to have passed without comment. Few administrations have placed so much stress on discontinuity, while being seen to align themselves closely with values which have traditionally been associated with reaction. This is reflected in proposals for controlling immigration, extending imprisonment, retraining parents, imposing statutory curfews and new controls on children and young people and its emphasis on individual responsibility and an extended role for the market in public policy. While mental health policy has traditionally tended to be treated as marginal and there are suspicions that it has been accorded a particularly inferior status in social policy by governments in recent years, it is essential to locate it in this broader political and policy context if we are to make sense of it.

New Labour and mental health

The dash for social reform has undoubtedly extended to mental health policy and provision. While the government's commitment to change in this context can be read as inherited from its Conservative predecessors (health and welfare reform were also priorities for Thatcher and Major), the form it has taken unquestionably reflects New Labour's particular approach to and conceptualisation of social policy.

In 1998, the new Labour Government launched its new plan, *Our Healthier Nation*, to promote health and improve the health and well-being of the worst off and least healthy in society and to improve their neighbourhoods. One of its four priority areas was mental health. In 1999, *Saving Lives: Our Healthier Nation* set national targets, aiming to reduce the death rate from suicide and 'undetermined injury' by at least a fifth by 2010.

All this must also be placed in the framework of National Health Service reform. First was the NHS Plan, with its stated commitment to patient and public participation. Next came the proposals for integration through the creation of 'health and social care trusts'. This was followed in 2001 by the Government's announcement of major plans 'shifting the centre of gravity in the NHS from Whitehall to frontline services . . . to liberate services.' The number of health authorities will be reduced from 99 to 30; regional offices abolished and financial control passed to primary care trusts which by 2004 will have control of 75% of the NHS budget. This shift to 'frontline staff (being) the architects of change is seen as the keynote of Labour's second term plans for health' (Wintour and Carvel, 2001). The Secretary of State for Health said:

> *Patients should have more information, more influence and more power. The balance of power in the NHS will shift decisively in favour of the patient.* (DoH, 2001)

We have yet to find out how this shift in power to patients and service users is to be achieved. What we do know is that frequent reorganisation, moves to fewer and larger authorities and developed management, create problems for participation and tend to result in problems of over-centralisation, as well as patchy local implementation.

Many changes have been taking place in mental health policy and practice. Specific government initiatives include:
- *Partnership in Action — New Opportunities for Joint Working between Health and Social Services* (1998), to improve collaboration and put service users' needs first;
- *The National Service Framework* (1999), setting out national standards for mental health as a basis for how money should be spent;
- *Who Decides?* (1999), concerned with key principles for making decisions on behalf of mentally incapacitated adults;
- *'Mental Health Czar'* (2000) established;
- *Reform of The Mental Health Act 1983,* Green Paper (1999); White Paper (2000);
- *Managing People with Severe Dangerous Personality Disorder* (1999) proposals and consultation. (Department of Health, 1998a & 1998b; 1999a, 1999b, 1999c; 2000; Home Office/Department of Health, 1999).

Two systems currently operate in statutory mental health services. These are:
- care management, mainly provided by local authority social services departments following the National Health Service and Community Care Act 1990 and
- the care programme approach (CPA) operating under the National Health Service since 1991.

Under the care programme approach, a mental health service user is intended to have their own 'care plan' similar to a local authority 'care package'. They should be involved in drawing up the care plan, be entitled to regular reviews of their plan and they should have a named key worker. Mental health workers have argued that a single system would improve the quality, coordination and continuity of support, and such a simpler system has begun to operate in a growing number of areas.

Multi-disciplinary community mental health teams have developed alongside the care programme approach with the aims of increasing the involvement of service users and working in a more holistic and integrated way. Teams can include psychiatrists, clinical psychologists, social workers, nurses, occupational therapists and others. At the same time their differing power, status and values mean that psychiatric approaches and the medical model often still rule. Service users are also concerned about the possible compromise of independence of social workers, particularly in the approved social worker (ASW) role, with its statutory powers for compulsory detention.

The launch of Primary Care Groups in April 1999 also has significance for mental health service users. Participation of service users in PCGs seemed initially to be limited. The introduction of Primary Care Trusts in England and Local Health Care Co-operatives in Scotland. PCTs and LHCCs raise some major challenges for meaningful user involvement, both because of their frequently large size and their potential for reinforcing the medical model in mental health and social care policy.

Both these emerging arrangements for practice and current policy proposals and developments also need to be considered in the context of broader policies. These include proposals:

• to change the roles and relationships between health and social services in the provision of social care;
• to review charging for long term care;
• for reviewing professional social work training and its funding;
• included within the NHS Plan;
• for addressing quality issues in the government's 'Quality Strategy for Social Care';
• for the introduction of new bodies for regulation and standard setting in social care — the General Social Care Council and the National Care Standards Commission.

The politics of dangerousness

The Government's new documents for mental health policy and provision emphasise a range of key concepts which it has similarly prioritised in other areas of social policy and for other service user groups. These ideas are at the heart of its stated project for social policy and social care. They include notions of: raising standards, improving quality, partnership, empowerment, social inclusion and participation and in some cases anti-discrimination. But in the context of mental health they are accompanied by another commitment — to 'public safety'. The idea of public safety has become the driving force in mental health proposals and policies. It is explicitly presented as such. However, ideas of partnership and involvement carry limited conviction tied to a philosophy of public safety which primarily conceives of mental health service users as a threat from which 'the public' needs to be protected and safeguarded.

Thus at the heart of all the massive changes which are taking place in mental health policy and practice are three big concerns which government has. These are based on a view of:

• mental health service users as dangerous
• the need to give top priority to 'public safety'
• the achievement of this by emphasising control and compulsory 'treatment'.

This is a sharp reminder of the traditional nature of mental health services. There is a crucial difference between mental health service users and most other groups of social care service users. While the rights of many people may be wrongly restricted by the quality and nature of social care, mental health service users, unlike other disabled people, are subject to legislation and provision which is intended and allowed to restrict their rights and freedom. *By law mental health service users' rights can be removed in the name of 'treatment'.* This puts them in a uniquely disadvantaged position. This issue is now dominating mental health policy and discussion.

The 1999 Green Paper, *Reform of The Mental Health Act 1983* and the subsequent White Paper (2000) both included provisions to extend compulsory treatment beyond hospital to people living at home through the introduction of 'community treatment orders'. The 1999 consultation document *Managing People with Severe Dangerous Personality Disorder* contained plans to lock up people given this label before they had actually been convicted of any offence.

It is not yet clear what form government proposals for mental health reform will ultimately take or what they will actually mean for service users/survivors on a day to day basis. But if the answer to how far they will actually go remains unclear, the direction in which they are heading is less open to doubt. The extension of control and compulsion lies at their heart. If the original liberatory goal of the shift from institution to community was to break the link between madness, distress and punitive and custodial regimes, the logic of present proposals is to extend surveillance, regulation, constraint and compulsion from within institutional walls to the wider world. It allows the mental health service user/survivor no place of safety or sanctuary.

The origins of policy
As we move into the third millennium, the climate for political and media debate about mental health service users is hostile and destructive (Mind, 2000). The government's mental health agenda and current political proposals for mental health policy and practice have been shaped by this negative climate. The emphasis is on control, on compulsion, on custody, on dangerousness, on segregation, on re-emphasising genetic and biochemical solutions; on stressing the separateness, 'otherness' and threat of mental health service users. The threat this poses for people's civil and human rights is disturbing. The particular threat for black and minority ethnic mental health service users is likely to be extreme. So far service users/survivors have had little or no involvement in developing government plans for reforms. While the government requires local health and social services to involve service users in their mental health plans and policies, it has not yet done the same itself to any significant extent.

If there is one event to which the thrust of present policy can be traced, it is the introduction of 'care in the community' or 'community care' in the early 1990s. The positive aim of community care was to close down the large institutions as Enoch Powell had proposed a generation earlier and wherever possible enable mental health service users/survivors to stay in their own homes or live somewhere nearby and have suitable support to do so. This support would be local or 'community-based' and would include both support from specialist workers and from the expansion of a wide range of mental health services 'in the community'.

Service users'/survivors' experience of community care was, to say the least, mixed. All the signs are that its inadequate funding by successive governments ruined the policy. This was made worse by continuing problems of poor communication, coordination and integration between different departments and agencies at both local and national levels.

However it was the *principles* not the practice of community care which came under attack. De-institutionalisation and decarceration represent radical and far-reaching policies in the context of madness and distress. Adopting them without proper resources and reorganisation could only be expected to be a recipe for disaster, particularly for service users/survivors left without adequate, appropriate or reliable support, or in some cases, even a roof over their heads. This issue, however, did not rate high on news values and did not become the news story. Instead the tabloid press blamed community care for members of the public being killed by mental health service users and a small number of tragic deaths became front page news and dominated media coverage of mental health policy and issues. This is despite the fact that it is more common for mental health service users to kill themselves or to die in questionable circumstances in the psychiatric system (Sayce, 2000).

The nature of the evidence base for the association of community care and the closure of psychiatric hospitals with increased threat and danger from mental health service users demands examination. The public safety argument which dominates government policy is rooted in a close alliance between the tabloid press and pressure groups like SANE. SANE and its director Marjorie Wallace have persistently argued that the decline in psychiatric hospital beds linked with community care is the cause of increased risk and danger to members of the public from mental health service users. Early in 1999, as part of a research study we were undertaking supported by the Joseph Rowntree Foundation, we made repeated calls to SANE to check the data that they had in order to track psychiatric hospital closures and bed numbers since the reforms. Their staff were friendly and helpful. We spoke to different members of staff in SANE's research, strategy and press departments. They told us that they had *no specific data* on hospital closures. They had no separate figures for hospital bed losses. The only statistics they had were the aggregated statistics for all settings including nursing homes produced by the Department of Health. As their head of strategy told us 'I don't think I have anything more detailed than the table from the Department of Health'. This is a worrying basis on which to mount a longstanding, high profile national campaign which has been extremely influential and helped set the terms of public and political debate. The definitive study of violence and homicide associated with mental health service users, published by the Royal College of Psychiatrists, shows no increase (and a slight fall) in such deaths since the implementation of community care (Taylor and Gunn, 1999).

While the goverment has emphasised the importance of 'evidence-based' policy and practice, this seems to have figured little in its formulation of mental health policy proposals. Instead these seem to have been shaped by fear of scandal and attack from the media. Mental health policy is heavily politicised. One of the early acts of New Labour's then Health Minister was to announce in the Daily Telegraph that 'Care in the community is scrapped' (9 January 1998). The Green Paper on mental health act reform was crucially shaped by advisers at the Number Ten Policy Unit rather than health ministers or civil servants. At a conference on mental health and the media, David Brindle, the Guardian's longstanding social services correspondent, stated that while publicly government ministers rejected the association of mental health service users, dangerousness and homicide, at private briefings, they and their spin doctors 'spun a different tune fuelling demands for a more custodial form of mental health care' (24 February 2000).

As far as mental health policy seems to be concerned, where the tabloids lead, government follows. Just before the 1997 general election, the Sun ran a banner headline over a two page feature calling it 'The real election issue'. The Labour Shadow Minister at the time, Tessa Jowell, in her contribution followed their lead publicly and stressed Labour's support for further controls on mental health service users. The new significance of the media's role in mental health issues and policies also needs to be related to the special role the press, particularly the tabloid press have played in recent years as part of the ideological and electoral apparatus of governments. We know that the tabloid press figured large both as an institution and line of communication in New Labour's political project first to be electable and then to be re-elected. We know it also figured as part of its concern to attract and retain the support of class and interest groups that old Labour traditionally did not concern itself with.

While it now looks as though the government intends to retain many aspects of the philosophy and practice of community care, large question marks are raised about the practicality of this, when control and compulsion now loom so large in policy proposals. Support and control do not sit comfortably together. Providing support for a group stereotyped as threatening and dangerous is unlikely to gain much political or public commitment. Service users/survivors and their organisations are concerned that the focus of policy will be on controlling people seen as a danger, rather than on ensuring adequate and appropriate support for the many, many more who want it. They expect many mental health service users to try and avoid the psychiatric system and 'go underground' rather than risk being compulsorily detained or 'treated' by it. Treatment and compulsion are seen as incompatible. Proper rights of appeal and independent advocacy and a right to support, currently lacking in proposals, are viewed as essential. The only treatment people may be guaranteed is electro shock (ECT) or neuroleptics (tranquillising drugs) under compulsion. There are fears that proposals for compulsion will discriminate especially against black and minority ethnic people. The scale of service users'/survivors' concerns has been reflected in the lobbies and demonstrations which they have both organised and been involved in (Common Agenda, 1999; 2000; Mind South East, 2000; Beresford, 2000).

While opposition to government mental health reform proposals has mainly been framed in moral and ethical terms because of the attack they constitute to mental health service users' civil and human rights, less often discussed but equally important is that they are unlikely to be workable. They may have populist appeal, but they are unlikely to provide the basis for practical policy.

Distress, discrimination and exclusion

While government proposals for mental health reform have dominated discussion over mental health policy and practice, it would be a mistake to confine our attention to them. Not only do mental health service users relate to mainstream services like housing, health, education and recreation (usually unequally), but they are also particularly affected by three particular policies. In addition to specific mental health policies, disability and income maintenance policies also impact upon them significantly. The emphasis which the Labour government placed on the policy of 'welfare to work' means that these last two policies are likely to have renewed significance for mental health service users/survivors for the foreseeable future. Now both Labour and Tory can be seen to be committed to claimants' integration into employment and removal from welfare.

Figures suggest that 85% of people with mental health problems don't have jobs. There are strong links between poverty, social deprivation and mental health service use. People with mental health problems are identified as having the highest rate of unemployment among disabled people. The level of income support is low and people who rely on it live in poverty (Bird, 1999; Mind/BBC, 2000). A longstanding problem is that policies for benefits have not necessarily pulled in the same direction as those for services. If the aim of mental health services is to provide support and help people live their lives, a complex and shaming benefits system which leaves people without an adequate or secure income will clearly have the opposite effect and be damaging for people's well-being and self-esteem.

The signs are that mental health service users also have more difficulty than people with physical or sensory impairments in getting and keeping disability benefits. These 'passport benefits' are very important since they can raise people's standard of living and quality of life. Qualifying for disability benefits may also depend on the acceptance of medical explanations of madness and distress. It may also depend on taking or being injected with prescribed drugs which may have damaging and dangerous effects.

While the government says it is committed to 'social inclusion' and highlights the problem of 'social exclusion', current thinking on and plans for mental health policy are likely to make things worse for mental health service users in two ways. First, they are bringing back old stereotypes of service users/survivors as unpredictable, strange and threatening. Second, mental health service users are also having difficulties with the government's key policy for combating social exclusion, 'welfare to work'. The government says it wants there to be 'work for those who can and security for those who can't'. The 'New Deal for Disabled People', in which many mental health service users are included, is part of this policy. But many mental health service users want a job *and* support. In practice many mental health service users are finding that this policy means being put under increasing pressure to get off benefits and get a job. This is likely to mean any job — whether or not they can manage full time employment, cope without support, or with the kind of low grade, low value work that is mostly on offer. Mental health service users are also still less likely to get — and increasingly at risk of losing — the non-means tested, non-contributory disability benefits which can lift them out of poverty and make their life more worthwhile and secure. Service users highlighted this point at a workshop on benefits at the Mental

Health Foundation's 'Big Alternative Conference' in spring 2000.

A policy in need of treatment?

The government's overall approach to mental health policy raises serious concerns because it appears to be neither evidence-based, consistent, workable nor even rational. It also fails by its own stated commitments to participation, social inclusion, anti-discrimination and human rights. If we consider the government in terms of the kind of psychiatric interpretations and diagnostic categories on which it seems to place ever greater reliance, the picture becomes even more disturbing.

If for one moment as service users we were in the psychiatrist's chair (temporarily suspending disbelief), how might we 'diagnose', as a case study, the Labour administration which embarked on the public safety project? The government's susceptibility to grandiose and unsuccessful projects (e.g. the millennium dome and bridge, ethical foreign policy and arms trade and a dubiously selected London mayoral candidate) suggest 'delusions of grandeur' associated with 'bipolar disorder'. Its frequent use of language without clear or shared meanings, failing at times to make sense (e.g. Department of Health, 1998a) raises suspicions of 'thought disorder' linked with 'schizophrenia'. 'Fixed and expressionless faces, with little or no eye contact (or a peculiar quality of eye contact)' and 'blunting of affect' (all associated with 'schizophrenia') seem almost to be trademarks of some of its key spokespersons and aides, while the 'reduction of the amount of spontaneous speech observed' (Thomas, 1997, p.22) as ministers were encouraged to be 'on message' and to 'sing from the same song book' have become characteristic features. While psychotic diagnostic categories may be most often brought to mind, indications of 'personality disorder' may also be suggested in the case of ministers linked with 'whispering campaigns' against colleagues, accused of having 'flawed personalities', or whose behaviour, whether in the context of house purchase or the operation of off-shore trusts, has been condemned as crossing the boundaries of criminality. While we would generally reject a medical model of madness and distress, we can begin to see how such a government's behaviour and preoccupations might lead some of its critics to see it as a suitable case for (urgent) treatment.

Making our own change

The strong reactionary strands in government mental health policy have special significance because they follow in the wake of massive progress in recent years challenging traditional medicalised individual approaches to madness and distress and developing alternative ideas, understandings, therapies and forms of support. This book and its predecessor are key sources for charting this progress. Here lies one of the true ironies of government modernisation. It looks like taking us backwards, when perhaps for the first time, genuine progressive alternatives are at last becoming available. Twenty years ago such progress could not have been predicted or hoped for. The psychiatric system survivors' movement has made a fundamental impact on psychiatric discourse even if there is still a reluctance to acknowledge this in much political, policy and professional debate.

Government proposals for mental health policy and practice look set to increase the obstacles in the way of realising the new user-led agendas. In our view this means that even more attention must be paid to how we work to make change and counter the oppressions that mental health service users/survivors continue to face. Traditional approaches to change, dominated by organisations for rather than controlled by service users/ survivors, offer little prospect of providing a way forward. More equal, more user-led approaches like those pioneered by the disabled people's movement are much more likely to be effective. There is a growing interest among survivors/service users in a rights-based approach to improving their lives. They are looking at how the Disability Discrimination Act, direct payments schemes and the new Human Rights Act may safeguard their rights, improve their quality of life and reduce the discrimination they face. Some mental health service users/survivors are developing new forms of direct action in order to bring about reform. They are also exploring social approaches to madness and distress (as disabled people have to disability) to replace old ideas about 'mental illness'. Here may be the route to finding successful ways of countering the populist presentation of madness and distress and of reshaping public and political responses to them.

References

Beresford, P. (2000) *Mental Health Issues, Our Voice In Our Future.* London: Shaping Our Lives/National Institute for Social Work

Bird, L. (1999) *The Fundamental Facts . . . All the latest facts and figures on mental illness.* London: Mental Health Foundation

Common Agenda (1999) New Mental Health Act...Direct from Hell, Special Green Paper Edition, *Common Agenda Newsletter, December.* London: Greater London Action on Disability

Common Agenda (2000) MPs Meet With Survivors, March 29 *Common Agenda Newsletter, May/June,* 1–2 London: Greater London Action on Disability

Department of Health (1998a) *Modernising Social Services: Promoting Independence, Improving Protection, Raising Standards* (White Paper). London: Department of Health

Department of Health (1998b) *Modernising Mental Health Services; Safe Sound And Supportive.* London: Department of Health

Department of Health (1999a).*National Service Framework for Mental Health.* London: Department of Health

Department of Health (1999b) *Reform Of The Mental Health Act 1983: Proposals for consultation* (Green Paper). London: Department of Health

Department of Health (1999c) *Draft Outline Proposals By Scoping Study Committee: Review of the Mental Health Act, 1983,* April. London: Department of Health

Department of Health/Home Office (1999) *Managing Dangerous People With Severe Personality Disorder* (Consultation Paper) London: Department of Health

Department of Health (2000) *Reform of the Mental Health Act 1983* (White Paper) London: Department of Health

Department of Health (2000) *The NHS Plan.* London: Department of Health

Department of Health (2001) Press Release 2000/0200, Wednedsay 25 April, Department of Health.

Dunn, S.(1999) *Creating Accepting Communities: Report of the Mind Inquiry into social exclusion and mental health problems.* London: Mind

Mind (2000) *The Daily Stigma: Counting the cost, mental health in the media,* February 9. London: Mind.

Mind/BBC (2000) *Mental Health Factfile,* January. London: Mind

Mind South East (2000) Mass Lobby At The House Of Commons

Mind South East (2000) *Newsletter, May.* London: Mind South East

Powell, M. (2000) New Labour And the Third Way In The British Welfare State: A new and distinctive approach? *Critical Social Policy, 20,1,* 39–60

Sayce, L. (2000) *From Psychiatric Patient To Citizen: Overcoming discrimination and social exclusion.* Basingstoke: Macmillan

Taylor, P. and Gunn, J. (1999) Homicides By People With Mental Illness: Myth and reality. *British Journal of Psychiatry, 174,* 9–14

Thomas, P. (1997) *The Dialectics Of Schizophrenia.* London: Free Association Books

Wintour, P. and Carvel, J. (2001) Labour's NHS Power Shift. The Guardian, 25 April, p.1.

CHAPTER 3

Integrating critical psychiatry into psychiatric training

DUNCAN B. DOUBLE

THERE IS AN ORTHODOX medical approach to the problems of interpreting and treating mental disorders. The argument of this chapter is that any challenge to this orthodoxy is suppressed by mainstream psychiatry. Over recent years, criticism of psychiatry has been marginalised as 'anti-psychiatry'. Voices against the harmful and inhumane tendencies within psychiatry are seen as disreputable. This chapter comments on this remarkable situation and argues that critics of psychiatry should be heard with more understanding and empathy. Self-questioning is required in psychiatric training.

Some psychiatrists are honest enough to acknowledge a rift in practice. For example, a psychiatrist, known for his support of user groups and critical approaches, was a visiting speaker at one of the regular fortnightly Tuesday evening meetings in Sheffield, which took place over many years under the auspices of Professor Alec Jenner of the Sheffield University Department of Psychiatry. Despite the overt radicalism of the speaker's talk, he confessed that as an academic psychiatrist responsible for the training of medical students and psychiatrists he adopted a required conventional mode in his teaching. He did not, however, believe in its content. In particular he thought that he had to teach certain requirements to enable trainees to prepare for the examination of the Membership of the Royal College of Psychiatrists. The unfortunate fact is that once many psychiatrists have passed their professional test, they still do not adopt a properly alert practice. Their sensitivities have been eroded by their training.

Similarly, a senior registrar in psychiatry, who had not long managed to obtain her first consultant psychiatrist appointment, once ruefully remarked to me that she had become 'irretrievably biological' in her approach to psychiatry (Double, 2001). Although this is regarded as an acceptable outcome of her training, she was not able to deal with any criticism of psychiatry. It is reasonable to expect psychiatric trainees to be able to consider the ideological implications of their practice.

Biological bias in psychiatry

Psychiatry is in danger of being defined by neurobiology. As an illustration,

Nurnberger (2000), in a review of *The Neurobiology of Mental Illness* by Charney *et al.*, (1999), noted that neurobiology was only represented in a few sections of the 1959 *American Handbook of Psychiatry*. As he remarks:

> *Few fields in medicine have experienced such a change in the underlying model of illness and treatment as did clinical psychiatry in the last part of the 20th century. Primary reasons for this development included the following: the overwhelming evidence of the efficacy of pharmacologic treatments, a growing appreciation of the heritability of psychiatric disorders, the standard use of objective, criterion-based diagnoses, and the ability to examine the structure and function of the brain directly.*

The primacy of these developments needs to be challenged. Nurnberger concludes by making grandiose claims for a textbook of neurobiology:

> *It will help them [practitioners] interpret the reports they will see in the future on genetic and neuroanatomical abnormalities in their patients. It will be of interest to physicians in other specialties who may wonder about the rationale for the use of anticonvulsants in patients with mood disorders, the interpretation of abnormalities on magnetic resonance imaging scans in patients with schizophrenia, or the use of the sleep laboratory in differential diagnosis. Teachers of clinical and basic neuroscience will use this book to convey the relevance of laboratory-derived concepts and methods to public health and human behavior. The discipline described here is a far cry from the psychiatry we grew up with. Sigmund Freud, a neurobiologist by training, would have been proud.*

Sigmund Freud, of course, created psychoanalysis. Freud met Charcot, the leading neurologist of his time, in Paris after he received a scholarship for research abroad in 1885. The importance of Charcot for Freud is obvious in that a lithograph of the painting 'Une lecon du Docteur Charcot a la Salpetriere' hung on the wall of his consulting room (Engelman, 1998). Moreover, Freud initially had a *Project for a Scientific Psychology* (Freud, 1895), and revealed in his letters to Fliess his motivation to conquer the mind (Masson, 1985). He had a notion of psychological determinism, but was confused (Rieff, 1966). But all this scarcely provides sufficient grounds for accrediting his heritage to neurobiology.

There has always been a conflict between somatic and psychological approaches in psychiatry. The tenets of biological psychiatry are not new, even if they have been reinforced by the introduction of a plethora of psychotropic medications over recent years. For example, Haslam in 1817 concluded that insanity is 'a corporeal disease'. The professional implications for him were clear, because it then made mental illness 'the peculiar and exclusive province of the *medical* practitioner' (his emphasis). He also naively admitted: '[F]rom the limited nature of my powers, I have never been able to conceive . . . *a disease of the mind.*' (Haslam, 1798, again his emphasis.)

Psychological approaches were also disparaged later in the nineteenth century (Clark, 1981). The insistence on somatic explanations of madness produced a resistance to overt psychologising. As anticipated by Henry

Maudsley: 'The explanation, when it comes, will not come from the mental, but from the physical side' (Maudsley, 1874).

At this basic level, modern mainstream psychiatry does not differ from Haslam and Maudsley in its views. Even though the essential conflict of the relation between mind and body remains as it was, the context is, of course, now different. Nurnberger describes four of the important recent developments in the first quote above and a critique of each of these conceptualisations will be provided in turn, viz. (1) the overwhelming evidence (or otherwise) of the efficacy of pharmacologic treatments; (2) a growing appreciation (or otherwise) of the heritability of psychiatric disorders; (3) the standard use (or otherwise) of objective, criterion-based diagnoses; (4) the ability (or otherwise) to examine the structure and function of the brain directly.

Bias in clinical trials

Randomised controlled trials have replaced uncontrolled studies and become accepted as the scientific 'gold-standard'. However, randomised controlled trials are too often assumed to produce unbiased evidence (Chalmers, 1998, see also Healy, this volume). The most methodically rigorous trials are associated with less treatment benefit than poor quality trials (Moher *et al.*, 1998). Even the best quality trials may still not completely eliminate bias because of difficulties in sustaining the two key elements of the method: that the trial is conducted 'double-blind', which means that neither subjects nor experimenters are aware of their group allocation so that their expectancies do not bias outcome; and that any inherent differences between groups are equalised by randomisation. Randomisation can be confounded because of drop-outs from the trial, leading to bias because of exclusions after randomisation.

One history of medicine is of doctors prescribing medication which is subsequently regarded as useless and often dangerous (Shapiro and Shapiro, 1997). The question is how much this situation continues into the present. Two examples will be considered: (i) the efficacy of antidepressants, including the problem of antidepressant discontinuation; and (ii) the efficacy of lithium.

The efficacy of antidepressants

Reviewing the research on antidepressant trials is a massive task. The first attempts to systematise the data, such as those by Morris and Beck (1974), looked at those trials published between 1958 and 1972 and found that tricyclic antidepressants were significantly more effective than placebo in 61 out of 93 group comparisons. Rogers and Clay (1975) concluded that the evidence for imipramine, the original antidepressant, was so strong that further trials of this drug were not justified in endogenous depression in non-institutionalised patients. Since these two reviews, many new antidepressants have been introduced, particularly the class of SSRIs (serotonin-specific reuptake inhibitors).

However, *New Scientist* could still report in 1998 that the benefits of antidepressant medication could be 'mostly in the mind' (Day, 1998). At least one third of the published clinical trials of approved antidepressants are negative for efficacy (Thase, 1999). The US Agency for Health Care Policy and Research (1999) produced a conservative lower limit to treatment efficacy for newer antidepressants using an intention to treat analysis of response rates of 50% for antidepressants and 32% for placebo in major depression. Antidepressants are not always effective and there is a considerable placebo response.

The double-blind methodology is inadequate in many antidepressant trials (Even *et al.*, 2000). Patients and doctors may be cued in to whether patients are taking active or placebo medication by a variety of means. In fact if treatment is clearly superior to placebo, this should be obvious to raters in the trial, making it not technically blind. Patients in clinical trials are naturally curious to ascertain whether they are in the active or placebo group, and may for example notice that placebo tablets they have been taking taste differently from medication to which they have previously become accustomed. Active medication may produce side effects which distinguishes it from inert medication. The difference between drug and placebo effect may be a true pharmacological effect, but the possibility that it is an enhanced placebo effect cannot be excluded (Kirsch and Sapirstein, 1998).

Using active drugs without apparent specific treatment effects as controls generally reduces the effect size of antidepressant treatment, maybe because bias is less likely to be introduced because of the detection of active effects in the control drug (Thomson, 1982). However, the adequacy of these active placebo trials can be questioned (Quitkin *et al.*, 2000).

The importance of the placebo response is relevant to problems in discontinuing medication. People may form attachments to their medications more because of what they mean to them than what they do. Psychiatric patients often stay on medications, maybe several at once, even though their actual benefit is questionable. Any change threatens an equilibrium related to a complex set of meanings that their medications have acquired. These issues of dependence should not be minimised, yet commonly treatment is reinforced by emphasising that antidepressants are not addictive. For example, the Defeat Depression Campaign of the Royal College of Psychiatrists criticised the general public for generally taking this view (Priest *et al.*, 1996). The general public might reasonably expect psychiatrists specialising in disorders of the mind to recognise psychological dependence, base their advice on clinical experience, and use their common sense (Double, 1997).

A sceptical view about the value of antidepressant medication is commonly rejected because it is regarded as undermining people's faith in their treatment. The issue is really about the scientific validity of claims for the efficacy of antidepressants. There is more uncertainty about this issue than many seem prepared to accept.

The efficacy of lithium
The reasoning behind the introduction of lithium into clinical practice was fallacious. Cade (1949) thought that mania may be caused by urea circulating in excess in the body. In an attempt to test this hypothesis he tested the effects of lithium urate, as this compound is the most soluble urate available. To determine whether lithium salts by themselves had any discernible effects, lithium carbonate was injected into guinea pigs and the animals became extremely lethargic and unresponsive to stimuli before once again becoming normally active after a few hours. This effect was almost certainly due to lithium toxicity. Even if what was being observed suggested that lithium may be of benefit in treating manic excitement, the association of ideas was

illogical and serendipitous.

Unsurprisingly then, such an observation was not taken forward at the time, although understandably the toxic effects of lithium were of concern. Also, lithium is the exception to the pharmaceutical industry-led introduction of psychotropic medication (Tansey, 1998). However, as noted by Kline in 1968:

> *Lithium, the 20-year old Cinderella of psychopharmacology, is at last receiving her sovereign due. Just plain old lithium . . . Only 9 papers or letters were published in the first 5 years reporting new cases and very few more in each of the next two 5-year periods, in contrast to some 10,000 papers on chlorpromazine in its first 15 years and more than 2,000 on LSD. This year, however, will probably witness the publication of more papers on the subject than in all the previous 19 years.* (p.558)

Schou *et al.*, (1954) tried lithium in several manic patients and were convinced of its value. Apparently, they took it more or less for granted that a drug that had a therapeutic effect during an ongoing manic episode must also prevent further episodes of mania (Schou, 1999). Cade (1949) had observed that lithium had no apparent beneficial effect on a small number of depressed patients. When it was reported that lithium ameliorated or prevented recurrences of depression the way was paved for the acceptance of lithium as a prophylactic agent for manic-depressive illness.

Moncrieff (1995, 1997) reviewed the controlled trial evidence of lithium and concluded that its efficacy has never been satisfactorily demonstrated. Jefferson (1998) has attempted to right a more conventional balance about the value of lithium. A meta-analysis of more recent placebo controlled lithium discontinuation studies did not find as great an effect of lithium as previous reviews (Baker, 1994). Non-specific factors do seem to be important as evidenced by the finding that rapid withdrawal is associated with higher relapse than gradual withdrawal. Furthermore, the largest recent trial to date has found no significant difference between lithium and placebo as measured by time to recurrence during maintenance treatment (Bowden *et al.*, 2000).

Lithium was introduced into practice on a wave of enthusiasm. Schou was involved in an influential early double-blind lithium discontinuation study, which had remarkably favourable results for lithium (21 placebo patients relapsed, none on lithium) (Baastrup *et al.*, 1970). Despite the lack of evidence of methodological weaknesses, it is difficult to believe that bias did not in some way affect the results as they are so strikingly favourable to lithium.

A sceptical re-evaluation is required to counter the overfavourable interpretation of the efficacy of lithium in the literature.

Overstating the genetic case

A common mistake is to implicate genetic transmission merely because mental illness runs in families. Twin studies and adoption studies are regarded as 'natural experiments' which enable an estimate to be made of the extent to which traits are familial because of shared genes, shared environment or a combination of both.

The work of the geneticists has been replete with uncritical dogmatic statements and lack of scientific rigour. For example, Kallmann (1938) presented a pair of twin girls born illegitimately to a domestic servant who died of tuberculosis soon after she left them to be brought up separately by two of her brothers who lived in different cities. Before they were ten they only saw each other a few times, but later met more frequently. One of the twins had a child aged 15 and was subsequently admitted to hospital in a 'catatonic stupor'. Twenty months later the other twin was admitted to the same hospital as she had become 'increasingly more and more helpless and emotionally indifferent'. Kallmann regarded this pair of twins as proof 'that definite somatogenic factors must count as dispositional determinants in the manifestation of a hereditary predisposition to schizophrenia'. As noted by Laing (1976):

> When one sees . . . [Kallmann's] . . . completely uncritical and naive approach to his data, there is no indication that his assertions about 'completely different environments' are any less naive; nor that he has more grasp of the pitfalls of retrospective data, or of reports from family members that may be equally biased due to fantasies held in common. . . . One can place no more confidence in Kallmann's assessments of 'concordance' of 'environment' than in those of life history and diagnosis. (p.118)

Moreover, although logically separate, Kallmann's 'scientific' presentation was combined with a eugenic campaign to prevent the propagation of the apparent genetic predisposition to schizophrenia. He stopped short of recommending compulsory sterilisation, except for the 'incorrigibles'. Yet his proposals to prevent breeding of people he calls schizophrenics are suspect.

Over recent years, a bewildering and apparently contradictory array of studies have reported links with various genes in schizophrenia (Moldin, 1997). In contrast, the identification and cloning of genes and the elucidation of chromosomal abnormalities has led to major progress in the molecular biology of genetic neuropsychiatric disorders, such as Huntington's disease, in which the abnormality of triplet repeat on chromosome four has now been demonstrated.

Multigene models of inheritance are still commonly regarded as the best model of familial transmission of schizophrenia (Tsuang *et al.*, 2000). There is speculation that the mapping of the human genome will help to put better treatments for psychiatric illness on the market and make discrimination a thing of the past (McGuffin and Martin, 1999). Despite the hype, accurate prediction may never be possible because of the complexity of the genetics of common disorders (Holtzman and Marteau, 2000). Scepticism about the overenthusiasm for genetic explanations is required.

The validity of psychiatric diagnosis
Operationalisation of diagnostic criteria was developed specifically to respond to criticisms of psychiatric classification (Blashfield, 1984). The primary motivation of these standardised, criterion-based definitions was to make diagnosis more consistent and reliable, initially for research (Feighner *et al.*, 1972). Clinically, diagnostic manuals have been developed through editions

of DSM-III, DSM-IIIR and DSM-IV (American Psychiatric Association, 1994) and ICD-10 (World Health Organisation, 1992). However, the most reliable of diagnostic criteria are not necessarily valid in the sense of measuring what they are supposed to measure. Diagnostic criteria do not solve the dilemma surrounding psychiatric classification.

The basic issue is about the meaning of psychiatric diagnosis. Single-word diagnoses do not necessarily help the understanding of a person's problems. The personal meaning of people's distress and the psychological and social origins of their difficulties are obscured by turning them into a simple diagnosis (Johnstone, 2000). In retrospect, the history of the development of diagnostic criteria over recent years has been little more than a professional discourse intent on justifying psychiatry. It has narrowed its scope and psychiatry needs to return to a biopsychosocial model, which was becoming more generally accepted by the 1950s before the widespread introduction of psychotropic medication (Wilson, 1993).

None of the above should be taken to mean that the reality of mental suffering is being denied. Thomas Szasz, in a plethora of books since his original *The Myth of Mental Illness* (1972), has argued for the logical inconsistency of a diagnosis of mental illness, as for him the term illness necessarily implies physical pathology. Therefore psychopathology cannot amount to illness. Such a view does seem overly rigid. Similarly, suggestions that terms such as schizophrenia are without any meaning (e.g., Boyle, 1990) can also seem to overstate the case. Diagnoses are no more than metaphorical use of language and there needs to be transparency about their use.

Searching for the neuropathology of mental illness
Modern neuroimaging methods have enabled relatively non-invasive *in vivo* studies of brain structure and function. There is a multitude of studies which report abnormalities in shape, size and functions in multiple anatomical regions of the brain, particularly related to the so-called neuropathology of schizophrenia. The working hypothesis of most investigators of schizophrenia is that it is a disease of neural connectivity caused by multiple factors that affect brain development (Andreasen, 1999). However, structural and functional cerebral abnormalities in schizophrenia are at best subtle rather than gross. The most consistent finding of lateral ventricular enlargement is modest and there is a large overlap with the normal population (Chua and McKenna, 1995).

Theories of neurotransmitter dysfunction arose following the introduction of psychotropic drugs at a time when few neurotransmitters had been discovered. Despite the subsequent discovery of a vastly more complex neurotransmitter network, psychiatrists still use such simplistic notions in their everyday management of patients when they explain that mental illness is due to 'chemical imbalance'. For example, the dopamine hypothesis of schizophrenia (dopamine overactivity in schizophrenic brains) arose because neuroleptic drugs, such as chlorpromazine, appear to act via an inhibition of dopamine receptors. However, measurements of dopamine metabolites *in vivo*, or of the transmitter and its receptors in post-mortem brain tissue, do not provide unequivocal evidence of a hyperactivity of dopaminergic neurotransmission in the disease, if only because it is difficult to disentangle the iatrogenic effects of the drugs themselves (Reynolds, 1989). Moreover, many of the newer drugs do not appear to work by dopamine antagonism, raising the question of the real nature of atypical antipsychotic medication.

Adolf Meyer (1951/2) was fond of seeing his philosophical approach to psychiatry, with its emphasis on the person, as an advance over the mechanistic philosophy of the 19th century. His work is currently largely neglected in the modern biological consensus in psychiatry. He warned against going beyond statements about the person to a wishful 'neurologising tautology' about the brain. Progress in understanding schizophrenia is more likely through rigorous and creative conceptualisation and evaluation of the evidence than uncritical application of neuroimaging methods. Reducing relations between people to objective connections seems to make them more manageable. Modern psychiatry has become so dominated by biologism that acknowledgement that there is a philosophical issue about the relationship between mind and brain is rare.

The discovery that the adult brain is capable of extensive reorganisation necessitates radical revision of traditional notions of anatomical fixity (Eisenberg, 1995). Biochemically the brain modifies its own responsiveness to incoming stimuli through neuromodulators. The human brain seems to be socially constructed in the literal sense that brain cytoarchitecture itself is fashioned by input from the social environment. Although this claim is an extrapolation from the evidence, it holds out hope for an integration of theory, even providing evidence for a Meyerian psychobiology.

The training of psychiatrists
Each of the four recent developments which Nurnberger regards as crucial to progress has been examined and found wanting as represented by mainstream psychiatry. The case for an extensive, national programme of training and supervision in order to disseminate a critical perspective on psychiatry is overwhelming. This is consistent with the ethos of involving users and user-groups in decision making and accountability, as survivors of mental health services tend to be critical of their treatment.

The lack of a whole-person way of understanding mental health problems originates in medical training. In particular, reductive causal analyses do not help to make intelligible the reasons for human action. Medical students are indoctrinated into a natural scientific perspective of basic biological processes. The issue is never raised about whether an understanding of human behaviour should take a form similar to the laws of natural science. Despite the obvious failings of positivism, its attraction is that it seems to avoid the complexities and uncertainties of psychological and social perspectives. Taken to its extreme, such an approach becomes irrational.

Once imbued with the idea that experimental natural science is an adequate discourse for a description of personal behaviour, medical students may take a mechanistic view of their treatment of patients. They are encouraged to see psychiatry as little different from medicine in this respect, although they do sense the uncertainties of mental health work and regard it as less rigorous and developed as a discipline. Still, the cause of a person's insane behaviour or other mental health problems is their 'chemical imbalance' or some other brain dysfunction, even if the mechanisms underlying this pathology seem less well understood than for other physical conditions.

The difficulty of communicating with disturbed and disturbing people can create defensive practice. Concentrating on the bodily complaints of people makes sense if they have a physical origin. Emotional complaints do not have to be addressed if they are reduced to their bodily substrate. Questions are avoided about why psychiatry interfaces with the law and human rights. An ethical approach to psychiatric practice can be difficult to sustain. The aim of social control may produce a lack of compassion in the care of people with mental disorder, and the history of psychiatry confirms the common degradation of patients. The health professional's own need for self importance can override the patient's problems.

These problems are not totally unique to psychiatric training. Much of the current criticism of medical professionalism is of an arrogance created because of the difficulties in engaging with people's suffering through illness. Claims are made for medical techniques which go beyond the evidence. Patients may have needless investigations and be overtreated. In an attempt to bolster professional interests, self-questioning is discouraged in the interests of certainty.

The modern use of the term 'anti-psychiatry' was introduced by David Cooper (1967). In general anti-psychiatry has been regarded as simply a passing phase in the history of psychiatry (Tantum, 1991). A more constructive approach is to place anti-psychiatry in its broader cultural context and see it in terms of its continuities (Gijswijt-Hofstra and Porter, 1998). The most consistent use of the term 'anti-psychiatry' derives from the recognition that psychiatry is not always the solution to mental illness; it may be the problem itself. The contemporary critique of psychiatry cannot dissociate itself from its history in anti-psychiatry. Its legacy may have foundered because some of its representatives were ultimately more interested in personal authenticity than carrying through their ideas in practice. Moreover, its message became confused because the movement included a wide range of different people, some of whom are essentially irreconcilable in their views. In particular, Thomas Szasz (1976) has been scathing in his censure of R.D. Laing. Laing never denied the reality of mental turmoil; merely contending that so-called mental illness was more understandable than generally assumed. It is the apparent denial of the reality of mental illness that allows the critique of psychiatric practice to be marginalised. Contemporary critical psychiatry needs to be clear that the concept of mental illness can be applied to psychological dysfunction (Farrell, 1979). The biological viewpoint is unjustifiable, as it assumes that mental illness is real in the physical sense. Anti-psychiatry is against psychiatry's excesses not anti-'mental illness'.

Psychiatrists in training need to be exposed to the ideological implications of their practice. Such a self-reflexive approach does not necessarily deny the need for the use of the Mental Health Act or the pragmatic use of medication. However, it may lead to the realisation of the importance of patient's rights as well as the assessment of risk, and the recognition of overreliance on medication.

In summary, the biomedical dominance of psychiatry needs to be challenged (Critical Psychiatry Network website). Psychiatric training needs to incorporate a critical perspective.

References

Agency for Health Care Policy and Research (1999) *Treatment of depression—newer pharmacotherapies.* Evidence report/Technology assessment: Number 7. Rockville: AHCPR

American Psychiatric Association (1994) *Diagnostic and Statistical Manual of Mental Disorders* (4th edition). Washington: APA

Andreasen, N. (1999) Understanding the causes of schizophrenia. *New England Journal of Medicine*, 340, 645–7

Baastrup, P.C., Poulsen, J.C., Schou, M., Thomsen, K. and Amdisen, A. (1970) Prophylactic lithium: Double blind discontinuation in manic-depressive and recurrent-depressive disorders. *Lancet*, ii, 326–30

Baker, J.P. (1994) Outcomes of lithium discontinuation: a meta-analysis. *Lithium*, 5, 187–92

Blashfield, R.K. (1984) *The classification of psychopathology. Neo-Kraepelinian and quantitative approaches.* New York: Plenum

Bowden, C.L., Calabrese, J.R., McElroy, S.L., *et al* (2000) A Randomized, Placebo-Controlled 12-Month Trial of Divalproex and Lithium in Treatment of Outpatients With Bipolar I Disorder. *Archives of General Psychiatry*, 57, 481–9

Boyle, M. (1990) *Schizophrenia: A scientific delusion?* London: Routledge

Cade, J. (1949) Lithium salts in the treatment of psychotic excitement. *Medical Journal of Australia*, 36, 349–52

Chalmers, I. (1998) Unbiased, relevant, and reliable assessments in health care. *British Medical Journal*, 317, 1167–9

Charney, D.S., Nestler, E.J. and Benjamin, B.S. (1999) *The neurobiology of mental illness.* New York: OUP

Chua, S.E. and McKenna, P.J. (1995) Schizophrenia — a brain disease? A critical review of structural and functional cerebral abnormality in the disorder. *British Journal of Psychiatry*, 166, 563–82

Clark, M.J. (1981) The rejection of psychological approaches to mental disorder in late nineteenth century British psychiatry. In *Madhouses, mad-doctors and madmen.* (ed. A Scull). London: Althone Press

Cooper, D. (1967) *Psychiatry and anti-psychiatry.* Tavistock Publications: London.

Critical Psychiatry Network website http://www.criticalpsychiatry.co.uk/

Day, M. (1998) Mostly in the mind. *New Scientist* 159 (11 July 1998)

Double, D.B. (1997) Prescribing antidepressants in general practice. People may become psychologically dependent on antidepressants. *British Medical Journal*, 314, 829

Double, D.B. (2001) Can psychiatry be retrieved from a biological approach? *Journal of Critical Psychology, Counselling and Psychotherapy*, 1, 2–6

Eisenberg, L. (1995) The social construction of the human brain. *American Journal of Psychiatry*, 152, 1563–75

Engelman, E. (1998) *Sigmund Freud. Vienna IX. Bergasse 19.* Wien: Universe

Even, C., Siobud-Dorocant, and Dardennes, R.M. (2000) Critical approach to antidepressant trials. Blindness protection is necessary, feasible and measurable. *British Journal of Psychiatry*, 177, 47–51

Farrell, B.A. (1979) Mental illness: a conceptual analysis. *Psychological Medicine*, 9, 21–35

Feighner, J.P., Robins, E., Guze, S.B., *et al.* (1972) Diagnostic criteria for use in psychiatric research. *Archives of General Psychiatry*, 26, 57–63.

Freud, S. (1895) Project for a scientific psychology. In: *Standard edition of the complete works of Sigmund Freud*. London: Hogarth Press

Gijswijt-Hofstra, M. and Porter, R. (1998) *Cultures of psychiatry and mental health care in postwar Britain and the Netherlands*. Amsterdam: Wellcome Institute

Haslam, J. (1798) *Observations on insanity*. London: Rivington

Haslam, J. (1817) *Considerations on the moral management of insane persons*. London: Hunter

Holtzman, N.A. and Marteau, T.M. (2000) Will genetics revolutionize medicine? *New England Journal of Medicine*, 342, 141–4

Jefferson, J.W. (1998). Lithium. Still effective despite its detractors. *British Medical Journal*, 316, 1330-1

Johnstone, L. (2000) *Users and abusers of psychiatry: a critical look at psychiatric practice*. (Second edition) London: Routledge

Kallmann, F.J. (1938) *The genetics of schizophrenia*. New York: J J Augustin

Kirsch, I. and Sapirstein, G. (1998) Listening to prozac but hearing placebo: a meta-analysis of antidepressant medication. *Prevention & Treatment* 1 Article 0002a, (http://journals.apa.org/prevention/volume1/pre0010002a.html (posted June 26, 1998)

Kline, N.S. (1968) Lithium comes of its own. *American Journal of Psychiatry*, 125, 558–60

Laing, R.D. (1976) A critique of Kallmann's and Slater's genetic theory of schizophrenia. In: Evans, R.I. *RD Laing. The man and his ideas*. New York: Dutton

Masson, J. M. (ed) (1985) *The complete letters of Sigmund Freud to Wilhelm Fliess 1887-1904*. Cambridge, Mass: Harvard UP

Maudsley, H. (1874) *Responsibilities in mental disease*. (2nd ed) London: Kegan Paul

McGuffin, P. and Martin, N. (1999) Behaviour and genes. *British Medical Journal* ,319, 37–40

Meyer, A. (1951/2) *Collected Papers*. Edited by Winters E. Baltimore: Johns Hopkins Press

Moher, D., Pham, B., Jones, A., Cook, D.J.,Jadad, A.R., Moher, M., Tugwell, P. and Klassen, T.P. (1998) Does quality of reports of randomised trials affect estimates of intervention efficacy reported in meta-analyses? *Lancet*, 352, 609–13

Moldin, S.O. (1997) The maddening hunt for madness genes. *Nature Genetics*, 17, 127–9

Moncrieff, J. (1995) Lithium revisited: a re-examination of the placebo-controlled trials of lithium prophylaxis in manic-depressive disorder. *British Journal of Psychiatry*, 167, 569–74

Moncrieff, J. (1997) Lithium: evidence reconsidered. *British Journal of Psychiatry*, 171, 113–9

Morris, J.B. and Beck, A.T. (1974) The efficacy of antidepressant drugs. A review of research (1958-1972). *Archives of General Psychiatry*, 30, 667–74

Nurnberger, J.I. (2000) Book review of *The neurobiology of mental illness* (by Charney DS, Nestler EJ & Benjamin BS). *New England Journal of Medicine*, 342, 1617

Priest, R.G., Vize, C., Roberts, A., Roberts, M. and Tylee, A. (1996) Lay people's attitudes to treatment of depression: results of opinion poll for Defeat Depression Campaign just before its launch. *British Medical Journal*, 313, 858–9

Quitkin, F.M., Rabkin, J.G., Gerald, J., *et al.* (2000) Validity of clinical trials of antidepressants. *American Journal of Psychiatry*, 157, 327–37

Reynolds, G.P. (1989) Beyond the dopamine hypothesis. The neurochemical pathology of schizophrenia. *British Journal of Psychiatry*, 155, 305–16

Rieff, P. (1966) *The triumph of the therapeutic*. Harmondsworth: Penguin

Rogers, S.C. and Clay, S.M. (1975) A statistical review of controlled trials of imipramine and placebo in the treatment of depressive illness. *British Journal of Psychiatry*, 127, 599–603

Schou, M. (1999) The early European lithium studies. *Australian and New Zealand Journal of Psychiatry*, 33, S39–S47

Schou, M., Juel-Nielsen, N., Stromgren, E. and Voldby, H. (1954) The treatment of manic psychosis by the administration of lithium salts. *Journal of Neurology, Neurosurgery and Psychiatry*, 17, 250–60

Shapiro, A.K. and Shapiro, E. (1997) *The powerful placebo. From ancient priest to modern physician*. London: John Hopkins Johns Hopkins University Press

Szasz, T.S. (1972) *The myth of mental illness*. Paladin: London

Szasz, T.S. (1976) 'Anti-psychiatry': The paradigm of a plundered mind. *New Review* 3(29) 3–14

Tansey, E.M. (1998) 'They used to call it psychiatry': Aspects of the development and impact of psychopharmacology. In: Gijswijt-Hofstra, M. and Porter, R. (eds) *Cultures of psychiatry and mental health care in post-war Britain and Netherlands*. Amsterdam: Wellcome Institute

Tantum, D. (1991) The anti-psychiatry movement. In: Berrios, G.E. and Freeman, H. (eds) *150 Years of British Psychiatry, 1841–1991* (eds). London: Gaskell

Thase, M. (1999) How should efficacy be evaluated in randomized clinical trials of treatments for depression? *Journal of Clinical Psychiatry*, 60, (suppl 4), 23–31

Thomson, R. (1982) Side effects and placebo amplification. *British Journal of Psychiatry*, 140, 64–8

Tsuang, M.T., Stone, W.S. and Faraone, S.V. (2000) Toward reformulating the diagnosis of schizophrenia. *American Journal of Psychiatry*, 157, 1041–50

Wilson, M. (1993) DSM-III and the transformation of American psychiatry: A history. *American Journal of Psychiatry*, 150, 399–410

World Health Organisation (1992) *The ICD-10 classification of mental and behavioural disorders*. Geneva: WHO

CHAPTER 4

Policing happiness

MARK RAPLEY

Julia: *So what does it mean if you have a mental handicap?*
Kathleen: *It means you get made fun of, like blind people.*

Todd and Shearn (1995, p. 21)

THE END OF THE twentieth century saw a remarkable transformation in the social construction of intellectual disability. Both in academic texts and political documents, a group of people produced at the start of the century as a biologically degenerate menace to society, and in most of its latter half as the incompetent recipients of necessarily lifelong care, came instead to be produced as consumers of services with individual wants, choices and preferences. While such a transformation may be understood as merely a reflection of the wider societal adoption of consumerist and individualist discourses[1] of the subject across western cultures in this period (Rapley and Ridgway, 1998), for people with intellectual disabilities this change in status — on the face of it a positive development — may not have been as benign as may be assumed at first blush.

Measuring[2]
It is, of course, a given of psy-complex[3] (Rose, 1985; 1990) practices that classification and quantification are an essential good. Operationalising and measuring hypothetical (mental state) constructs is the hallmark of modernist psychological science and is justified by the assertion that it is in this way — and this way only — that we can reliably, validly and objectively come to grips with the world, and the cognitive contents of persons within it. Of necessity, or so the argument goes, carving up the phenomenological world into readily measurable chunks requires the construction of devices which pre-categorise experience in a standardised form — a form which is, hence, comparable across persons. Such devices — psychological tests, inventories and questionnaires — are, at least in the canonical literature, routinely portrayed as *essentially neutral scientific objects* which offer an otherwise unobtainable purchase on any and all aspects of human subjectivity. We can, or so the psy-complex assures us, sensibly measure people's intelligence,

anxiety, personality, sexual orientation, depression, career aptitudes and so on (and on and on) with instruments which veridically represent the reality of these states of being in the world, reliably and validly, for all persons. In much the same way that a tape measure will faithfully and unproblematically measure the height of any person against whom it is laid, so too — and with similarly little political significance — will psychological tests read off the true nature of persons to whom they are applied, in universally meaningful terms.

There is now a substantial body of work which suggests that this insistence on *a priori* categorisation in the social sciences, a practice which reaches its peak in the psychometric endeavour, is not only epistemologically flawed[4] (and thus inevitably methodologically compromised) but also has far-reaching political ramifications[5]. That people with intellectual disabilities may, sensibly, be said to have been invented by the development of the apparatus of the intelligence quotient, suggests the potential seriousness of the consequences, Binet's good intentions notwithstanding. Furthermore, while the psychometrics literature discusses (at length) the possibility that people may be less than desirably compliant with testing — indeed some may go so far as to fake their responses or display other vexatious response biases[6] — the possibility that psychological testing is far from a neutral technology for its recipients, or that the process of testing may indeed be an aversive procedure *per se*, does not appear to be seriously considered.

'Quality of life'

The (often implicit) thesis of the psy-complex, that any and all aspects of subjectivity are measurable, and that *all* aspects of subjectivity are essentially private, is well illustrated by the development of interest in the notion of 'Quality of life' (or QOL as it is often known) in the academic psychological and intellectual disability research communities in the 1980s and 1990s. A concept which began life as an index of the general economic and social well-being of national communities (Schalock, 1990) was transformed by the mid-1990s into another piece of individualised mind-stuff, the — by now measurable — quantity of which possessed by any given individual or, for audit purposes, by a collection of individuals, could be described by the mid-1990s as 'the ultimate criterion for the effectiveness of social care delivery' (Perry and Felce, 1995, p. 1).

Psy-complex interest in QOL took place against the backdrop of the emergence of the general notion of quality in commercial, professional and public life in the 1980s and 1990s. The relatively sudden appearance of quality in so many different managerial discourses invites a sustained analysis for which there is no room here.[7] Borrowed from the language of business, the idea that QOL was a sensible outcome measure of human service practices or medical interventions — despite little in the way of a clear theoretical specification of the necessary linkage between a vast range of disparate service activities and consumers' happiness — produced, in short order, an exponentially expanding literature. So extensive and chaotic is the QOL literature that Cummins (1996) — one of the leading international researchers in the area — states simply that familiarity with it all is now an impossibility. Indeed a preliminary literature search by Antaki and Rapley (1996b) found 'Quality of life' cited as a keyword in 1,400 articles published between 1992 and mid-1995 alone. Typical examples are surveys of the quality of life of people with HIV (Revicki, *et al.,* 1995), adolescents with 'schizophrenia' (Swales, *et al.*, 1995); medical patients with advanced cancer (Kaasa, *et al.*, 1993) and comparative analyses of the quality of life of people with intellectual disabilities living in differing forms of residential care (e.g. Perry and Felce, 1995). QOL, in the form of the 'Quality Adjusted Life Year', has also become a measure used to guide differential medical treatment/no treatment decisions (see Baldwin, Godfrey and Propper, 1990 for a review). Such medical uses of the construct have made QOL assessment literally a matter of life and death (Wolfensberger, 1994).

If human services' employment of the notion of QOL is thus (potentially, lethally) consequential for the individual it is also, as Perry and Felce (1995) have suggested, consequential for the institution providing services to those individuals. The aggregated QOL of service recipients is now a routine site for the evaluation of the delivery of health and social care, features prominently in organisationalmission statements, attracts institutional funding and technical support, and has been promoted as an appropriate index (e.g. Heal and Sigelman, 1990) for use in inter-service 'league table' quality comparisons and bureaucratic decision-making.

QOL measurement is then a serious business as far as service providers and academic researchers are concerned. The psy-complex has expended major efforts in attempting to define and operationalise QOL, and in developing a multiplicity of technologies for measuring the quantity of 'it' the recipients of human services 'have'. While at least two of these efforts in the intellectual disability field have been, in psychometric terms at least, remarkably successful (Schalock and Keith's (1993) *Quality of Life Questionnaire* and Cummins' (1997) *Comprehensive Quality of Life Scale – Intellectual Disability*)[8] a number of fundamental questions remain to be addressed. Given the individual and institutional ramifications of the use of the concept, and the seductiveness of scientific-sounding scores on psychological scales[9], clarity about what quality of life means is essential. So what is quality of life? In whose terms is quality of life to be defined? If the necessary and sufficient components of quality of life can be consensually defined *a priori*, is the provision of such a life the proper purpose of human services? If the provision of such a life *is* a proper purpose, whether it is feasible, and whether the routine measurement of the quality of life of service recipients is a desirable service activity, remain open questions. In the remainder of this chapter, and drawing upon a series of QOL and open interviews with people with intellectual disabilities, I shall focus primarily on the issues of what a life of quality might consist in, and in whose terms such a life is to be understood.

So what is 'quality of life'?

A number of writers critical of the reifying and homogenising tendencies of the psy-complex (e.g. Boyle, 1990) have pointed to the dangers of using lay constructs as scientific terms. 'Quality of life' would appear to be a prime candidate for the exercise of such caution. It is a term both redolent with everyday reference and also sufficiently imprecise, in lay discourse, to function most commonly as a content-free 'motherhood' category in the persuasive rhetoric of politicians, human service executives and real estate agents. The very imprecision which grants the term its rhetorical force — and consequent political utility — in these contexts (well, who would buy a policy position, a hip replacement or a house which did not promise to enhance their quality of life?) is precisely what should — as others such as Taylor (1994) have also argued — lead to the rejection of the use of the term as a scientific one. As Taylor argues, consideration of the overall quality of people's lives may be a very useful sensitising notion in human services. However, the standardisation of such consideration as QOL (be it mind-stuff or service practice outcome) is incommensurable with both the person-centred focus supposedly driving service practices (Individual Program Plans and the like) and the individualist discourse (the trope of consumers with choices, for example) which legitimates them.

Such counsel has, however, not been heeded. Rather, the psy-complex has, through the use of its usual rigorous procedures, sought to define, to reify and to operationalise a term which, like all other social categories, is granted meaning locally and contingently[10]. In so doing, while this literature shows signs of coalescing around a single quasi official'definition of QOL[11], two general working definitions — as instanced by schedules and questionnaires designed to measure 'it'—have emerged. Broadly speaking, as Antaki and Rapley (1996a) put it: 'Where there is debate, it is over the [degree of] overlap or separation, for traditional psychometric purposes, between the "subjective" and the "objective".' Schalock, Keith and Hoffman (1990, p. 15), for example, contend that 'quality of life is necessarily subjective and cannot be inferred strictly from objective measures of life conditions', whereas other writers have suggested that a wide range of objective factors may be employed to gauge quality of life (e.g. Hughes *et al.*, 1995). Some, then, believe that it can only be assessed by asking the person directly (where possible); others doubt that such subjectivity is to be trusted, and prefer observable measures. Crudely: one school will want to ask how happy you are; the other will want to ask you or your guardians whether you have a job, a key to your house, and fresh linen every week, and will calculate your happiness from that.

In this debate one further, and highly significant, difference emerges. The difference in emphasis turns (implicitly) on the social status of people with intellectual disabilities as members of a common cultural order, and raises issues that have as yet to be adequately addressed. In brief, the *QOL.Q* presupposes that people with intellectual disabilities are outside the common cultural order and that any estimation of the quality of their lives should reflect this state — hence questions which seek information about the possession of keys to the door and whether staff decide how personal income is to be spent — whereas the *ComQol-ID* stipulates the inherent commonality/homogeneity of QOL across IQ levels (and, implicitly, social standing) and seeks the same information from people with intellectual disabilities as from their 'unimpaired' peers. While coherent arguments may be put for both of these positions, and, in their own terms, they may be seen to have intellectual merit, both also make a number of presuppositions which entail difficult political questions.

Firstly it is presupposed that there is such a thing inside peoples' heads as a 'QOL' state and that this is measurable, as such, by the administration of standardised measures. Secondly, it is assumed that the questions which researchers have devised to measure this state have relevance to the persons being questioned — in the case of *ComQol-ID*, that QOL is, essentially, the same *thing* for Fred Jones, resident of a long-stay institution for 30 years and described by the psy-complex as 'having' an IQ of 46, as it is for comfortable middle-class members of the salariat. In the case of the *QOL.Q* the assumption is that, while there are some universal determinants of QOL (adherence to the Protestant work ethic is perhaps the clearest example), there are also a series of characteristics of intellectual disability services which are, *ipso facto*, the matters of most relevance to the people in receipt of them. In both cases, of course, what QOL *is*, is determined *a priori* by the researchers: the only role for respondents is to be measured and recorded as 'having' a greater or lesser amount of it. The third, and perhaps most troubling, presupposition is that QOL measurement is inherently benign: that measuring peoples' QOL is in their best interests, and that testing itself is of no greater consequence — either immediately or in the longer term — than having one's temperature taken. Taken together these assumptions combine to present the psy-complex as not only knowing precisely what a 'normal' quality of life is, but also as having the (reliable and valid) tools with which to measure (deviations from) it. QOL measures then offer the psy professions a means to monitor the provision of, and individuals' success in achieving, a life of quality; a protocol for the policing of happiness.

Testing

The QOL measurement literature serves to promote the idea that assessing the QOL of people with intellectual disabilities can have nothing but positive outcomes. The exercise may, perhaps, be of some value — at least to the extent that it offers a normatively silenced group the opportunity to comment on matters that may be of some importance to them. However, balanced against this is the very real possibility that the administration of such measures is not experienced as the well-meaning and solicitous enquiry after happiness that it is promoted as being[12], but rather is experienced as threatening and unpleasant; as an encounter approximating interrogation.

In the extract below, taken from the opening moments of the administration of the *QOL.Q*, Arthur — whose quality of life was being measured as part of an audit of the residential service in which he lives — makes *his* understanding of the nature of the questioning to come explicit. In Line 3 (arrowed) Arthur's question about the 'hardness' of the questions he is to be asked would seem to suggest that, for him, this encounter is not a cosy chat about his happiness, but is instead another test.

Extract 1: Code: CA/KK/CD (From Rapley and Antaki, 1996)[13]

1	I	erm (...) and I'd ↑like you to ↑answer some questio::ns to tell me how you
2		feel about the ⌈(unintell)
3→	AR	⌊they're not 'ard ones are they (.)
4	I	not very⌈hard
5	AR	⌊no:o
6	I	no (.) and ↑if you don't understand ↓them Arthur you can just tell me (.)
7	AR	yeus

8	I	and I'll I'll say them differently (.)
9	AR	ym
10	I	↑ok? (.) erm (...) let's °see (wharr) else° ↑erm (...) ↑there's no right or
11		wrong answers ↑Arthur↓ (.)
12	AR	mm
13	I	it's just to tell me how you ↓feel about ↑things
14	AR	m↑yes
15	I	allright? and we (.) we can take as ↑long as time as you ↓need↑
16	AR	↓ye:hm↑=
17	I	so there's no ↓hurry ⌈(..) °do you have any° ↓ques↑tions? (.)
18		⌊(paper shuffling)
19	I	to ↓ask ↑me?
20	AR	ye: ↑e:r↓:::s
21	I	what would you like to ↓ask me
22→	AR	I ↑like being I like being er (..) in 'ere (.)
23	I	you ↑like being =
24→	AR	(living) in 'ere like I like living in 'ere

That the reassurances offered by the interviewer (in lines 5–17) are not heard as such, and that he understands that his test results may be used by other people to inform decisions affecting the quality of his life, is made clear in lines 22 and 24. Rather than 'asking a question' as invited by his interviewer (ll. 17–21), Arthur uses the opportunity to make very clear, at the outset of the interview, that he is happy living where he is. Leaving no room for uncertainty on the interviewer's part, he repeats 'I like living in 'ere' three times. Why might this be? It is, I think, hard to avoid reading this exchange as other than a worried Arthur taking pains to state his understanding of the encounter. He knows, he is telling us, that his answers to a set of test questions are highly consequential. He is aware that his continued residence in his house is on the line. He fears that the likely upshot of a poor performance is being relocated. 'I like living in 'ere', then, may be heard as conveying that his 'quality of life' interview in some way scares him. Unfortunately, however, 'do you like living here' does not feature as a specified item on the questionnaire schedule, so this particular datum — despite its apparent importance to the quality of Arthur's life — must be disregarded in calculating his QOL score.

Talking quality of life
The formalised measurement of QOL is evidently readily understood, by people described as intellectually disabled, as a testing session. Furthermore, *by virtue of* the protocols of standardised psychometrics, formal measurement must ignore matters that are clearly of importance to interviewees. However, rather than approaching the quality of people's lives as a matter for psychometric rigour, if people with intellectual disabilities are themselves asked about the things that make a difference, a clear and repeatedly identified set of concerns (as Arthur has already shown us) eloquently emerge. Most of these concerns are, unfortunately, entirely unrepresented in official measures of QOL.

In Extract 2, taken from a series of unstructured interviews with people with intellectual disabilities about 'what is important in your life', Simon talks about his relationship with his partner, Tina, and her parents' interference in their lives.

Extract 2: (PK/SM/MR1997)

1	Simon:	Tina's not allowed to have a baby
2	Int:	She's not allowed to have a baby
3	Simon:	Tina's mum and dad said
4	Int:	They have said, OK, Tina's mum said
5	Simon:	They say it's not fair for the baby
6	Int:	Not fair for the baby. Is that because you have a handicap
7	Simon:	Yes. They not talk to us. They make up the mind for themselves
8	Int:	They didn't talk to you about it
9	Simon:	They told us after
10	Int:	Do you want to have children. Is it something you would like
11	Simon:	I can't have children. I've been fixed
12	Int:	You've had a vasectomy
13	Simon:	Yes
14	Int:	Whose idea was that
15→	Simon:	Tina's Mum. Tina's Mum. She said you 'can't have
16→		children because you're handicapped'

It is hard to know how, sensibly, one might go about expressing the detailed quality of Simon's fraught relationship with Tina's parents numerically. While it is easy to imagine a QOL questionnaire item called 'relationship with extended family' (perhaps with a five-point Likert scale anchored on 'good' and 'terrible') to measure this important variable, it is difficult to see how reporting Simon's experience as '5' could be anything but insulting. It is, further, surely to traduce the complexity of the narrative here — raising as it does issues of coerced sterilisation, explicit and non-negotiable parental control, and denial of adult sexuality, among others — to reduce Simon's experience to a set of scores. Not, of course, that existing QOL measures recognise matters such as coerced sterilisation as being relevant to the quality of a person's life.

Similarly, while measures like the *QOL.Q* attempt to take account of some of the organisational consequences of intellectual disability (staff decision-making and the like), any recognition of the effects on the quality of peoples' lives of having a discreditable, handicapped, identity is entirely absent from formalised measures of QOL. In Extract 2, Simon made it clear that he understood that the reason for his enforced sterilisation was *because he has an intellectual disability*: that his disqualification from control over matters he saw as central to the quality of his life was warranted by the fact of his identity as a disabled person. In Extract 3, again, humiliation and abuse feature prominently in Simon's account of the quality of his working life. His job is another site for degradation on account of his membership of a stigmatised category of persons: he is of 'a different sort'.

Extract 3: (PK/SM/MR97)

1→	Simon:	The supervisor made fun of me
2	Int:	He made fun of you
3	Simon:	He said never get a car licence, not me. I not pass
4	Int:	But you did
5	Simon:	Yes I did
6	Int:	Why do you think that is. Why do you think the
7		supervisors are like that
8 →	Simon:	They say us handicapped are a different sort
9	Int:	So if you're handicapped, you're not good enough to do
10		things
11	Simon:	Yes
12	Int:	What do you think of that
13	Simon:	It's not true

It is not difficult to recognise that the routine experience of humiliation, degradation and abuse by virtue of one's identity may have a negative effect on the quality of one's life. But, again, these everyday experiences, repeatedly identified by people with intellectual disabilities as diminishing the quality of their lives, do not feature in the calculations of the psy-complex. We are to take it, presumably, that these things do not really matter.

Conclusions

The quality of someone's life is, surely, best understood as a locally constructed, intersubjectively achieved, assessment of a set of highly individual circumstances. It is not a pre-existing construct-in-the-head of variable quantity. Whatever meaning the term 'quality of life' has is essentially socially produced, localised and contingent: such meaning is traduced by measurement. The psy-complex conceptualisation, operationalisation and measurement of QOL has, in contrast, treated QOL as a largely unproblematic, relatively static, cognitive component of persons. Current endeavours are then primarily conducted on (and in) the terms of the psy-complex/research establishment. The measurement of QOL overlooks both the essential arbitrariness (where they are not irrelevant) of the issues about which decisions are sought, and the forced nature of the 'choices' made on scales designed to quantify happiness. The instruments employed in the policing of happiness by the psy-complex thus produce a life of 'quality' by virtue of having a key to the door, belonging to a club or making some of one's own life decisions unaided by staff. That these happiness quanta often tend to underpin the status quo in service provision is merely, of course, an adventitious spin off. But in so doing these instruments exclude fundamental concerns raised by people with intellectual disabilities in discussion of issues affecting the quality of their lives. Existing 'Quality of life' measures ignore what might, naively, be thought to be at least marginally important matters. Unrecognised are such issues as:
- Enforced sterilisation,
- The denial of adulthood and the absence of opportunity for the exercise of power;
- The routine experience of stigma, belittlement and rejection;

- The routine denial of everyday competence by powerful others;
- The appreciation of 'having' an identity as 'disabled';
- A recognition that this identity matters, is done *in interaction with others*, and that the nature of these interactions is inseparable from the 'quality' of a life.

What intellectual disability often means then — as Kathleen's observation at the start of the chapter reminds us — is a life not of quality, but of mockery and marginalisation. If the psy-complex is to take the quality of the lives of people with intellectual disabilities seriously, then perhaps concerns such as these represent a place to start.

Acknowledgement
Many thanks to Susan Hansen for her critical reading of earlier versions of this chapter.

References
Antaki, C. and Rapley, M. (1996a) Questions and answers to psychological assessment schedules: Hidden troubles in 'Quality of Life' interviews. *Journal of Intellectual Disability Research*, 40, 5, 421–37

Antaki, C. and Rapley, M. (1996b) 'Quality of Life' talk: The liberal paradox of psychological testing. *Discourse and Society*, 7, 3, 293–316

Baldwin, S., Godfrey, C. and Propper, C. (eds.) (1990) *Quality of Life: Perspectives and Policies*. London: Routledge

Boyle, M. (1990) *Schizophrenia: A Scientific Delusion?* London: Routledge

Burman, E. (Ed.) (1990) *Feminists and Psychological Practice*. London: Sage

Cummins, R. A. (1996) The domains of life satisfaction: An attempt to order chaos. *Social Indicators Research*, 38, 303–32

Cummins, R. A. (1997) *Comprehensive Quality of Life Scale — Intellectual/Cognitive Disability, 5th edition: Manual*. Melbourne, School of Psychology, Deakin University

Edwards, D. (1997) *Discourse and Cognition*. London: Sage

Edwards, D., Ashmore, M., and Potter, J. (1995) Death and Furniture: The rhetoric, politics, and theology of bottom line arguments against relativism. *History of the Human Sciences*, 8, 2, 25–49

Fairclough, N. (1993) Critical Discourse Analysis and the marketisation of public discourse: The universities. *Discourse and Society*, 4, 133–59

Felce, D. and Perry, J. (1993.) *Quality of Life: A contribution to its definition and measurement*. Mental Handicap in Wales — Applied Research Unit, University of Wales College of Medicine

Heal, L.W. and Sigelman, C.K. (1990) Methodological issues in measuring the Quality of Life of individuals with mental retardation. In, R.L. Schalock (ed.) *Quality of Life: Perspectives and Issues*. Washington, D.C: American Association on Mental Retardation

Hopkins, N., Reicher, S., and Levine, M. (1997) On the parallels between social cognition and the 'new racism'. *British Journal of Social Psychology*, 37, 305–29

Houtkoop-Steenstra, H. (2000) *Interaction and the Standardised Interview: The Living Questionnaire*. Cambridge: Cambridge University Press

Hughes, C., Hwang, B., Kim, J.H., Eisenman, L.T. and Kilian, D.J. (1995) Quality of Life in applied research: A review and analysis of empirical measures. *American Journal on Mental Retardation*, 99, 623–41

Kaasa, S., Malt, U., Hagen, S., Wist, E., Moum, T. and Kvikstad, A. (1993) Psychological distress in cancer-patients with advanced disease. *Radiotherapy and Oncology*, 27, 193–197

McHoul, A. and Rapley, M. (2000) Sacks and (Clinical) Psychology: *Clinical Psychology Forum*. 142, 3–11

Newnes, C., Holmes, G. and Dunn, C. (eds) (1999) *This is Madness: A critical look at psychiatry and the future of mental health services*. Ross-on-Wye: PCCS Books

Perry, J. and Felce, D. (1995) Objective assessments of Quality of Life: How much do they agree with each other? *Journal of Community and Applied Social Psychology*, 5, 1–21

Potter, J. (1996) *Representing Reality: Discourse, Rhetoric and Social Construction*. London: Sage

Potter, J. and Wetherell, M. (1987) *Discourse and social psychology: Beyond attitudes and behaviour*. London: Sage

Rapley, M., and Antaki, C. (1996) A conversation analysis of the 'acquiescence' of people with learning disabilities. *Journal of Community and Applied Social Psychology*, 6, 207–27

Rapley, M. and Antaki, C. (1998) 'What do you think about...': generating views in an interview. *Text,* 18, 4, 587–608

Rapley, M. and Ridgway, J. (1998) 'Quality of Life' talk and the corporatisation of intellectual disability. *Disability and Society*, 13, 3, 451–71

Rapley, M., Kiernan, P. and Antaki, C. (1998) Invisible to themselves or negotiating identity? The interactional management of 'being intellectually disabled'. *Disability and Society,* 13, 5, 807–28

Revicki, D. A., Wu, A. W. and Murray M. I., (1995) Change in clinical status, health-status, and health utility outcomes in HIV-infected patients. *Medical Care*, 33,173–82

Rose, N. (1985) *The Psychological Complex: Psychology, Politics and Society in England 1869–1939*. London: Routledge and Kegan Paul

Rose, N. (1990) *Governing the Soul: The Shaping of the Private Self*. London: Routledge

Schalock, R.L. (1990) Attempts to conceptualise and measure Quality of Life. In R.L. Schalock (ed.) *Quality of Life: Perspectives and Issues*. Washington, D.C: American Association on Mental Retardation

Schalock, R. L. and Keith, K. (1993) *Quality of Life Questionnaire*. Worthington, OH. IDS Publishing Corporation

Schalock, R.L., Keith, K.D., and Hoffman, K. (1990) *Quality of Life Questionnaire: Standardization Manual*. Hastings: NE. Mid-Nebraska Mental Retardation Services

Swales, J. M. and Rogers, P. S. (1995) Discourse and the projection of corporate culture: the Mission Statement. *Discourse and Society*, 6, 223–42

Swales, T. P., Findling, R. L., Friedman, L., Kenny, J. T., Cola, D. and Schulz, S. C. (1995) Quality-of-life in adolescents with schizophrenia. *Schizophrenia Research*, 15, 221

Taylor, S.J. (1994) In support of research on Quality of Life, but against QOL. In D.Goode, (Ed.) *Quality of Life for Persons with Disabilities: International Perspectives and Issues*. Cambridge, MA: Brookline Books

Todd, S., and Shearn, J. (1995) *Family secrets and dilemmas of status: Parental management of the disclosure of 'learning disability'*. Cardiff: Welsh Centre for Learning Disabilities – Applied Research Unit

Todd, S., and Shearn, J. (1997) Family dilemmas and secrets: Parents' disclosure of information to their adult offspring with learning disabilities. *Disability and Society*, 12, 3, 341–66

Wolfensberger, W. (1994) Let's Hang Up 'Quality of Life' as a Hopeless Term. In Goode, D. (Ed.) (1994) *Quality of Life for Persons with Disabilities: International perspectives and issues.* Cambridge, MA: Brookline Books

Notes

[1] A discourse can be understood as an organised way of speaking of some aspect of experience. Potter and Wetherell (1987) describe discourses as 'interpretative repertoires': constellations of grammatically and semantically coherent terms which collectively provide particular interpretations or descriptions of the way the world is. A clear and problematic example is the use of medical discourse (with its talk of 'signs', 'symptoms' and 'illness') to describe psychological distress.

[2] See McHoul and Rapley (2000) for a more extended discussion of the problems entailed by the fetish for quantification in psychology.

[3] The term 'psy-complex' refers to all those professions associated with 'mental health' and may be read as synonymous with the term 'psychiatry' in Newnes, Holmes and Dunn (1999).

[4] See, for example, Potter (1996), Edwards (1997), Houtkoop-Steenstra (2000), Edwards, Ashmore and Potter (1995) for general discussion of the issues and Antaki and Rapley (1996a; b) for a detailed analysis of a specific QOL measure.

[5] The continuing succour to racism offered by the standard methodological commitments and practices of psychology is an obvious example (see Hopkins, Reicher and Levine, 1997). Burman (1990) and other feminist writers have also drawn attention to the deleterious consequences of the psychological project of quantifying and measuring 'sex-differences'.

[6] See Rapley and Antaki (1996) for an examination of the notion of the 'acquiescence bias' of people with intellectual disabilities.

[7] See, for example, Fairclough (1993) for an analysis of the marketing of 'educational quality' in universities; Swales and Rogers (1995) for analysis of the 'mission statements' of American companies; and Rapley and Ridgway (1998) on the relationship between notions of quality in economic rationalist discourse and in intellectual disability research and policy.

[8] The *QOL.Q* is a 40-item questionnaire which measures both objective circumstances and subjective perceptions of satisfaction with life in terms of four factors: (Satisfaction; Competence/Productivity; Social Belonging and Empowerment/Independence). The *ComQol-ID* is a psychometrically more complex instrument which also measures objective circumstances and subjective perceptions of satisfaction in seven areas (Material well-being, Health, Productivity, Intimacy, Safety, Place in community and Emotional well-being) but provides for the subjective weighting of objective factors by their level of importance to the individual. Broadly speaking the *QOL.Q* can be said to measure how happy people are in normalisation-congruent service settings, whereas the *ComQol-ID* provides for a direct comparison of (aspects of) life satisfaction between people with an intellectual disability and 'normals'.

[9] While standard psy-complex practices of describing persons with an intellectual disability as 'having a QOL score of 73', or of calculating that the 'mean QOL score of group home *x* is 77.5', seem discursively unproblematic, one wonders how middle class professionals would take to describing their own satisfaction

with the world in such terms. 'My QOL today is 73.75' is, of course, an outlandish formulation.

[10] Amusingly, there is some evidence to suggest that if ordinary people are asked to define 'Quality of Life' by researchers they do not understand the question. See Rapley and Antaki (1998).

[11] Perhaps the most widely recognised definition is that by Felce and Perry (1993, p13) viz. 'Quality of life is defined as an overall general well-being which comprises objective descriptors and subjective evaluations of physical, material, social and emotional well-being together with the extent of personal development and purposeful activity all weighted by a personal set of values'

[12] The *QOL.Q*, for example, explicitly enjoins its administrators to adopt a relaxed and conversational approach.

[13] Extracts are transcriptions of audiotaped interviews. Transcription conventions for extract 1 are those developed by Gail Jefferson. Other extracts employ a simplified transcription.

CHAPTER 5

What people need to know about the drug treatment of children

PETER R. BREGGIN, M.D.

IN THE UNITED STATES, non-medical therapists—especially psychologists and counsellors—play a pivotal role in decisions about the appropriateness of prescribing stimulant medication to children. Advocates of stimulant medication frequently try to 'educate' school mental health professionals to make them more enthusiastic about diagnosing Attention Deficit/ Hyperactivity Disorder (ADHD) and encouraging medication.

In North America, a giant social experiment is being carried out. A large proportion of school age children are being given psychoactive medications to control their behaviour. One recent study of several school districts disclosed that 7 per cent of children were being given stimulant drugs by the school itself each day and another found that 10% of children were receiving stimulants at home and school (Marshall, 2000). Yet another study has shown a three-fold increase in the drugging of preschool toddlers with stimulants (Zito *et al.* 2000). No official statistics on prescription drug use are kept in the United States, but probably at least 5–6 million of 50 million school age children are taking stimulant drugs, while another million at least are taking other drugs as well.

In addition to stimulants children are commonly given multiple psychiatric drugs. Often the stimulant drug is the gateway drug to others. After being put on methylphenidate (Ritalin) or amphetamine (Adderall, Dexedrine), the child develops adverse drug reactions that are mistaken for a worsening of the child's 'mental disorder'. If the child becomes depressed, as commonly occurs on stimulants, an antidepressant is added. If the child becomes manic or psychotic, a mood stabilizer or an antipsychotic drug is added. Often these drugs have not been approved for children by the U.S. Food and Drug Administration. Sometimes they haven't even been approved for psychiatric purposes at all[1].

Drug advocates in North America have become fond of observing, 'Your child's depression has emerged under drug treatment' or 'The medication brought out your child's underlying bipolar disorder.' In fact, the drugs

Footnote [1] overleaf

themselves are causing severe disorders in millions of children in the United States.

Meanwhile, as the children's market becomes saturated in North America, drug company marketing and drug advocates are turning their attention to Europe and Australia. As a result, England and Australia in particular are noticing a rise of the use of drugs in treating children.

Often this escalation of drugs takes place in the complete absence of any psychosocial interventions, such as family counselling and therapy, or an improved educational programme. Often the parents and the teachers mistakenly believe that the child suffers from a 'biochemical imbalance' or 'crossed wires in the head', so that psychosocial interventions are viewed as irrelevant or ineffective compared to medication.

Most recommendations for stimulant drugs in the United States originate from schools. School psychologists and counsellors are in particular need of a more thorough understanding of the mechanism of action of stimulants, as well as their many adverse effects. Until recently, most of the information has been generated by individuals with strong vested interests in what may be called the ADHD/stimulant lobby.

Drawing largely on double-blind placebo-controlled clinical trials and on animal laboratory research, I will focus on the emotional and behavioural effects of dextroamphetamine (e.g., Dexedrine, Adderall), methamphetamine (Desoxyn, Gradumet), and methylphenidate (Ritalin). Emphasis will be placed on two relatively ignored areas: the mechanism of action that enforces specific behaviours, and adverse drug effects on the central nervous system, mental life, and behaviour of the child. An overview of all adverse reactions will also be provided.

The mechanism of action: effects on animals

Stimulant drugs lend themselves readily to suppressing behaviours that are unwanted in the classroom or family situations, and for enforcing obsessive-compulsive behaviours that adults desire in the classroom or the family. Animals, like children, have spontaneous tendencies to move about, to explore, to innovate, to play, to exercise, and to socialize. Dozens of studies have shown that stimulant drugs suppress all of these spontaneous tendencies, sometimes completely inhibiting them (reviewed in Breggin, 1998; 1999b,c). In effect, the animals lose their 'vitality' or 'spirit'. They become more docile and manageable.

Animals, like children, resist boring, routine, rôte, or meaningless tasks. As documented in dozens of laboratory studies, stimulant drugs enforce these behaviours in animals, producing what is called *stereotypy* or *perseveration* in animal research. In human research it is called obsessive-compulsive or over-focused behaviour. For example, instead of struggling to escape a cage, the animal will sit relatively still, carrying on rôte, useless

---

[1] In November 1998 I was invited by the National Institutes of Health (NIH) to be the scientific expert on 'Risks and Mechanism of Action of Stimulant Drugs' at the 'Consensus Development Conference on ADHD and its Treatment.' This led to the publication of extensive reviews on the mechanism of action and adverse reactions of stimulant drugs (Breggin, 1999a, b, c). These sources can provide the reader with more detailed information and additional citations to the literature.

behaviours, such as compulsive grooming, chewing on its paws, or staring into the corner. If the drugged animal does move about, it will pace a constricted area in a purposeless manner.

In summary, in animals, stimulant drugs (1) suppress spontaneous and social behaviours, rendering them more submissive and manageable, and (2) enforce perseveration or obsessive-compulsive over-focusing.

The mechanism of action: emotional and behavioral effects on children
The effects of stimulants on children are identical to those in animals. This is not surprising since the basic biochemical or neurological impact is the same. Similarly, the effects on children are the same regardless of the child's mental state or diagnosis.

Drawing on double-blind studies (Breggin, 1999b,c), Table 1 lists the adverse drug reactions (ADRs) of stimulant drugs that lend themselves to being easily mistaken for improvement in the child. The chart is divided into three categories of stimulant ADRs: (1) obsessive-compulsive ADRs, such as over-focusing, cognitive perseveration, inflexibility of thinking, and stereotypical activities; (2) social withdrawal ADRs, such as social withdrawal and isolation, reduced social interactions and responsiveness, and reduced play; and (3) behaviourally suppressive ADRs, such as compliance, reduced curiosity, reduced spontaneity, and behaviours that are subdued, depressed, apathetic, lethargic, and bland. Some studies have shown that most children become sad and unhappy, lethargic, and disinterested in others while taking stimulant drugs.

Stimulants commonly cause obsessive-compulsive behaviours, including over-focusing, that are similar to stereotypy in animals. In one study involving a single small dose of methylphenidate on the day of the experiment, over-focusing in 42% of children was disclosed. Another found that 25% of children on methylphenidate developed obsessive-compulsive ADRs. A thorough study of the subject found that 51% of children taking methylphenidate and dextroamphetamine developed obsessive-compulsive ADRs. Some children exhausted themselves raking leaves or playing the same game over and over again. The authors of these and related studies note that these behaviours are sometimes considered improvements in the classroom.

More extreme emotional and behavioural effects
Swanson *et al.* (1992) reviewed 'cognitive toxicity' produced by methylphenidate. They summarized the more extreme effects on children:

> *In some disruptive children, drug-induced compliant behavior may be accompanied by isolated, withdrawn, and overfocused behavior. Some medicated children may seem 'zombie-like' and high doses which make ADHD children more 'somber', 'quiet' and 'still' may produce social isolation by increasing 'time spent alone' and decreasing 'time spent in positive interaction' on the playground.* (Swanson et al., 1992, p.15)

Arnold and Jensen (1995) also comment on the 'zombie' effect caused by stimulants:

> *The amphetamine look, a pinched, somber expression, is harmless in*

itself but worrisome to parents, who can be reassured. If it becomes too serious, a different stimulant may be more tolerable. The behavioral equivalent, the 'zombie' constriction of affect and spontaneity, may respond to a reduction of dosage, but sometimes necessitates a change of drug. (p.2307)

The 'zombie' effect is mentioned by a number of other investigators. It is a more extreme manifestation of the supposedly 'therapeutic' effect that makes a child more compliant, docile, and easier to manage. When a child seems more compliant in class or seems to attend more readily to boring, rôte activities, the child is experiencing an adverse drug reaction. The seeming 'improvement' is an expression of a continuum of drug toxicity with the zombie effect at one extreme. The toxicity is considered 'therapeutic' unless it becomes so extreme that the child seems bizarre or disabled.

Excitatory adverse effects
As already described in detail, routine stimulant doses given to children or adults commonly cause ADRs that seem paradoxical, such as depression, lethargy, and apathy (see Tables 1 and 2).

Stimulants also cause more classic signs of over-stimulation or excitation, such as anxiety, agitation, aggression, and insomnia, as well as manic psychoses and seizures. Often the stimulant ADRs occur in combination with the more suppressive effects, as in a mixture of agitation and depression. Frequently stimulants cause tachycardia and cardiac arrhythmias, and can even weaken heart muscle. The U.S. Food and Drug Administration has received many reports of methylphenidate-induced heart attack.

The overall list of stimulant ADRs is much too extensive for inclusion in this paper. Table 2 draws on several independent sources to present an overview (Breggin, 1999a: c). Many doctors seem unaware of the varied nature of stimulant ADRs. Often they mistake these drug reactions for the surfacing of new psychiatric disorders in the child and mistakenly increase the dose or add further medications, instead of stopping the stimulants.

Gross and irreversible brain dysfunction
In addition to the many serious central nervous system ADRs that are apparent in the child's behaviour, stimulants also cause gross brain dysfunction. Methylphenidate (Ritalin), for example, in routine doses causes a 23%–30% drop in blood flow to the brain in volunteers. All stimulants directly disrupt at least three neurotransmitter systems (dopamine, norepinephrine, and serotonin). There is strong evidence that stimulant-induced biochemical changes in the brain can become irreversible. In regard to amphetamine and methamphetamine, research demonstrates that clinical doses can lead to loss of receptors and cause cell death (for example, Melega *et al.* 1997a, b). A study by Nasrallah and others (Nasrallah *et al.* 1986) demonstrated that adults develop atrophy of the brain after being treated with stimulants as children.

Through a combination of anorexia and disruption of growth hormone, stimulants also inhibit growth, including the growth of the brain. Bathing a child's growing brain in toxic chemicals must ultimately impair its development.

Stimulants are highly addictive. The U.S. Drug Enforcement Administration and the International Narcotics Control Board place methylphenidate, amphetamine, and methamphetamine into Schedule II along with cocaine and morphine as the most addictive drugs used in medicine. Recent studies indicate that children who are treated with Ritalin will have a higher rate of stimulant addiction (including cocaine) as young adults (Lambert and Hartsough, 1998). The DEA and the International Narcotics Control Board have both issued warnings about the danger of widespread stimulant prescription in North America. The United States uses 90% of the world's methylphenidate.

Typical of addictive drugs, stimulants often cause withdrawal or rebound. Rebound commonly occurs after only one or two doses in normal children, and it can last many hours and even days. During rebound, the child's original ADHD-like symptoms may become worse than before the drug was ever taken. Even when children do not become addicted to stimulants, they often give them away or sell them to friends who abuse them. Stimulants commonly cause tics and other abnormal movements, and sometimes these become irreversible. Often the tics occur along with obsessive-compulsive symptoms. Too often, drug-induced ADRs lead mistakenly to the prescription of other psychiatric drugs rather than to the termination of the stimulant.

ADHD and the rationalization of stimulant effectiveness

The concept of ADHD was developed to rationalize a pre-existing motivation within medicine and psychology to use stimulant drugs to control the behaviour of children. From the beginning, the focus was on classroom settings in which one-to-one attention was unavailable. ADHD as a diagnosis evolved as a list of various behaviours that make classroom control more difficult and that require attention from teachers or other adults. Almost any behaviour that tries a teacher's ability or patience, or drains a teacher's energy and attention, has been put into the diagnosis. The official criteria for ADHD in the *Diagnostic and Statistical Manual of Mental Disorders, IV* (American Psychiatric Association,1994) are thus behaviours that interfere with an orderly, quiet, controlled classroom. The first criterion under *hyperactivity* is 'often fidgets with hands or feet or squirms in seat' and the second is 'often leaves seat in classroom or in other situations in which remaining seating is expected'. The first criterion under *impulsivity* is 'often blurts out answers before questions have been completed' and the second is 'often has difficulty awaiting turn'. Under *inattention* the first criterion is 'often fails to give close attention to details or makes careless mistakes in schoolwork, work, and other activities'.

None of the ADHD criteria are relevant to how the child feels. Mental and emotional states, such as anxiety or depression, are not included.

All of the behaviours in the ADHD diagnosis are commonly displayed by children in groups where they feel frustrated, anxious, bored, or abandoned. Individually, each of the behaviours represents normal developmental stages. Of course, the behaviours can become exaggerated. A child can become extremely hyperactive, impulsive, or inattentive. These behaviours, even when extreme, do not constitute a syndrome — a consistent pattern of symptoms related to a specific cause. Instead, they reflect a normal child's response to varying kinds of severe stressors.

Talking Back to Ritalin (Breggin, 1998) catalogues dozens of 'causes' for ADHD-like behaviour. Most commonly, the behaviours are displayed by a normal child faced with boredom, frustration, fear, or some other kind of stress. The child may be suffering from physical or emotional abuse, lacking in parental discipline, or witnessing conflict in the home. Sometimes the child is too far behind in class, sometimes too far ahead of class. Invariably, the child is in need of special attention that is not being provided. More rarely, the child may be suffering from a genuine physical disorder, such as a head injury or thyroid disorder, that requires special medical attention rather than stimulant medication.

However, whatever the case, no good comes from applying the fraudulent diagnosis ADHD. Each child needs to be evaluated individually in the context of the family, school, and community, and each child needs improved relationships with parents, teachers, and other adults.

ADHD as conflict

ADHD-like behaviours in a child almost always indicate a *conflict* between the child and adults in the child's life, especially adult expectations for submissive, conforming, or compliant behaviour. When we diagnose the child, we simply blame the weakest member of the conflict.

Instead of leading to diagnosis of the child, ADHD-like behaviours in children should focus attention on the need for changes in the behaviour of the adults in the conflict. The seemingly exaggerated hyperactivity, impulsivity, or lack of attentiveness in the child can and should become a signal for the adults to find, identify, and respond to the child's genuine needs for rational discipline, unconditional love, play, exercise, and engaging education.

An effective teacher or parent in reality does what I am suggesting. He or she uses signs of hyperactivity, impulsivity and inattention in a youngster to indicate the need for greater, more focused adult attention on the child's needs.

Stimulant drugs, as we have seen, flatten the child's behavioural signal system. The child literally becomes *neurologically unable* to express feelings of boredom, frustration, distress, or discomfort. The child becomes too neurologically impaired to display hyperactivity, impulsivity, or inattention. Adults can then feel justified in teaching the class or managing the group without attending to the child's individual and often varied needs.

Evidence for ineffectiveness

Reviews by stimulant drug advocates routinely demonstrate that stimulants have no positive long-term effects whatsoever on any aspect of a child's behaviour. In the short-term (a few weeks or months) they can suppress behaviour, but they do not improve academic performance or learning. Based on the most extensive review in the literature, Swanson (1993, p.44) concluded:

• *Long-term beneficial effects have not been verified by research.*

• *Short-term effects of stimulants should not be considered a permanent solution to chronic ADHD symptoms.*

• *Stimulant medication may improve learning in some cases but impair learning in others.*

• *In practice, prescribed doses of stimulants may be too high for optimal effects on learning [to be achieved] and the length of action of most stimulants is viewed as too short to affect academic achievement.*

Swanson (1993, p.46) also summarized: 'No large effects on skills or higher order processes': teachers and parents should not expect significantly improved reading or athletic skills, positive social skills, or learning of new concepts. Defining short-term as 7–18 weeks, Swanson declared: 'No improvement in long-term adjustment': teachers and parents should not expect long-term improvement in academic achievement or reduced antisocial behaviour.

Similarly, Popper and Steingard (1994) state: 'Stimulants do not produce lasting improvements in aggressivity, conduct disorder, criminality, education achievement, job functioning, marital relationships, or long-term adjustment' (p.745).

Richters *et al.* (1995), from the National Institute of Mental Health (NIMH), conclude: 'the long-term efficacy of stimulant medication has not been demonstrated for *any* domain of child functioning.' They conclude that there is no evidence for even short-term positive effects on academic performance.

More recently, the National Institute of Mental Health (NIMH) conducted a giant six-centre fourteen month study in North America that purported to show that stimulant drugs are superior to other methods of treatment (MTA, 1999). The research failed to meet the two most basic scientific criteria for clinical trials; it lacked both a double-blind and placebo controls. It was essentially a giant impressionistic study conducted by highly biased investigators. Yet a careful analysis of the data still disclosed that stimulants offer no advantage to children in any aspect of their behaviour or the psychosocial development (Breggin, 2000b).

Conclusion

Stimulant drugs have two basic effects on animals and children regardless of their mental status. First, stimulants reduce all spontaneous and social behaviour. This makes the child more docile, submissive, and manageable. Drug advocates call this compliance. Second, stimulants enforce perseverative, obsessive-compulsive, or over-focused behaviour. This makes it easier to force the child to do rôte, boring activities. These twin *toxic* effects are readily misinterpreted as improved behaviour in highly structured or controlled environments where children are given insufficient or inappropriate attention, and where their genuine needs are being ignored. As a result of toxicity, stimulants suppress a child's behaviour in a global fashion that has nothing to do with any diagnosis or disorder.

Stimulant drugs also produce a wide variety of other adverse effects. By causing anorexia and by disrupting growth hormone, they suppress the growth of the body, including brain size and development. They cause severe biochemical imbalances in the developing brain that can become permanent. They often worsen ADHD-like symptoms and can cause psychoses.

The ADHD diagnosis is tailored to justify the use of stimulants for the behavioural control of children, especially in groups where they receive insufficient or inconsistent attention from adults. When children do become hyperactive, inattentive, and impulsive in an extreme fashion, it should be taken as a sign that they need more rational and caring attention from adults.

By suppressing emotional and behavioural signals of distress and conflict, stimulants allow adults to ignore the needs of children in favour of creating a controlled environment. Meanwhile, stimulants do not improve academic performance and provide no long-term improvement in *any* aspect of a child's behaviour or life.

The massive drugging of children in North America does not indicate that increasing numbers of children have mental disorders. Instead, it reflects on social conditions within the United States and Canada. Above all else, it indicates a willingness to subdue children as a substitute for identifying and meeting their genuine needs for improved family and school life.

In May, 2000, however, some of America's most powerful attorneys began a series of fraud and class action suits against the manufacturer of Ritalin, Novartis. The suits charge Novartis with conspiring to fraudulently over-promote the ADHD diagnosis and Ritalin treatment. The American Psychiatric Association and CHADD, a parents' group that has drug company support, are named as co-conspirators. The suits are being taken seriously because they are being brought by attorneys with great resources, determination, and experience—the same attorneys who successfully took on the tobacco industry in the United States. They are planning a decisive legal assault on the drugging of America's children. I helped to formulate these law suits which were inspired by *Talking Back to Ritalin* (Breggin, 1998) (These developing legal events are described on www.breggin.com)

It is not certain what impact these class action and fraud suits will have on countries other than the United States. On the one hand, such a vast array of legal power is likely to make drug companies and doctors more cautious about their claims for ADHD and Ritalin. On the other hand, the American suits may drive the drug companies to expand their markets in Europe and elsewhere outside North America. The National Institute for Clinical Excellence (NICE) has for example, recently given its approval to the use of Ritalin in Britain.

Professionals must be prepared to stand up and be counted in opposition to the drugging of children for behavioural control. Psychologists, counsellors, and therapists should strongly discourage the use of stimulant drugs for treating 'ADHD' and other emotional or behavioural problems that surface in the classroom or in the home. Instead, more effort should be made to identify and to address the genuine individual needs of the children in our families and schools.

**Table 1: Stimulant Adverse Drug Reactions (ADRs) Potentially
Misidentified as 'Therapeutic' or 'Beneficial' for Children
Diagnosed with ADHD**

Obsessive Compulsive ADRs	Social Withdrawal ADRs	Behaviourally Suppressive ADRs
Stereotypical activities Obsessive-compulsive behaviour Perseverative behaviour Cognitive perseveration Inflexibility of thinking Over-focusing or excessive focusing	Social withdrawal and isolation General dampening of social behaviour Reduced social interactions, talking or sociability Decreased responsiveness to parents and other children Increased solitary play Diminished play	Compliance, especially in structured environments Reduced curiosity Sombre Subdued Apathetic; lethargic: tired, withdrawn, listless, depressed, dopey, dazed, subdued and inactive Bland, emotionally flat Depressed, sad, easy or frequent crying Little or no initiative or spontaneity Diminished curiosity, surprise or pleasure Humourless, not smiling Drowsiness Social inhibition with passive and submissive

From Breggin (1999b), reprinted by permission of Springer Publishing Co.
(Citations omitted.)

Table 2: Summary of Adverse Drug Reactions (ADRs) Caused by Methylphenidate and Amphetamines

Cardio-Vascular	Central Nervous System	Gastro-intestinal	Endocrine or Metabolic	Other	With-drawal and Rebound
Palpitations Tachycardia Hypertension Arrhythmia Chest pain Cardiac arrest	Psychosis with hallucinations Depression and mania Hostility and aggression Withdrawal, decreased social interest, apathy Excessive brain stimulation with convulsions Insomnia Agitation, anxiety Impaired cognition Dyskinesias, tics, Tourette's Nervous habits (e.g., picking at skin, pulling hair) Compulsions Zombie-like behaviour	Anorexia Nausea Vomiting Stomach ache, cramps Dry mouth Constipation Abnormal Liver function tests Bad taste Diarrhoea	Pituitary dysfunction, including growth hormone and prolactin disruption Weight loss Growth suppression Disturbed sexual function	Blurred vision Headache Dizziness Hyper-sensitivity reaction with rash, con-junctivitis or hives	Insomnia Evening crash Depression Overactivity and irritability Rebound worsening of ADHD-like symptoms

Modified from Breggin (1999a), reprinted by permission of Springer Publishing Co.

References

American Psychiatric Association (1994) *Diagnostic and statistical manual of mental disorders* (Fourth Edition). Washington, D.C.: APA

Arnold, L.E. and Jensen, P.S. (1995) Attention-deficit disorders. In H. I. Kaplan and B. Sadock (Eds.) *Comprehensive textbook of psychiatry* (Fourth Edition). Baltimore: Williams & Wilkins

Breggin, P. R. (1993) *Toxic Psychiatry: Drugs and electroconvulsive therapy: The truth and the better alternatives.* London: Fontana

Breggin, P. R. (1998) *Talking back to Ritalin.* Monroe, Maine: Common Courage Press

Breggin, P. R. (1999a) Psychostimulants in the treatment of children diagnosed with ADHD: Part I—Acute risks and psychological effects. *Ethical Human Sciences and Services, 1,* 13–34

Breggin, P. R. (1999b) Psychostimulants in the treatment of children diagnosed with ADHD: Part II—Adverse effects on brain and behaviour. *Ethical Human Sciences and Services, 1,* 213–41

Breggin, P .R. (1999c) Psychostimulants in the treatment of children diagnosed with ADHD: Risks and mechanism of action. *International Journal of Risk and Safety in Medicine, 12,* 3–35

Breggin, P. R. (2000a) *Reclaiming our children: A healing solution for a nation in crisis.* Cambridge, Massachusetts: Perseus Books.

Breggin, P. (2000b). The NIMH multimodal study of treatment for attention-deficit-hyperactivity disorder: A critical analysis. *International Journal of Risk & Safety in Medicine, 13,* 15–22

Breggin, P.R. and Cohen, D. (1999) *Your drug may be your problem: How and why to stop taking psychiatric medications.* Cambridge, Massachusetts: Perseus Books.

Lambert, N.M. and Hartsough, C.S. (1998). Prospective study of tobacco smoking and substance dependence among samples of ADHD and non-ADHD subjects. *Journal of Learning Disabilities 31,* 533–44

Marshall, E. (2000, August 4) Duke study faults overuse of stimulants for children. *Science, 289,* 721

Melega, W.P., Raleigh, M.J., Stout, D.B., Huang, S.C. and Phelps, M.E. (1997a) Ethological and 6-[18F]fluoro-L-DOPA-PET profiles of long-term vulnerability to chronic amphetamine. *Behavioural Brain Research, 84,* 258–68

Melega, W.P., Raleigh, M.J., Stout, D.B., Lacan, G., Huang, S.C. and Phelps, M.E. (1997b) Recovery of striatal dopamine function after acute amphetamine- and methamphetamine-induced neurotoxicity in the vervet monkey. *Brain Research, 766,* 113–20

MTA Cooperative Group. (1999) A 14-Month randomized clinical trial of treatment strategies for attention-deficit/hyperactivity disorder. *Archives of General Psychiatry, 56,* 1073–86

Nasrallah, H., Loney, J., Olson, S., McCalley-Whitters, M., Kramer, J. and Jacoby, C. (1986) Cortical atrophy in young adults with a history of hyperactivity in childhood. *Psychiatry Research 17,* 241–46

Popper, C.W. and Steingard, R.J. (1994) Disorders usually first diagnosed in infancy, childhood, or adolescence. In: R. Hales, S. Yudofsky and J. Talbott (Eds.) *The American Psychiatric Press textbook of psychiatry* (Second Edition). Washington, D.C.: APA

Richters, J.E., Arnold, L.E., Jensen, P.S., Abikoff, H., Conners, C.K., Greenhill, L.L., Hechtman, L, Hinshaw, S.P., Pelham, W.E. and Swanson, J.M. (1995) NIMH collaborative multisite multimodal treatment study of children with ADHD: I.

Background and rationale. *Journal of the American Academy of Child and Adolescent Psychiatry, 34,* 987–1000

Swanson, J.M. (1993, January 27-29) Medical intervention for children with attention deficit disorder. *Proceedings of the Forum on the Education of Children with Attention Deficit Disorder,* pp. 27–34. Washington, DC: U.S. Department of Education, Office of Special Education and Rehabilitation Services and Office of Special Education Programs, Division of Innovation and Development.

Swanson, J.M., Cantwell, D., Lerner, M., McBurnett, K., Pfiffner, L. and Kotkin, R. (1992) Treatment of ADHD: Beyond medication. *Beyond Behavior, 4, 1,* 13–16 and 18–22

Zito, J.M., Safer, D .J., dosReis, S., Gardner, J.F., Boles, J., and Lynch, F. (2000) Trends in the prescribing of psychotropic medications to preschoolers. *Journal of the American Medical Association, 283,* 1025–30

CHAPTER 6

The SSRI suicides

DAVID HEALY

THIS CHAPTER IS about the potential for inducing suicide inherent in a group of antidepressant drugs called the selective serotonin reuptake inhibitors (SSRIs) of which Prozac (fluoxetine), Seroxat (paroxetine) and Lustral (sertraline) are the best known. These drugs act to block the reuptake of the neurotransmitter serotonin into nerve endings. There is now a considerable body of evidence that while these drugs may be helpful for some people, they may be fatal for others. Despite this evidence, neither the companies concerned nor the regulators of medicines in Britain appear prepared to issue any warnings or encourage any monitoring of those who may be taking these drugs.

The SSRIs were developed in the mid-to-late 1970s, continuing through the 1980s. As part of their development programme, pharmaceutical companies gave SSRIs to healthy volunteers in what are called phase 1 studies. These studies are designed to test whether drugs can be safely given to human beings. In the case of the SSRIs, some of these studies were concerned with traditionally important safety issues such as the impact of the drugs on cardiac or respiratory functions. Others were concerned with mechanical issues such as the length of time the drug spent in the system, the means by which it was excreted and possible interactions with other drugs. Yet other studies will have been concerned with questions such as the impact of the drugs on bodily systems from neuroendocrine profiles to pupillary diameters. Astonishingly, none of these studies were designed to establish the behavioural toxicity of any of these compounds. In the course of these studies, an undetermined number of volunteers became agitated, a proportion of whom almost certainly became suicidal (MCA, 2000). Few of these phase 1 studies have been published and of those published none have included details of these reactions.

The agitated responses of healthy volunteers at the time may have been explained away in terms of the odd responses that are produced when drugs such as these are given to 'normal brains'. People who are depressed, it was probably argued, could be expected to respond differently. After all, these drugs were supposedly designed to treat depression and not to be given to non-depressed (normal) people.

However the SSRIs as it turned out were never effective for the kinds of melancholic depression that clinicians were treating in the 1960s and 1970s, that required hospitalisation. Initial trials of SSRIs in these patient populations showed that many such patients responded with marked agitation and that few got well on for example fluoxetine. Despite this, Prozac (fluoxetine) was launched in January 1988 in America for the treatment of depression and it came without warnings that it could make either the severely depressed, or those who were minimally depressed or simply stressed, agitated and suicidal. During the 1990s, this brand name has had all the prominence Valium once had. Prozac was marketed as non-addictive compared to the benzodiazepines and as safer in overdose than older antidepressants (Healy, 1997).

In February 1990, Teicher and colleagues (Teicher, Glod and Cole, 1990) reported an emergence of suicidality on Prozac. This report was followed by others (Hoover, 1990; King, *et al.*, 1991; Wirshing *et al.*, 1992; Dasgupta, 1990; Masand, Gupta and Dwan, 1991; Rothschild and Locke, 1991; Creaney, Murray and Healy, 1991). Many of these involved cases in which the problem emerged on exposure to the drug (challenge), cleared up when the drug was discontinued (dechallenge), and re-emerged on re-exposure (rechallenge). This is a widely accepted indicator of a strong causal link between a drug and some effect (Healy, Langmaack and Savage, 1999). The investigators were senior figures, including leading authorities on akathisia, a drug-induced state of restless dysphoria, which by then was seen as the primary mechanism whereby Prozac induced suicidality.

Eli Lilly, the makers of Prozac, responded by analysing their clinical trial database and claimed that this indicated that Prozac reduced rather than induced suicidal ideation (Beasley *et al.*, 1991). This analysis, covering 3,065 patients, had the appearance of scientific rigour. No mention was made of the fact that the 3,065 patients had been drawn from a trial database of over 26,000 patients, nor that within those trials analysed up to 5% of patients had dropped out for akathisia-like symptoms, nor that benzodiazepines were co-prescribed with fluoxetine to minimise drug-induced agitation, nor that some of the trials analysed had been rejected by the FDA for registration purposes (Beasley, 1994; Tollefson, 1999).

The Lilly response to criticisms that the methods used in their analysis were flawed (Healy, 1991) was dismissive (Beasley, 1991) but it has since become apparent that internally they had previously recognised just this. As of September 1990, Lilly scientists wrote: '[these] trials were not intended to address issue of suicidality' (Heiligenstein, 1990). While aspects of the problem were debated in mainstream journals and there was support for the possibility of treatment-emergent suicidality (Mann and Kapur, 1991; Power and Cowen, 1992), Lilly's analysis appeared to settle the question within academic circles. Whenever the issues were raised thereafter (Healy, 1994; Bond, 1998), they drew a swift response from Lilly (Nakielny, 1994; Beasley, 1998). Subsequent silence tells us nothing about how satisfactorily the issues had been addressed.

Akathisia emerged early as a problematic side-effect of psychotropic drugs leading to suicide (Healy and Savage, 1998). It is pernicious as the main complaints may be of strange feelings or impulses; these are liable to be regarded as evidence of the underlying problem unless clinicians are suitably suspicious (Van Putten, 1975; Van Puttten *et al.*, 1981). Until the advent of

Prozac, akathisia was only associated with major tranquillisers, where it was linked to suicide (Drake and Ehrlich, 1985) and suicide-homicide (Schulte, 1985). But in the case of these drugs, the patients at risk were largely closely supervised inpatients, who were on immobilising drug regimens that degraded their capacity to act.

Akathisia appeared in early studies with Prozac at a 25% rate (Lipinski *et al.*, 1989). Nevertheless, throughout the 1990s, Lilly's published view was that 'any association between this symptom [akathisia] and suicide is not proven', that there was no evidence that Prozac was more likely to lead to akathisia 'any more than other antidepressants' and that 'clinical trial data has failed to confirm the hypothesis that some patients treated with an antidepressant who develop akathisia experience treatment emergent suicidality' (Nakielny, 1994). What were primary care prescribers, many of whom would have had no education on or experience of akathisia, to make of these denials?

Cause and effect?

By 1994, over 160 American Prozac lawsuits had been filed, a number of which led to substantial settlements (Cornwell, 1996). As of October 1999, more than 2,000 Prozac-associated suicides were recorded on the FDA's ADR system, which is thought to capture 1–10% of serious adverse events. Of these over 500 had clear indicators of akathisia and in this sample there is an equal male-female suicide ratio unlike the normal 4 males to 1 female ratio (FDA). According to FDA statutes, indicators of possible causation even if there is no consensus on the issue should lead to warnings. In fact, although company monitors had from 1990 'assigned Yes, reasonably related on several reports', Lilly turned the burden of proof upside down by adopting a strategy of blaming the 'patient's disorder and not a causal relationship to Prozac' (Heiligenstein, 1990/1999): 'its in the disease not the drug' (Daniels, 1991/1999).

The academic community appeared not to recognise a problem here, even though some of the earliest clinical studies reporting problems had involved children being given Prozac for obsessive-compulsive disorder, i.e. who were not depressed (King *et al.*,1991). This oversight may have arisen because during this period, randomised clinical trials (RCTs) were actively portrayed by Lilly as a 'gold standard' as regards cause and effect linkage and Lilly's meta-analysis had apparently demonstrated that there was no linkage between Prozac and treatment-emergent suicidality.

RCTs are not the gold standard for determining cause and effect for adverse effects, for reasons outlined below. But as a further point, germane RCT evidence on the issue was not published. As of 1986, Lilly's clinical trial database was showing rates of 12.5/1000 patients attempting suicide on fluoxetine, versus 2.5/1000 patients on placebo and 3.8/1000 patients on reference antidepressants (Lilly, 1986). This data remained unpublished and unreported to the FDA. There are other unpublished collections of figures from clinical trials consistent with this finding. As of 1991, for instance, Pfizer's clinical trials of sertraline in major depressive disorder showed a relative risk of 1.9 for sertraline versus placebo (Healy, 2000b). An increased relative risk of 2.0 or greater is usually taken as indicating a cause for concern. In this case given that some suicidal patients are likely to have been made less suicidal by treatment, a figure of much less than 2.0 should indicate problems. In fact, there are two sets of published figures showing a relative risk for SSRIs compared to reference antidepressants greater than 2.0 (Kasper, 1997; Jick, Dean and Jick, 1995).

Epidemiological studies

Epidemiological studies are studies that survey large sections of a population. They may contribute on issues of drug-induced injury to estimates of frequency and risk. Few studies of this kind have been conducted to look at the question of antidepressants and suicide. There has been only one study relevant to the issue of SSRIs and suicide. This examined suicides associated with over 172,000 antidepressant scripts in British primary care and reported a relative risk of completed suicide on Prozac that was 2.1 times the risk for the reference antidepressant dothiepin, an older tricyclic antidepressant associated with a substantial risk of lethality in overdose (Jick, Dean and Jick, 1995).

The first point is what did not happen after publication of this study. It was easily replicable with a larger dataset but no other studies appeared. New drugs come to the marketplace in groups; one gets a set of SSRIs, rather than a set of diverse antidepressants. If the problems were class based, for which there was in fact evidence (Lane, 1998), no competing company would have any incentive to pursue the issue. The lack of any response to the Jick study suggests just such a situation.

Just as the Beasley meta-analysis could be undertaken, so can pharmaceutical companies also produce supportive 'epidemiological' studies. Lilly cite three. The first (Fava and Rosenbaum, 1991) was a prescription-event-monitoring rather than an epidemiological study, whose results re-analysed indicate that Prozac is 3 times more likely than placebo to induce suicidality (Teicher, Glod and Cole, 1993). The second (Warshaw and Keller, 1996) was a naturalistic prospective study of 654 anxious patients, in which the only suicide occurred on Prozac, undercutting claims that depression was the cause of the problem. The third was another prospective naturalistic study, instituted a decade before Prozac's launch in which only 185 patients got Prozac (Leon *et al.*,1999). It was not designed to detect this problem and its designers were mostly deceased at the time of this 'reanalysis'. All three studies, however, have been used as of 1999 to support claims that Prozac does not cause suicide.

In fact, despite company claims that Prozac was the most researched psychotropic drug in history, from Teicher's first reports, no new research to answer the questions raised by the early clinical studies was published. The lack of research for any SSRI in this area is comparable to the lack of research undertaken by tobacco companies on the hazards of smoking.

One way of minimising concerns about the Jick study (Jick, Dean and Jick, 1995) is to set its Prozac suicide figures (187/100,000 patient years — this cumbersome figure refers to the number of suicide attempts from a given number of patients extrapolated up to the figure that might be likely from one year's exposure to a drug) against conventional figures that depression produces suicide rates of 200–600/100,000 patient years. However these latter figures for depression were derived from studies of hospitalised patients. In fact as of 1995, no one knew what the suicide risk for primary care depressions was. There was reason to suspect that it had to be considerably lower than 187/100,000 patient years or else British annual suicide figures would not add up. It has since become clear from various sources, including an analysis of a database of half a million patients (2,500,000 patient years), that the suicide risk for primary care depressions in the United Kingdom cannot exceed 40/100,000 patient years (Boardman and Healy, 1999).

Lilly (Tollefson, 1997) cite a Swedish study as indicating a 79-fold increased suicide risk in depression compared to normal (790/100,000 patient years). This figure refers to hospitalised cases of depression. The figure from the same study for suicide risk in non-hospitalised depressions was 0/100,000 patient years (Hagnell, Lanke and Rorsman, 1981). If the figure for primary care depressions does not differ substantially from the general population figure, the Jick study suggests a risk that unmonitored treatment with Prozac will increase suicide risk to something like the same extent that cigarette smoking increases the risk of lung cancer (a 10-fold increase in risk). But the impact of treatment cannot be monitored properly if physicians are not adequately warned about potential hazards.

From the Jick, Kasper and unpublished Lilly data outlined above, it can be estimated that 1/1000 patients will commit suicide on Prozac and 1/100 will attempt suicide over the rate that would have occurred if the condition for which the drug were given had been left untreated. Given that there have been in excess of 1 million individuals who have taken Prozac in the UK since its launch, this gives figures of 1 patient per week committing suicide since its launch and 1 per day attempting suicide. Could a problem on this scale pass undetected? At these rates few general practitioners, hospital consultants or coroners (150 in England and Wales) would ever see more than one case of suicide every few years, so a problem on this scale could be missed. Overall national suicide rates remain the same, despite the great increase in antidepressant prescribing that might otherwise have been expected to reduce them (see Kelly and Rafferty, 1999).

Randomised clinical trials (RCTs) and legal jeopardy

The emphasis on RCTs, meta-analyses and epidemiological studies obscures the fact that neither RCTs nor epidemiological studies were required to prove cause and effect in this case. This had already been proven by the initial controlled clinical studies. RCTs and epidemiological studies, however, require enormous resources and the goodwill of academic investigators, thereby putting the potential to contest the issues out of reach for most people. This effectively also minimises company liabilities from not warning patients of potential treatment risks.

Clinical trials of the type done to test whether a treatment works or not have never been used legally to establish causation for drug-induced adverse effects for good reasons. The adverse effects of psychotropic agents may be elicited by spontaneous reports, systematic checklists or detailed interviewing by senior clinicians. Lilly have supported a study which demonstrates that spontaneous reports underestimate side-effects by a six-fold factor (Rosenbaum *et al.*, 1998). Systematic checklists are the best that could be expected from current clinical trials which, while notionally conducted under the aegis of senior investigators in some settings, are often in fact run by junior medical or untrained non-medical personnel (Stecklow and Johannes, 1997; Eichenwald and Kolata, 1999; Boseley, 1999). In such settings, spontaneous reporting is the method employed for determining adverse events.

A further bizarre twist arises in the case of the SSRIs and suicidality. Akathisia is in fact not codable under current spontaneous reporting systems. As a result, the most authoritative compendium on psychotropic drugs (Ayd, 1996) can state that 'fluoxetine's propensity to cause akathisia is widely recognised' and the physiological mechanisms by which this happens are relatively well understood (Heslop and Curzon, 1999), yet Lilly's published database of 42 side effects of Prozac does not mention akathisia (Plewes, Koke and Sayler, 1997). This is the case, even though, prior to its launch, Prozac had been associated with akathisia and agitation, occurring with sufficient frequency and intensity to lead to internal company recommendations that benzodiazepines be co-prescribed with Prozac in clinical trials.

Consider also, emotional flatness or blunting. This side-effect reported frequently by patients on Prozac is arguably all but intrinsic to the mode of action of the SSRIs, which generally reduce emotional reactivity (Healy and Healy, 1998). It has been reported in observational studies, where it has been linked to other potentially harmful behaviours (Hoehn-Saric, Lipsey and McLeod, 1990). But nothing resembling emotional blunting appears in the clinical trials side-effect database for Prozac. Nor is treatment-emergent suicidal ideation recognised by any code in current clinical trial systems. It is not recorded as a side effect of Prozac in the Lilly database.

There are, therefore, problems with current side-effect data. If RCT-based side-effect profiles were used just for marketing purposes, there might be little problem with this state of affairs. These profiles have, however, also been used in academic debate and for legal purposes to deny that claimed adverse effects are happening (Nakielny, 1994; Beasley, 1998). Because of this, the participation of patients in clinical trials using these methods potentially puts the entire national community in legal jeopardy, as the absence of data produced by current methods is taken in practice as evidence that the agent does not cause effects consistent with injuries to a patient.

This is a problem that could be readily remedied. If UK ethical committees were to insist that consent forms for trials included a statement that side-effects collected by current methods could be used for marketing but for no other purposes, the present poor arrangements could continue without posing a threat of legal jeopardy to all of us. Alternatively, ethical committees could request better side-effect collection methods, which would both enhance the scientific information provided by clinical trials and minimise the risks of jeopardy. As many important trials are now multinational and must adhere to the same protocols, these simple manoeuvres would have an immediate international effect. Many companies would be happy to adopt such arrangements.

An ethical crisis?

Ethical committees came into existence because the process of recruitment of patients to clinical studies was not transparent (Rothman, 1991). Beecher's review of these practices in 1966 indicated a situation where it was likely that some abuses were happening or could happen (Beecher, 1966). A similar situation applies today to the use of data emerging from clinical trials.

Since the early 1980s pharmaceutical corporations have grown greatly. They are now managed by managers who rotate in from non health-care corporations. It is clear that some corporations, such as tobacco corporations, have avoided research on the advice of their lawyers that to engage in such research would increase their legal liability (Glantz *et al.*, 1996). Pharmaceutical corporations are advised, in some instances, by the same law firms offering this advice to tobacco corporations. If the advice is the same, it risks striking at the heart of prescription-only arrangements.

Prescription-only arrangements were aimed at protecting consumers by having medical practitioners as their advocates. They were established at a time when it was unthinkable to question the proposition that a doctor would put the interests of their patients above all others. The general understanding is that companies will provide appropriate information in good faith to doctors. This information comes largely from clinical trials. Because of this arrangement, there are no strong consumer groups in the health care arena. Elsewhere corporations, such as Nintendo, post warnings of possible convulsions on computer game systems. In medicine, the Prozac story indicates companies can evade the need to post a warning by invoking the duty of the physician to outline the risks of treatment. In such an instance, prescription-only arrangements risk becoming a vehicle to deliver adverse medical consequences with near legal impunity.

Denouement?

We recently reported the results of a clinical study in twenty healthy volunteers comparing the effects of sertraline, a selective serotonin reuptake inhibitor (SSRI) and reboxetine, an agent with no effects on the serotonin system. One of the outcomes of this study was that two volunteers became severely agitated and suicidal (Healy, 2000a). The relative risk for volunteers becoming suicidal on sertraline compared with the normal state of affairs was 2000 to 1. Other studies of healthy volunteers reporting even higher rates of marked agitation and probable suicidality, within days of starting an SSRI, exist on file with the Medicines Control Agency in Britain, who have characterised the adverse events involved as severe (Healy, 2000b). These results however remain unpublished and were not known to us at the point of application for ethical permission for the above study.

In the light of these healthy volunteer studies, ethical committees in this country would have significant problems sanctioning studies with SSRIs in healthy volunteers without well-thought out arrangements for warning volunteers and monitoring their progress. The agencies, which insure such studies for university departments, might have even greater problems insuring subjects, even subjects who have been warned about possible hazards and who are being monitored.

In 1993, in the course of studies with sertraline in children, an 8-year old boy with obsessive-compulsive features developed suicidality and mutilated himself severely. The clinical investigator attributed this to the sertraline the child was taking (Pfizer, 1996). Pfizer, when reporting this to the Food and Drug Administration in May of 1996, noted that '[drug]- induced activation is a plausible explanation for the emergence of suicidal behavior in our patient' (Pfizer, 1996). They invoked earlier reports of similar findings on fluoxetine (King *et al.*, 1991).

Despite the difficulties ethical committees or insurers might have letting medical or nursing personnel take an SSRI, and despite frank admissions of causality filed with regulatory authorities, these drugs remain available without warnings in this country. They are in fact being prescribed to an ever-larger number of people, who are more accurately seen as suffering from stress reactions or adjustment disorders rather than depression. In addition, they are being prescribed for an ever-larger number of children. Among primary care physicians, who are the largest prescribers of these drugs, some recognise the hazard and monitor appropriately but many, perhaps a majority, do not. Enquiries from companies will lead to a denial of the problem. The situation is extraordinary, perhaps unparalleled in therapeutics.

There are a number of other extraordinary features to this situation. The initial reports of drug-induced agitation or akathisia came 45 years ago; they were notable because this reaction led to suicides in individuals who had no history of mental illness, taking reserpine for hypertension (Healy and Savage, 1998). Despite this and despite acknowledgment by senior figures in the field that akathisia is probably the greatest hazard of psychotropic agents, there has only once in the past 45 years been a symposium at a major meeting in the English-speaking world dedicated to this problem.

Finally, it has recently emerged that Lilly have purchased the marketing rights on a patent of a derivative of fluoxetine, R-fluoxetine. This has been patented on the basis that it may, but is less likely to, induce akathisia and suicidality than the parent compound (Prozac) (Young, Barberich and Teicher, 1998). Given the basis of the patent, this compound if marketed in several years' time will presumably have to come complete with warnings. It is not clear how regulators and companies could tolerate a situation in which such an agent would come with warnings while older, more hazardous agents do not have a warning. But neither is it clear given legal actions currently in train, how such an inconsistency can be avoided. The situation is unprecedented and in my view grotesque.

References

Ayd, F. Jr (1996) *Lexicon for Psychiatry, Neurology and Neuroscience*. Baltimore: Williams & Wilkins

Beasley, C. (1991) Fluoxetine and suicide. *British Medical Journal*, 303, 1200

Beasley, C. (1994) Deposition in Fentress et al vs Eli Lilly, May 17th, 18th 1994

Beasley, C.M. (1998) Suicidality with fluoxetine. *CNS Drugs*, 9, 513–14

Beasley, C.M., Dornseif, B.E., Bosomworth, J.C., Sayler, M.E., Rampey, A.H. and Heiligenstein J.H. (1991) Fluoxetine and suicide: a meta-analysis of controlled trials of treatment for depression. *British Medical Journal*, 303, 685–92

Beecher, H.K. (1966) Ethics and clinical research. *New England Journal of Medicine*, 74, 1354–60

Boardman, A. and Healy, D. (1999) Suicide rates in primary affective disorders in primary care. Presented at British Association for Psychopharmacology annual meeting Harrogate July

Bond, A.J. (1998) Drug induced behavioural disinhibition: incidence, mechanisms and therapeutic implications. *CNS Drugs*, 9, 41–57

Boseley, S. (1999) Trial and error puts patients at risk. *Guardian* July 27th p. 8

Cornwell, J. (1996) *The Power to Harm*. London: Viking Penguin

Creaney, W., Murray, I., and Healy, D. (1991) Antidepressant induced suicidal ideation. *Human Psychopharmacology*, 6, 329–32

Daniels (1991/1999) Memo 15/4/91, to Leigh Thompson coaching for a television appearance. In Forsyth vs Eli Lilly, Plaintiffs' exhibit 123

Dasgupta, K. (1990) Additional case of suicidal ideations associated with fluoxetine. *American Journal of Psychiatry*, 147, 1570

Drake R.E., and Ehrlich, J. (1985) Suicide attempts associated with akathisia. *American Journal of Psychiatry*, 142, 499–501

Eichenwald, K., and Kolata, G. (1999) Drug trials hide conflict for doctors, *New York Times* May 16th pages, 1, 28, 29; A doctor's drug studies turn into fraud. *New York Times* May 17th pages 1, 16, 17

Fava, M., and Rosenbaum, J.F. (1991) Suicidality and fluoxetine: is there a relationship? *Journal of Clinical Psychiatry*, 52, 108–11

Food and Drug Administration. Adverse Drug Reaction data can be accessed on www.FDA.gov

Glantz. S.A., Bero, L.A., Hanauer, P., and Barnes, D.E. (1996) *The Cigarette Papers*. Berkeley: University of California Press

Hagnell. O., Lanke, J., and Rorsman, B. (1981) Suicide rates in the Lundby study: mental illness as a risk factor for suicide. *Neuropsychobiology*, 7, 248–53

Healy, D. (1991) Fluoxetine and suicide. *British Medical Journal*, 303, 1058

Healy, D. (1994) The fluoxetine and suicide controversy. *CNS Drugs*, 1, 223–31

Healy, D. (1997) *The Antidepressant Era*. Cambridge, Massachusetts: Harvard University Press

Healy, D. (2000a) Emergence of antidepressant induced suicidal ideation. *Primary Care Psychiatry*, 6, 23–28

Healy, D. (2000b) Deposition in Miller vs Pfizer. March 29th 2000

Healy, D. and Healy, H. (1998) The clinical pharmacological profile of reboxetine: does it involve the putative neurobiological substrates of wellbeing? *Journal of Affective Disorders*, 51, 313–22

Healy, D., Langmaack, C., and Savage, M. (1999) Suicide in the course of the treatment of depression. *Journal of Psychopharmacology*, 13, 106–11

Healy, D., and Savage, M. (1998)Reserpine exhumed. *British Journal of Psychiatry*, 172, 376–78

Heiligenstein, J. (1990/1999) Plaintiff's exhibit 110 in Forsyth vs Eli Lilly, Memo dated 14/9/90 from Lilly's Dr J Heiligenstein to Dr L Thompson 1990/1999

Heslop, K.E., Curzon, G. (1999) Effect of reserpine on behavioural responses to agonists at 5HT–1A, 5HT–1B, 5HT–2A and 5HT–2C receptor subtypes. *Neuropharmacology*, 38, 883–91

Hoehn-Saric, R., Lipsey, J.R., and McLeod, D.R. (1990) Apathy and indifference in patients on fluvoxamine and fluoxetine. *Journal of Clinical Psychopharmacology*, 10, 343–45

Hoover, C. (1990) Additional cases of suicidal ideation associated with fluoxetine. *American Journal of Psychiatry*,147, 1570–71

Jick, S., Dean, A.D., and Jick, H. (1995) Antidepressants and suicide. *British Medical Journal*, 310, 215–18

Kasper, S. (1997) The place of milnacipran in the treatment of depression. *Human Psychopharmacology*, 12 (suppl 3), S135–41

Kelly, C., and Rafferty, T. (1999) Effect of increased antidepressant prescribing on suicide rate in Northern Ireland. *Psychiatric Bulletin*, 23, 484–86

King, R.A., Riddle, M.A., Chappell, P.B., Hardin, M.T., Anderson, G.M., and Lombroso, P. (1991) Emergence of self-destructive phenomena in children and adolescents during fluoxetine treatment. *Journal of American Acad Child & Adolescent Psychiatry*, 30, 171–76

Lane, R.M. (1998) SSRI-induced extrapyramidal side effects and akathisia: implications for treatment. *Journal of Psychopharmacology*, 12, 192–214

Leon, A.C., Keller, M.B., Warshaw, M.G., Mueller, T.I., Solomon, D.A., and Coryell, W. (1999) Prospective study of fluoxetine treatment and suicidal behavior in affectively ill subjects. *American Journal of Psychiatry*, 156, 195–201

Lilly (1986) Memo re suicides and suicide attempts October 1986. Forsyth vs Eli Lilly, Plaintiffs' exhibit 73

Lipinski, J.F., Mallya, G., Zimmerman, P., and Pope, H.G. (1989) Fluoxetine induced akathisia: clinical and theoretical implications. *Journal of Clinical Psychiatry*, 50, 339–42

Mann, J.J. and Kapur, S. (1991) The emergence of suicidal ideation and behavior during antidepressant pharmacotherapy. *Archives of General Psychiatry*, 48, 1027–33

Masand, P, Gupta, S., and Dwan, M. (1991) Suicidal ideation related to fluoxetine treatment. *New England Journal of Medicine*, 324, 420

Medicines' Control Agency. (2000) Correspondence between David Healy and Dr Keith Jones

Nakielny, J. (1994) The fluoxetine and suicide controversy. A review of the evidence. *CNS Drugs*, 2, 252–53

Pfizer (1996) Exhibit 40 in Miller vs Pfizer, Suicide Related behaviour in children and adolescents in the sertraline OCD clinical development program, May 23, pp 17, 18 & 20

Plewes, J.M., Koke, S.C., and Sayler, M.E. (1997) Adverse events and treatment discontinuations in fluoxetine clinical trials: an updated meta-analysis. *European Neuropsychopharmacology*, 7, S169

Power,A.C., and Cowen, P.J. (1992) Fluoxetine and suicidal behavior. Some clinical and theoretical aspects of a controversy. *British Journal of Psychiatry*, 161, 735–41

Rosenbaum, J.F., Fava, M., Hoog, S.L., Ashcroft, R.C., and Krebs, W. (1998) Selective serotonin reuptake inhibitor discontinuation syndrome: a randomised clinical study. *Biological Psychiatry*, 44, 77–87

Rothman, D. (1991) *Strangers at the Bedside. A History of how Law and Bioethics transformed Medical Decision Making.* New York: Basic Books

Rothschild, A.J., and Locke, C.A. (1991) Re-exposure to fluoxetine after serious suicide attempts by 3 patients: the role of akathisia. *Journal of Clinical Psychiatry*, 52, 491–93

Schulte, J.R. (1985) Homicide and suicide associated with akathisia and haloperidol. *American Journal of Forensic Psychiatry*, 6, 3–7

Stecklow, S., and Johannes, L. (1997) Questions arise on new drug testing. Drug makers relied on clinical researchers who now await trial. *Wall Street Journal*, August 15th

Teicher, M.H., Glod, C., and Cole, J.O. (1990) Emergence of intense suicidal preoccupation during fluoxetine treatment. *American Journal of Psychiatry* 147, 207–10

Teicher, M.H., Glod, C.A., and Cole, J.O. (1993) Antidepressant drugs and the emergence of suicidal tendencies. *Drug Safety*, 8, 186–212

Tollefson, G. (1997) Expert witness statement in trial of Forsyth vs Eli Lilly. U.S.D.C. Hawaii, Civil Action no 95–00185 ACK

Tollefson, G. (1999) Witness. Trial testimony in Forsyth vs Eli Lilly

Van Putten, T. (1975) The many faces of akathisia. *Comp Psychiatry*, 16, 43–7

Van Putten, T., May, P.R., and Marder, S.R. (1981) Subjective responses to antipsychotic drugs. *Archives of General Psychiatry*, 38, 187–90

Warshaw, M.G., and Keller, M.B. (1996) The relationship between fluoxetine use and suicidal behavior in 654 subjects with anxiety disorders. *Journal of Clinical Psychiatry* 57, 158–66

Wirshing, W.C., Van Putten, T., Rosenberg, J., Marder, S., Ames, D., and Hicks-Gray, T. (1992) Fluoxetine, akathisia and suicidality: is there a causal connection? *Archives of General Psychiatry*, 49, 580–81

Young, J.M., Barberich, T.J., and Teicher, M.H. (1998) US Patent number 5, 708,035. January 13th

CHAPTER 7

'I've never said "No" to anything in my life': helping people with learning disabilities who experience psychological problems

BIZA STENFERT KROESE AND GUY HOLMES

UNTIL THE 1980s, residential services for people with learning disabilities were predominantly hostel or hospital based. Many adults lived in rural long-stay hospitals far away from the rest of society. These institutions were run by doctors (psychiatrists) and nurses and although there were opportunities for vocational and recreational activities, the over-riding ethos was based on a medical model where the inmates were considered to be patients and therefore ill. As there are no cures for learning disabilities, patients were destined to stay in hospital until death. They were at the mercy of strict rules, regulations and routines whereby other people decided when they were to get up, when to wash, when to eat, what to wear, and who to befriend.

Living in such deprived, highly controlled environments created severe psychological disturbances for many people. Some became chronically institutionalised, losing all initiative and joy in life. Others developed very disturbed behaviours, for example self-injuring, being aggressive to people and property, or spending long periods of every day engaged in the same repetitive behaviour. Because contact with relatives (who could have acted as advocates) was rare and patients could not speak up for themselves and were therefore very vulnerable, it was not uncommon for medical and other health professionals to try out experimental (and sometimes unethical) treatments. New types of psychotropic medication, behaviour therapy regimes (such as token economies) and treatments based on punishment and isolation (such as time out) were introduced without ethical or empirical considerations. Sometimes people were used as guinea-pigs for research purposes unrelated to their problems. In the 1950s in Sweden, for example, the inmates of a hospital were used to test out whether sweets really decayed teeth. The study involved a large number of adults with learning disabilities being given (on a daily basis) very large, sticky sweets which were hard to chew and impossible to swallow.

Interventions that, on the surface, were relevant to people's problems were rarely aimed at improving psychological wellbeing. Rather, they were intended to control or change a person's behaviour. The medical or scientific approach did not involve discovering what the person might be feeling or thinking, whether they felt they had a problem, and if they did, what they thought might be causing it and what help they might want. Instead, third parties (usually ward staff) would be asked for their impressions and opinions. It was not unusual for the clinician not to see the patient before prescribing drugs or a behavioural regime. There was no collaborative relationship between the clinician and patient. The patient would not usually be informed of the treatment programme (let alone be asked for informed consent). Some behaviourists explicitly argued against informing the person of how the behaviour programme would work as it was unnecessary for the treatment's success (see Lovett, 1985). Even if information was given and consent sought, it was often done in such a way that the explanations were superficial and the person was made to feel that they had no choice but to consent.

The lives of people with learning disabilities and the services set up to help them are still tainted by many of these problems, although a great deal has changed in the last two decades. In the 1980s, most large British institutions started to close down and there are now very few large long-stay hospitals and hostels. Social role valorisation (e.g. Wolfensberger, 1998) has had a major influence and has made us consider a learning disability not as an illness but a label which can be more handicapping than any organic condition. Social role valorisation is an approach to service delivery that tries to help devalued people (devalued through, for example, disability, age, or social standing) to achieve or regain a valued role in their family and in their community. The physical settings and the activities and opportunities available are therefore very important, as are the ways in which people are grouped and the language that is used to describe them. People are devalued if they are housed in old, large, segregated buildings, are given menial, meaningless tasks, spend most of their time in large groups, and are labelled by others (e.g. 'low-grade', 'epileptic', 'schizophrenic', 'OAP').

The medical model of service delivery has been particularly prone to devaluing, dehumanising and isolating people in care. The use of diagnosis in mental health and learning disabilities services has resulted in simplistic labelling, resulting in the neglect of personal needs over the scientific pursuit of treatment and cure. In this chapter we offer a critique of psychiatric diagnosis, medication and some types of individual psychological therapy as means of helping people with learning disabilities who experience psychological problems, and make some recommendations about how they may be more appropriately helped.

The problems with psychiatric diagnosis

The validity of classifying people by psychiatric diagnosis is highly questionable (see Boyle, 1999). Because there are no physical tests or scans to confirm a mental illness, diagnosis is solely done by clinical interview, a process that is notoriously unreliable and prone to bias (Kutchins and Kirk, 1999). These problems are accentuated when psychiatric diagnoses of people with learning disabilities are made (see Stenfert Kroese, Dewhurst and Holmes (2001) for a comprehensive review). People with learning disabilities may have difficulties describing their experiences, and there are often discrepancies between their own reports and third party reports of their problems (e.g. Moss *et al.*, 1996). Behaviours which are classified as symptoms of an underlying mental illness may be nothing of the sort (see Box 1 and Box 2). People with learning disabilities often have different ways of understanding the world and sometimes have less clear distinctions between dreams, fantasies, vivid thoughts on the one hand and observable events on the other (Stenfert Kroese *et al.*, 1998). The power imbalance between the person who makes the diagnosis and the diagnosed accentuates people with learning disabilities' tendency to acquiesce and their own descriptions of their experiences are reinterpreted as psychiatric symptoms. What are labelled as symptoms of mental illness (e.g. the negative symptoms of schizophrenia — social withdrawal, underactivity, emotional blunting, slowness of thought and action, and poverty of speech) may be due to factors relating to a person's learning disability (e.g. neurological damage), the impoverished environment they live in, or the effects of tranquillising medication (see later). Given these difficulties it is not surprising that research on the prevalence of mental illnesses in people with learning disabilities has revealed widely differing rates (e.g. Fraser and Nolan, 1994; Sturmey, Reed and Corbett, 1991). Discussion in the literature about whether there is under- or over-diagnosing misses the point: given the lack of validity and reliability of psychiatric diagnoses and complications regarding their use with this population, it is our opinion that psychiatric diagnosis should be dropped as a way of analysing the lives and experiences of people with learning disabilities.

Box 1: The man with bats in his body

John was referred as it was thought that he was having a psychotic breakdown. He had started to wear women's clothes and talk of having bats flying around in his body. Half an hour into the interview I realised he was describing feeling nervous. An hour in I finally asked 'You don't mean you've got butterflies, do you?' 'That's it, Guy! That's it!' he shouted. The 'women's clothes' turned out to be an apron that he liked to continue wearing after he finished washing up as it made him feel like he had a job.

Box 2: Nigel talks

Nigel was referred to psychology because some of the staff in his day centre thought that he was hearing voices. When I met Nigel, he would sometimes turn to his right and mutter something. When we got to know each other better, he was able to explain that he was telling himself to shut up or to 'stop'. Nigel has a lot of obsessional thoughts and repetitive behaviours and in order to try to control these he often talks to himself and tells his 'obsessional self' to be quiet. This sometimes works for him and allows him to get on and do other things.

The problems with psychotropic medication

Despite these problems with psychiatric diagnosis, there is a large body of literature that shows high rates of prescription of psychotropic medication for people with learning disabilities (see Stenfert Kroese, Dewhurst and Holmes, 2001). For example, Kiernan *et al.* (1995) found 48% of a large (N = 695) sample of adults and children with learning disabilities and challenging behaviours resident in hospitals and community settings in England were prescribed psychotropic medication. Prescription rates of the most powerful drugs (the anti-psychotics or major tranquillisers) are particularly high. In one review, Branford (1996) described their use as 'excessive, inappropriate and potentially harmful' (p. 358). These drugs are often used without a psychiatric diagnosis for people who have challenging behaviours or mild anxiety-related problems (Fleming *et al.*, 1996). Despite their name, the drugs immobilise rather than tranquillise people (Healy, 1997). Their side effects are considerable (BMA & RSPG, 2000) and may be misinterpreted as (or worsen) existing neurological and interpersonal problems. They can make you dribble, have seizures, have contorted body movements, make your tongue feel swollen and your speech slurred, and make you look odd as you become 'stone-faced' and have other parkinsonian symptoms. They cause hormonal and sexual problems. They can make it difficult to concentrate and hard to be motivated or energised to do anything. They can make you feel disorientated and affect co-ordination and movement to such an extent that it becomes difficult to walk. People are less inclined to get out of bed, let alone engage in the community, when taking these drugs. Services are often set up to help people with learning disabilities to be more active and take part in social activities. It seems odd that one part of a service creates the type of problems that another part is funded to alleviate. Some of the side effects are unpleasant but can go unnoticed, as they are difficult for non-verbal people to report, for example nausea, blurred vision, internal agitation.

People with learning disabilities are not always given regular drug reviews, and sometimes end up on a mixture of different drugs, the side-effects profile of which may be complicated (Etherington *et al.*, 1995). They are also more likely to be given the cheaper, older ('dirtier') drugs (Fleming *et al.*, 1996). Given that people with learning disabilities are by definition already cognitively impaired, the fact that these drugs can cause dementia and irreversible neurological conditions such as tardive dyskinesia is particularly tragic.

The above discussion has concentrated on one class of drug in the adult population, but the issues are equally applicable to other types of drugs (e.g. anti-depressants, anti-convulsants) or other groups of people (e.g. children with learning disabilities, older adults with dementia). There is a lack of evidence in the literature that psychotropic medication is helpful for people with learning disabilities (Crabbe, 1994), and considerable evidence that it is used as a general sedative rather than as a specific treatment for an identified disorder (e.g. Aman and Singh, 1983; Royal College of Psychiatrists, 1998). Many people are given several different drugs and often more than one brand of drug from the same drug group, despite warnings against this practice in the British National Formulary (BMA & RSPG, 2000).

We now describe people as having challenging behaviours (rather than labelling them as aggressive or having behaviour problems) in order to emphasise that their behaviours challenge *us*. The term should remind us of the inevitable relationship between people's behaviour and the environment in which they find themselves, and of the *challenge* that is before us to give the people concerned the quality of life that is their due. Sadly, the evidence suggests that one of our most common responses to that challenge has been to use medication that sedates and immobilises.

People who work in the field of learning disabilities, including members of all the caring professions, are rarely given sufficient (if any) training in the adverse effects of medication and tend to see medication as a solution to a problem rather than a cause of one. Stopping or reducing medication can be a difficult and lengthy process due to withdrawal effects (see Stenfert Kroese, Dewhurst and Holmes (2001) and Lehmann, this volume). It would be far better if people were helped in a different way.

The problems with psychology

Craig Newnes, in a review of the history and modern practice of clinical psychology, asked the question 'Which is more important: to help people or to practice science on them?' (Newnes, 1996). The history of psychology is associated with the development of measures which have classified people and assigned that group a devalued social status. At its most extreme, this helped the Nazis commit genocide against (or in their phrase, grant a mercy killing to) all the people in Germany classified as having a mental handicap. As Pilgrim and Treacher (1992) have pointed out, the history of psychology, right back to its founding fathers (people like Galton, Pearson, Spearman and Cattell) has explicitly or implicitly been linked to eugenics. Tests and assessments devised by psychologists have long been associated with labelling and excluding people from services or mainstream society rather than identifying things that people want and need in order to have better lives. For example, Binet's intelligence test was used to identify the 'feeble minded' in order to segregate them into special schools. As IQ tests developed they were used to identify and lend scientific credibility to the sterilisation of people who scored low on those scales (Rose, 1989).

Psychological therapy with people with learning disabilities is historically rooted in medically influenced conceptualisations of problems (sometimes referred to as the pathological approach), that is, an emphasis on the eradication of the pathology (illness) rather than a concentration on strengths and building on a person's positive characteristics. In order for the latter approach to be successful, the person has to be viewed holistically, not in the manner in which a surgeon may only see a defective appendix and have no interest in the person as a whole.

Behavioural approaches to challenging behaviours have accompanied psychiatric diagnosis and share much of its characteristics as the problem is identified and labelled by an expert professional, is seen as rooted in the individual, and a treatment is prescribed with the aim of cure. Treatments have often involved doing things (often unpleasant things that are given ethical legitimacy by calling them programmes rather than punishment) to the individual rather than bringing about environmental change. This has tended to involve stopping a behaviour that third parties (rather than the person him/herself) find annoying or disturbing. Clinical practice and academic literature is dominated by treatment programmes aimed at decreasing 'undesirable' behaviours and increasing 'desirable' ones, without any attempt to find out what the person wants. Indeed, whether people feel that they have a problem, and what they might want to do about it, is rarely explored. It is important to remember that there are very few self-referrals to therapeutic learning disability services.

People with learning disabilities are usually thought of as a group incapable of giving informed consent. Thus, little attempt has been made to explain the adverse consequences of any psychological therapy offered. Recently, simplistic cognitive-behavioural programmes, where people are taught to control their own actions, have come alongside traditional behavioural treatments. A shift is being made from external control to internal control, where people have to tell themselves what to do and what not to do rather than be told (or rewarded and punished) by others. Although this may have led to some clients attaining greater autonomy, it still serves the purpose of social control (see for example Box 3). Therapies which aim to uncover personal meaning are still rare (Lovett, 1995). Only a select band of the wide range of therapies available to the non-learning disabled population have been offered or tried with people with learning disabilities.

Humane, warm, caring and respectful individual therapy undoubtedly goes on, but without a 'reasonable world' to enter outside the consulting room, the benefits of such therapy will at best be limited (Gunzburg, 1974). Clients may end up in confusing situations where, for example, they may be encouraged to be assertive and independent by therapists, only for this to bring them into conflict with carers or relatives who do not value these traits. Worse than this, many people with learning disabilities continue to suffer physical, sexual and emotional abuse and neglect, in childhood and adulthood, something which services have permitted or been unable to prevent.

Box 3: The woman who learned to be good: an example of self-management (from Gardner *et al.*, 1983).

Trainer:	Sue, what did you do?
Sue:	I yelled at Joyce. (self-monitoring)
Trainer:	Right, Is that good adult behaviour or not adult worker behaviour?
Sue:	Not adult worker. (self-evaluation)
Trainer:	Yes. What would a good adult worker do?
Sue:	Work quietly. (puts finger to lips)
Trainer:	Good! So what are you going to do next time?
Sue:	Ignore Joyce and work quietly. (self-redirection)
Trainer:	Great, Sue! Show me how you work quietly.
Sue:	(Demonstrates)
Trainer:	Good worker, Sue! You're working quietly. I'll bet you're happy when you're acting like a good adult worker! Now when you're ready to be a good worker, flip over your card and set your timer.

Ways forward

Given the chequered history of psychiatry and psychology in helping people with learning disabilities, and the more effective and humane ways that people associated with the social role valorisation and advocacy movements have helped, a case can be made for not having designated services for people with learning disabilities. People would then access services available to the general population. Of course, those services are not necessarily going to treat people humanely and respectfully either. Wolfensberger has written eloquently about how dangerous society can be for members of societally devalued groups (Wolfensberger, 1987). For example, people with learning disabilities regularly get substandard care in general hospitals, and are allowed to die in what is conceptualised as a merciful outcome (Wolfensberger, 1992).

Similarly, equality of access to mainstream psychiatric services does not equate with improvements in quality of life. We do not believe that psychiatric diagnosis is a useful way to conceptualise the problems of people with learning disabilities or a valid base from which to decide how best to help them alleviate their difficulties. It is well known that impoverished environments, neglect, physical and sexual abuse, powerlessness, not being listened to or understood, and a myriad of other factors that can characterise the lives of people with learning disabilities lead to psychological problems. Labelling such people as mentally ill is an additional stigma they could do without.

People currently taking psychotropic medication need to have the number of drugs they are taking and dosage of those drugs regularly reviewed, with the aim of reducing and stopping medication regimes where the adverse effects outweigh the benefits. People need to be much better informed about the short-term and permanent adverse effects of psychotropic medication, whether they are carers, relatives, advocates or the clients themselves. In our opinion, everyone who works with people with learning disabilities shares some responsibility if their clients are on high doses of medication and have a quality of life that is damaged by unwanted effects of their medication. Regular multi-disiplinary reviews can be useful, but it is clear that without a shift in attitude, which enables non-medical staff, advocates or the clients themselves to question medication regimes, these meetings will not result in major changes.

Rather than be prescribed psychotropic medication, a range of alternatives should be considered. We need to find effective yet humane ways of helping people with learning disabilities. Carrying out good therapeutic work can be quite a challenge for a number of reasons. People's limited ability to express and comprehend language can complicate the therapeutic process. However, a common language can be learned which may use non-verbal communication (such as drawing, mime, role-play and video) to convey important issues. We need to be better at finding out what people with learning disabilities think about certain issues, what is important to them, and what sort of help they want. It takes time to find out about these so it is important that therapists do not 'treat' people who they do not know.

A wide range of supports and therapies can help people experiencing psychological difficulties (for example, see Newnes, Holmes and Dunn, 1999) and people with learning disabilities ought to have opportunities to benefit from all of these. Approaches which allow all parties to rethink some of the existing patterns of communication and power are particularly pertinent in this context. As such approaches are extremely complex and demanding there is perhaps a role for workers who have specialist training and extensive experience in working with people with learning disabilities. However, rather than remaining in a segregated service, these specialists must concentrate on close co-operation with generic services in order to allow easy, safe and effective access to them.

Those offering help need to adapt and build on the recent movements that aim to improve people's quality of life (see Rapley, this volume, for a critique of this concept), give people with learning disabilities a more powerful voice, and challenge ignorant and stigmatising attitudes. Some of the best services have moved from a focus of the professional expert identifying the clients' problems to a focus on what clients want and how workers might best assist them to get what they want. The emergence of advocacy schemes all over the country and the genuine efforts made to ensure user representation on various planning and research bodies are witness to this.

People need to be given more information about the types of help available and alternatives that they may want to consider. If they cannot give informed consent then an independent advocate, preferably one who knows the client really well, should be involved who can advise the client and professional as to what the client's best interests are. This applies whether it is medication or psychological therapy that is being considered.

In order to facilitate the process of people giving informed consent, we have recently begun to give clients who have been referred to the clinical psychology department clear and simple information booklets about what to expect from sessions with a psychologist (e.g. 'we do not give pills to people'). The leaflet has clear illustrations and prompts people to give their opinions. We emphasise that people can say 'no' if they don't want to see us. One client responded: 'I've never said no to anything in my life', illustrating how much we still need to do in order to help some people to gain the skills and confidence to be assertive. One leaflet cannot change a lifetime of subservience.

People need to consider the climate in which they work and how willing and able they are to be constructively critical of each other. When bad practice is observed, there is a need to speak out (see Box 4). At the same time, we all need to be aware of our own strengths and limitations and engage in regular self-evaluation, as well as seek out the opinions of others, not least our clients.

> **Box 4: Reasons to be angry**
>
> Peter moved to a brand new house with very friendly female staff after having struggled on his own in a flat for a number of years. He was very happy in his new home but things went wrong when three other men moved into the house. The staff had less time to spend with Peter and became a bit impatient with him. He in turn became bad-tempered and angry. As a consequence he was put on medication which made him even angrier as it made his hands shake and his mouth dry. Because he did not want to take any more medication, the staff started to hide his pills in his food. Peter went into a rage when he found a blue pill in his Mars bar. He was referred to psychology for 'anger management'. After hearing his story, a meeting was held with the staff and with the psychiatrist and it was decided that instead of Peter managing his anger, the obvious solution to all the problems was for us to be more considerate of Peter's needs and respond to what he was asking for. It will take some time before Peter will be able to trust us again.

There needs to be an acceptance that people with learning disabilities cannot be 'cured'. Indeed, they don't need to be. They are valuable members of our society who have a great deal to contribute. We have both learned much from our contact with people with learning disabilities, including significant lessons about what is and what isn't important in human contact. Being good with words doesn't always count for much. Psychologists tend to worship intelligence but have little to say about love, respect, kindness, equality of opportunity, and insightfulness that is not rooted in the intellect. Indeed, we have learned more about these things from people with learning disabilities than from any training course, textbook or colleague.

References

Aman, M. and Singh, N. (1983) Pharmacological intervention. In: J. Matson and J. Mulick (eds.) *Handbook of Mental Retardation*. Oxford: Pergamon Press

Boyle, M. (1999) Diagnosis. In: C. Newnes, G. Holmes and C. Dunn (eds.) *This is Madness: a Critical Look at Psychiatry and the Future of Mental Health Services*. Ross-on-Wye: PCCS Books

Branford, D. (1996) A review of antipsychotic drugs prescribed for people with learning disabilities who live in Leicestershire. *Journal of Intellectual Disability Research*, 40, 358–68

British Medical Association and Royal Pharmaceutical Society of Great Britain (2000) *British National Formulary*. London: BMA & RSPG

Crabbe, H. (1994) Pharmacotherapy in mental retardation. In: N. Bouras (ed.) *Mental Health in Mental Retardation: Recent Advances and Practices*. Cambridge: Cambridge University Press

Etherington, J., Sheppard, L., Ballinger, B. and Fenton, G. (1995) Psychotropic drugs in a hospital for intellectual disability: the story of 18 years. *Mental Handicap Research*, 8, 184–93

Fleming, I., Caine, A., Ahmed, S. and Smith, S. (1996) Aspects of the use of psychoactive medication among people with intellectual disabilities who have been resettled from long-stay hospitals into dispersed housing. *Journal of Applied Research in Intellectual Disabilities*, 9, 194-205

Fraser, W. and Nolan, M. (1994) Psychiatric disorders in mental retardation. In: N. Bouras (ed.) *Mental Health in Mental Retardation: Recent Advances and Practices*. Cambridge: Cambridge University Press

Gardner, W.I., Cole, C.L., Berry, D.L.and Nowinski, J.M. (1983) Reduction of disruptive behavior in mentally retarded adults. A self-management approach. *Behavior Modification*, 7, 76–96

Gunzburg, H.C. (1974) Psychotherapy. In: A.M. Clarke and D.B. Clarke (eds*)* *Mental Deficiency. The Changing Outlook* (3rd edn.). London: Methuen & Co.

Healy, D. (1997) *Psychiatric Drugs Explained* (2nd ed.). Guildford: Mosby

Kiernan, C., Reeves, D. and Alborz, A. (1995) The use of anti-psychotic drugs with adults with learning disabilities and challenging behaviour. *Journal of Intellectual Disability Research*, 39, 263–74

Kutchins, H. and Kirk, S. (1999) *Making Us Crazy: DSM – the Psychiatric Bible and the Creation of Mental Disorders*. London: Constable

Lovett, H. (1985*) Cognitive Counselling and Persons with Special Needs. Adapting Behavioral Approaches to the Social Context*. New York: Praeger

Lovett, H. (1996*) Learning to Listen: Positive Approaches and People with Difficult Behavior*. London: Jessica Kingsley

Moss, S., Prosser, H., Ibbotson, B. and Golding,D. (1996) Respondent and informant accounts of psychiatric symptoms in a sample of patients with learning disability. *Journal of Intellectual Disability Research*, 40, 457–65

Newnes, C. (1996) The development of clinical psychology and its values. *Clinical Psychology Forum*, 95, 29–34

Newnes, C., Holmes, G., and Dunn, C. (eds.) (1999) *This is Madness: A Critical Look at Psychiatry and the Future of Mental Health Services*. Ross-on-Wye: PCCS Books

Pilgrim, D. and Treacher, A. (1992*) Clinical Psychology Observed*. London: Routledge.

Rose, N. (1989*) Governing the Soul*. London: Routledge

Royal College of Psychiatrists (1998) *Management of Imminent Violence. Clinical Practice Guidelines: Quick Reference Guide*. London: Royal College of Psychiatrists

Stenfert Kroese, B., Cushway, D. & Hubbard, C. (1998) The conceptualisation of dreams by people with intellectual disabilities. *Journal of Applied Research in Intellectual Disabilities*, 11, 146–55

Stenfert Kroese, B., Dewhurst, D. and Holmes, G. (2001) Diagnosis and drugs: help or hindrance when people with learning disabilities have psychological problems? *British Journal of Learning Disabilities*, 29, 26–33

Sturmey, P., Reed, J. & Corbett, J. (1991) Psychometric assessment of psychiatric disorders in people with learning difficulties (mental handicap): a review of measures. *Psychological Medicine*, 21, 143–55

Wolfensberger, W. (1987) *The New Genocide of Handicapped and Afflicted People*. Syracuse, NY: Training Institute for Human Service Planning, Leadership and Change Agentry (Syracuse University)

Wolfensberger, W. (1992*) A Guideline on Protecting the Health and Lives of Patients in Hospitals, Especially if the Patient is a Member of a Societally Devalued Class*. Syracuse, NY: Training Institute for Human Service Planning, Leadership and Change Agentry (Syracuse University)

Wolfensberger, W. (1998) *A Brief Introduction to Social Role Valorization* (3rd edn.). Syracuse, NY: Training Institute for Human Service Planning, Leadership and Change Agentry (Syracuse University)

CHAPTER 8

Coming off neuroleptics

PETER LEHMANN

COMING OFF PSYCHIATRIC drugs, especially neuroleptics (also known as anti-psychotics and major tranquillisers), is not an issue for typical psychiatrists, drug companies or family organisations sponsored by drug companies with a vested interest in solving family problems with drugs. They all want to have more, preferably life-long, drug treatment. In many US states there have been court-decisions and law-amendments to permit permanent, often violent, use of neuroleptics in people's communities.

On the other hand, there are more and more reports about the damage caused by neuroleptic use. Many forms of professional action, even within the context of health promotion, might unintentionally enhance the process of marginalisation of recipients of neuroleptics (Lehtinen, Riikonen and Lahtinen, 1997). According to thousands of reports, neuroleptics and other psychiatric treatments can cause a deterioration of health. So it is no accident that the world's biggest organisation of people who have been treatment-objects of psychiatrists has decided to call itself, 'European Network of (ex-) Users and Survivors of Psychiatry'. The term 'survivor' refers to those who have mainly experienced psychiatric diagnosis and treatment as a danger to their health and life. The term 'user' refers to people who have mainly experienced psychiatric diagnosis and treatment as helpful in their specific situation. These definitions are often misunderstood: to survive psychiatry does not mean that psychiatrists are being accused of intentionally killing people; but it does mean that diagnoses such as schizophrenia and psychosis, which very often have a depressing and stigmatising effect leading to resignation and chronic hospitalisation, must be prevented. Drug-effects such as neuroleptic malignant syndrome, tardive dyskinesia, febrile hyperthermia, pneumonia, asphyxia, and other dystonic or epileptic attacks, which can pose a danger to health and sometimes cause death even after small and single doses, have to be survived, in order for people to have a real choice in going on taking neuroleptics or to withdraw. Kerstin Kempker, a German survivor of psychiatry, in her book *Mitgift — Notizen vom Verschwinden* (*Dowry of poison — Notes from disappearing*) shows the indifference of the majority of psychiatric workers to the harm psychiatry can do. For example, they elected the German psychiatrist Uwe H. Peters as leader of their professional psychiatric organisation even when he is known to have treated young people with insulin, coma, electroshock, neuroleptics and antidepressants apparently without informed consent (Kempker, 2000).

Liver damage, pigmentation of inner organs, eye and brain damage, chromosome damage, receptor-changes, modification of the personality and 'broken-wing' syndrome are other possible dangerous effects of psychopharmacological treatment. Increased incidence of breast cancer caused by drug-connected increases in the level of the sexual hormone prolactin is discussed in the American Journal of Psychiatry (Halbreich, Shen and Panaro, 1996). But who cares? All these damaging effects are caused by all sorts of neuroleptics; very potent ones, less potent ones, the older typical ones and the newer atypical ones. Differences of damage-causing potential are secondary, for example the most common damage from typical neuroleptics like haloperidol arises from changing the dopamine-D_2-metabolism, observable as movement-disorders; the most common damage from atypical neuroleptics like clozapine is a change in the metabolism of special subtypes of dopamine-receptors, dopamine-D_1 and -D_4, seen as producing or increasing psychotic syndromes of organic origin medium and long-term (Chouinard and Jones, 1980; 1982; Ungerstedt and Ljungberg, 1977). Surveys of medical literature on the withdrawal problems of neuroleptics can be found in *Wie Chemie und Strom auf Geist und Psyche wirken* (*The effects of chemistry and electricity on the human mind and psyche*: Lehmann, 1996a, pp. 99ff.) and *Wie Psychopharmaka den Koerper veraendern* (*How psychotropic drugs change the body*: Lehmann, 1996b, pp. 405ff.). There are many good reasons to decide to come off neuroleptics.

Withdrawal risks of neuroleptics

In the USA and Europe there are some remarkable court decisions bringing compensation for drug-damaged people, sometimes with sums of more then one million US$, on the grounds that there were no attempts made to help people withdraw from the medication over many years. Lacking information about the risk of dependency will soon no longer be a valid defence in these cases, even if psychiatric workers deny vehemently that dependence on neuroleptics occurs. International psychiatric journals are full of reports about massive withdrawal problems from neuroleptics. Physical and psychic withdrawal-symptoms may bring about — in itself unnecessary — continued psychopharmacological treatment (Lehmann, 1996b). The most obvious way to prevent tardive dyskinesia is to limit the use of neuroleptics (Jenner and Marsden, 1983).

The silence concerning withdrawal-symptoms, rebound-effects, supersensitivity-effects, receptor-changes, and tardive psychoses has fatal consequences for users of psychiatry. They cannot act in an appropriate way because they eventually misjudge the problems. Even psychiatric workers have the same difficulties; in withdrawal-studies there is no distinction between true relapse and withdrawal problems (Gilbert, Harris, McAdams and Jeste 1995; Woggon, 1979). There is a lack of scientific rigour, a problem frequently replicated within psychiatric practice. There are, however, many positive experiences of self-determined withdrawal; developing a system to support self-determined withdrawal would enhance the prospects of (ex-

)users and survivors of psychiatry. When individuals have come to their own decision to stop taking psychoactive drugs, it is important that they inform themselves about the many problems that can arise during withdrawal.

Withdrawal symptoms are diseases or problems that were never experienced before treatment with psychoactive drugs or not to such an extent. Knowing exactly what to expect during withdrawal from neuroleptics should enable the person and those who are helping him/her to assess problems realistically and to react appropriately, in order to bring the withdrawal process to a positive outcome. In addition to the usual withdrawal symptoms, another problem often arises: temporary rebound symptoms (sometimes more intense reappearance of the original symptoms present before treatment).The appearance of these somewhat mirror-like rebound symptoms makes it particularly difficult to see the difference between the withdrawal symptoms and the original problems. It should be taken into consideration (as it should be before starting such a treatment) when coming off neuroleptic drugs that hypersensitivity (delirium, withdrawal-related psychoses) is a serious risk. Sleeplessness, mental disturbance, symptoms of the central nervous system, muscular and motor disturbances and troublesome and even lethal disorders of the autonomous nervous system have to be taken into account, leading medical professionals to recommend gradual withdrawal.

There is a significant risk of developing tolerance and becoming dependent on (minor) tranquillisers even after a short period of treatment with a low dose. Severance from tranquillisers can be a dangerous matter with rebound phenomena and powerful, sometimes life-threatening withdrawal symptoms such as convulsions. Other risks are long ongoing depression and suicidal tendencies, anxiety, delirium, and psychoses, which can lead to the risk of continuous or repeated psychiatric drug treatment using progressively stronger and more harmful substances. Withdrawal from neuroleptics (major tranquillisers) is not basically different from withdrawal from other psychoactive drugs, but in addition to the usual withdrawal symptoms (agitation, anxiety, confusion, headaches, lack of concentration, eating and sleeping disorders, increased heartbeat rate, fainting, vomiting, diarrhoea, and sweating) rebound- and hypersensitivity-symptoms can become a problem. This is particularly true for the relatively recent, atypical neuroleptics such as clozapine (Leponex), olanzapine (Zyprexa), remoxipride (Roxiam), risperidone (Risperidal, Rispolin), sertindole (Serdolect), and zotepine (Nipolept).

R. Ekblom of Ullerak Hospital in Uppsala, Sweden, and his colleagues are the authors of a report on supersensitivity psychoses discernible immediately after withdrawal from clozapine. They state that normal relapses are highly unlikely to immediately follow withdrawal. They relate the case of a 23 year-old man who, after being observed to be 'emotionally withdrawn and subject to olfactory hallucinations' was given haloperidol and other neuroleptic drugs. Due to unbearable motor and muscular disturbances which can be the effects of these drugs, they changed to clozapine. 22 months later he developed a dangerous alteration in his blood; the neuroleptic had to be stopped immediately. The psychiatrists recount:

Twenty-four hours later his clinical picture changed dramatically. He became tense and restless with intensive auditory hallucinations, hearing voices which ordered him to crawl on the floor and to hit people. He also exhibited persecutory ideas and ambivalence. During his psychotic experiences he was well aware of the fact that he was ill. Thioridazine was given (commercially best known as Mellaril and Melleril, P.L.) *in doses of up to 600 mg/day, but his symptoms only gradually diminished and did not disappear.* (Ekblom, Eriksson and Lindstroem,1984, p. 293)

Uninformed, isolated and therefore defenceless individuals are understandably afraid to be sent back to the hospital and to be forcibly treated with neuroleptics, so they go on taking neuroleptics at the insistence of their psychiatrists or their families.

Rudolf Degkwitz, former President of the German Association for Psychiatry and Neurology, has repeatedly reported on withdrawal symptoms — not publicly, but in specialised journals:

We now know that it is extremely difficult, if not impossible, for many of the chronic patients to stop neuroleptics because of the unbearable withdrawal-symptoms. (Degkwitz and Luxenburger, 1965, p. 175 [Translation by P.L.])

George Brooks, psychiatrist at the Waterbury Centre, Vermont, says:

The severity of the withdrawal symptoms may mislead the clinician into thinking that he is observing a relapse of the patient's mental condition. (Brooks, 1959, p. 932)

How to come off neuroleptics
Desire, will-power and patience are of extreme importance in coming off psychoactive drugs. The rule of thumb is: do not overdo it, be aware that quick changes in the body's metabolism can cause severe withdrawal symptoms.

We should also be aware that persons coming off psychiatric drugs are weakened, particularly when they have just gone through withdrawal. Even if they are symptom-free, their nervous system is not yet stabilised. Only a person who is completely cured can take on new tasks.

A magic recipe for coming off psychoactive drugs does not exist. It might be that they must be reduced gradually and, if necessary, under medical supervision. Since it is very unusual to come off neuroleptic drugs in a sheltered ward, there are many alternative factors of great importance: contact persons, integration into self-help groups, social relations, access to less harmful substances to help calm severe symptoms (Ochsenknecht, 1993) as well as a disillusioned view of psychiatry. No matter what the conditions of one's life at the time of severance from psychiatric drugs, it is vital to persevere and to gradually pull oneself out of the mire. Others can only support. The decision to live a life free of mind-invading substances must ultimately be the patient's.

A series of articles by people who have freed themselves from dependency on neuroleptics and very often additional antidepressants, lithium, carbamazepine and (minor) tranquillisers as well as by those who helped these people professionally show that it is possible to stop taking psychoactive drugs without ending up in the treatment-room of a physician or in a psychiatric institution (Lehmann, 1998a). (Ex-)users and survivors of psychiatry who particularly feared the possibility of relapsing into psychiatry have found their own solutions such as autogenic training, social living and working together, examination of the meaning and nature of madness, avoidance of stressful (family) relationships, searching for the sense of life, living closer to nature, swimming, jogging, therapeutic bodywork, yoga, meditation, spiritual practice, prayer, constructive monologues (affirmation) and — this is particularly important — precautionary measures in case of the return of the original psychosocial problems.

There is no patent recipe for excluding problems when coming off or withdrawing psychiatric drugs: the uniqueness of individuals, their problems and their possibilities mitigate against any hope of a generalised approach. The survey of factors described by survivors as being essential for successfully withdrawing illustrates the diversity of strategies and needs[1].

If any problems are looming, the reduction of doses by degrees is the best way to decrease withdrawal risks. This is especially important if a psychiatric drug has been taken for more than one or two months. Optimally, all the necessary factors for successful withdrawal would be present simultaneously: a responsible attitude, a paced of coming off which matches the dose and duration of drug treatment, supportive environments, appropriate assistance, qualified specialists and a supporting self-help group.

But as a rule you can assume that the circumstances while coming off are the opposite of optimal. In the worst cases there is no other possibility than to help oneself get out of the jungle of psychopharmacologic addiction. Ulrich Lindner, a retired theologian, philologist and historian living in the Black Forest, and attempting to withdraw, has been taught how by his brother who has experiences of withdrawal. Gerda W.-Z., writer, translator and publisher of poems and short stories and also living in the Black Forest, encourages:

We are on our own, called upon to live in a responsible way. We are not only sentenced by others, muzzled by others. We always have more forces (and self-helping forces, too) available than we might have thought in dark days. (Lehmann, 1998a)

Some argue that as a condition for success it is important to see through the incompetence and the low probability of effective help from medics prescribing psychiatric drugs, to give up illusions about their help and to separate oneself from the doctor or psychiatrist as well as from an understanding of life-problems as illness. 'I gave away 21 valuable years of my life and hoped in vain for an improvement or a cure', says the German Bert Goelner, who worked as a type-setter for many years, now in early retirement (disabled); he is also founder of a self-help group for people with compulsive difficulties.

[1] References to individual experiences of withdrawal are taken from Lehmann, P. (ed.) (1998a) *Psychopharmaka absetzen — Erfolgreiches Absetzen von Neuroleptika, Antidepressiva, Lithium, Carbamazepin und Tranquilizern.* Berlin: Antipsychiatrieverlag. English translation due 2002.

Finally he says: 'Notice your harm and be your own therapist — help yourself or nobody helps you' (Lehmann, 1998a).

To make coming off successful in the long term, it is essential to refuse to adapt to unpleasant situations; this can mean leaving a burdensome environment as well as quitting an unsuitable relationship. Getting crazy is a sign showing the necessity of a change, says Maths Jesperson, board-member of the Swedish organisation of (ex-)users and survivors of psychiatry and researcher at the University of Lund (faculty of theatre-science): 'Madness is no illness to be cured. My madness came to call in a new life for me' (Lehmann, 1998a).

Those who learn to take feelings seriously, to follow their instincts and to take notice of and to react to warning signals of a developing crisis escape the danger of psychiatric drugs being prescribed for a second time. Thus developing a calm response to burdensome circumstances in life, patience, courage and determination and the understanding that harm and hurt are inherent to life was helpful for some survivors. Now they admit their mistakes and accept relapses without despairing immediately. So Tara-Rosemarie Reuter, born in the Federal Republic of Germany and having experienced a bipolar perception of herself and the world when she was 40 years old, writes: 'Relapses are needed to refine the instrumentarium. How should we learn if not that way?' (Lehmann, 1998a).

These people have learned to live through fearful situations and to reduce deep-seated anxieties. Wilma Boevink, working as a researcher at the Department of Care and Rehabilitation at the Trimbos-Institute in Utrecht, The Netherlands, reports:

> *During the years I developed the courage to face what I tried to cover with all my dependencies. I fought the monsters of my past, and to be able to do this, first I had to admit them and look into their eyes. (...) You have to find the courage to confess to yourself how things went so far.* (Lehmann, 1998a)

The sooner (ex-)users and survivors of psychiatry developed an understanding of the connection between violence or abuse and their difficulties, understood mad and troubling symptoms and reacted in alternative ways to crises, the easier it was for them to break off emotional involvement from life problems and deal with them. The hunt that is started after the end of an acute phase — madness or depression — has a preventive character, as the German Regina Bellion, former cleaning-woman, factory-worker, haute-couture sales-woman, teacher, waitress, now living in early retirement, says: 'Who gets down to understanding her psychotic experiences afterwards obviously does not run into the next psychotic phase that soon.' (Lehmann, 1998a)

Some people regard it as a fundamental condition to notice their own (co-)responsibility for their lives, their problem-burdened past and their responsibility for their future (see, for example, Coleman, 1999). Carola Bock, in the former German Democratic Republic working as an industrial accountant, in early retirement since 1991, says self-critically:

> *Today I know that I am partly to blame for the states of crisis because I acted wrong and was no angel at all. I often tried to solve my problems in*

heavy-handed way, and I had not collected enough experience of life either. (Lehmann, 1998a)

The necessity to take care of healthy and regular sleeping habits is said to be a key component of self-responsibility for some authors. First of all, a sensible and fulfilling occupation — a paid job or a hobby-like activity (especially writing) — as well as love and friendship add to the positive outlook on life which makes it much easier to come off psychiatric drugs (cf: Davey, 1999). Not to lose ground in argument, but to defend oneself and to be able to talk about delicate things is decisive, too. Friendships prove their value if the contact is continued during a crisis.

As long as they make an open non-invasive interchange of personal problems possible, self-help groups are as useful as friendships. Moreover, self-help groups build the scope for mutual advice and for the spread of information about possible damage caused by psychiatric drugs and problems with coming off: 'Most important were the conversations with (ex-)users and survivors of psychiatry who had comparable experiences and a similar attitude towards the world', reports Nada Rath, co-founder of the German national organisation of (ex-)users and survivors of psychiatry. For the English woman Una Parker, retired school teacher and member of Mindlink and ECT Anonymous, co-counselling meant the end of the danger of psychiatric drugs and electroshocks:

> *It has made a very great difference to me, and I think that the support I have had from regular co-counselling sessions not only kept me out of the psychiatric system but also helped me be much more effective in my life.* (Lehmann, 1998a)

Homeopathic decontamination, alleviation of withdrawal problems with naturopathic remedies (e.g. Saint John's wort, valerian), body- and psychotherapy, conversations in groups, sports, meditation, praying, shamanic practices and much more can additionally help with reducing problems of coming off and withdrawing.

The importance of a non-discriminating relationship between a person who wants to come off and a professional helper is underlined by Erwin Redig, who spent several years in psychiatry in Belgium and died in 1999 after a forced commitment to a psychiatric hospital:

> *This support will not come from the people that declared you ill. This support must be sought amongst people that look upon you with other eyes, that have honest appreciation and true interest.* (Lehmann, 1998a)

Professional helpers note their human presence and their availability in the critical moments of coming off as a prerequisite for effective support. But the (ex-)users and survivors of psychiatry have to do their share in overcoming the problems that can appear when coming off, too. Constanze Meyer, psychologist and psychotherapist, working in private practice as well as a counsellor in a women's centre for substance abuse in Berlin, knows that this is not always easy:

These solutions all normally need much time and an active confrontation with the person's own situation, attitudes and patterns of behaviour. (Lehmann, 1998a)

The more afraid the (ex-)users and survivors of psychiatry are when coming off, the more important becomes the relationship based on trust with the professional helper and, 'the patient knows that he/she can rely on the therapist if there is any trouble' (natural healer Klaus John from Northern Germany). Elke Laskowski, natural healer, indicates the interplay between specialist and human offerings: 'Of course, conversation and offering the patient the opportunity to call at any time have an incomparable therapeutic effect' (Lehmann, 1998a).

Anxieties should be relativised (and in that way reduced) by accurate specialist information about risks of psychiatric drugs and coming off them. It is not very surprising that practices used during the withdrawal process, like acupuncture, are often highly regarded in reports of people who have experiences with psychiatric drugs. Other measures, for example a complete change of diet or a considered use of other drugs, are, because of the frequent problems with getting on well without psychiatric drugs, also worth trying by people who want to come off.

When the body is finally free of psychoactive substances and the system is cleansed, former vitality probably will return. The belief that their stay in psychiatric treatment was just an unfortunate incident which is best forgotten, causes many to push away the thoughts, feelings and behaviours that got them into treatment in the first place.

This can be dangerous. People who were forced into psychiatric treatment should ask themselves how they can change their lives so that the psychosocial problems that led to their psychiatrisation can be diminished.

People who ask their doctors for psychoactive drugs should first ask themselves whether their needs — perhaps a need for peace, relief, attention, understanding, acknowledgement — could not be better taken care of without exposing their body to these risky and dangerous chemicals.

Alternatives and measures to encourage withdrawal
Karl Bach Jensen, the former chair of the European Network of (ex-)Users and Survivors of Psychiatry, developed responsible political demands to enhance the situation of people who made the decision to withdraw from neuroleptics:

> *To disagree with the conventional concept of mental illness and the need for synthetic psychoactive drugs — especially when prescribed for long term daily use or even for life — doesn't mean to close your eyes or to deny the real problems many people experience.* (Jensen,1998, p. 343)

Jensen's point is not that the society shouldn't care at all or that people should be locked up and left alone when they go crazy or out of their mind. A fundamental characteristic of alternative mental health services, he continues, would be to help people to cope with their problems by use of mutual learning processes, advocacy, alternative medicine, proper nutrition, natural healing, spiritual practice, etc. For example, alternative pharmacy knows a lot about herbs and homeopathic medicine which can help the body and mind to relax and regain its balance. There might not be that much financial profit in these things, but it is the future.

In this field, (ex-)users and survivors of psychiatry could play an important role as staff members and consultants, having the knowledge of what helped them. Such services linked with a positive subcultural identity and dignity could be provided by the public or with public financial support by the (ex-)user/survivor-movement itself giving people the space to meet and create their own lives (see Lindow, 1999). If people are locked up to save their life or to prevent them from doing serious damage to others, nobody should have the right to force upon them any kind of treatment. As a defence against involuntary treatment, Psychiatric Wills or advanced directives — with instructions about the kind of treatment a person wants or doesn't want if it comes to involuntary commitment — should be legally adopted by all states and nations. Alternative systems and decentralised services to meet the needs of people experiencing mental health problems would minimise and in the long run make use of synthetic and toxic psychiatric drugs needless. Until the final abolition of these drugs, a lot of people need help and support to withdraw from them.

An integrated part of building a future ecologically- and humanistically-oriented social system would be the renunciation of toxic substances in nature, the environment, the food chain and in medicine. The renunciation of the deployment of chemical toxins in the psychosocial field could be developed under the following aspects: (Ex-)users and survivors of psychiatry should raise awareness in the public, amongst professionals and consumers, about the inhuman, dangerous and negative cost-benefit outcome of long-term administration of synthetic psychiatric drugs. So (ex-)users and survivors of psychiatry should:

- oppose and fight international recommendations and national laws legitimising forced psychiatric treatment, especially legally-enforced conditions of long-term treatment in the outpatient sector,
- collect and promulgate knowledge about withdrawal problems and how to solve them,
- develop special services and havens for people to overcome dependency on psychiatric drugs,
- ensure that people are informed about the risks of injury and dependency when psychiatric drugs are initially prescribed,
- secure damages for pain and suffering and compensation for disability caused by prescribed psychiatric drugs,
- develop methods, systems, services and institutions for acute, short-term and long-term help and support not depending on the use of synthetic psychiatric drugs at all.

Services mentioned by Jensen are included in the aims of the European Network of (ex-)Users and Survivors (Lehmann, 1998b; Lehmann, 1999). One of these new services is the Berlin Runaway-House, an antipsychiatric project with a long history (Wehde, 1992; Hoelling 1999), whose staff reflect on the risks of psychiatric drugs. This antipsychiatric institution can provide a good shelter to withdraw from neuroleptics too, says Kerstin Kempker, member of the staff of the Berlin runaway-house (see her book *Flucht in die*

Wirklichkeit — Das Berliner Weglaufhaus: Escape into reality — The Berlin Runaway-House; Kempker 1998). When even the World Health Organisation and the European Commission are pleading for the development of innovative mental health policies in consultation with all stakeholders including users, for developing new non-stigmatising and self-help approaches and mental health legislation based on human rights, emphasising freedom of choice (World Health Organization/European Commission, 1999, p. 9f.), optimists may see a chance of providing services (ex-)users and survivors of psychiatry world-wide are waiting for. But even if all these plans are only sentences on worthless paper, people will go on to do what they always did (and what physically ill people do in the exactly same way with prescribed medicine); decide for themselves whether or not to take drugs. Others might guess how high the rate is of true relapse and the rate of withdrawal problems, which are misunderstood as relapses; but it is clear that many withdrawals would have a better outcome if there were knowledge about problems and opportunities to withdraw, more help and less fear, and more knowhow and more positive examples on the side of the users.

References

Brooks, G.W. (1959) Withdrawal from neuroleptic drugs. *American Journal of Psychiatry* 115, 931–32

Chouinard, G. and Jones, B.D. (1980) Neuroleptic-induced supersensitivity psychosis. *American Journal of Psychiatry* 137, 16–21

Chouinard, G. and Jones, B.D. (1982) Neuroleptic-induced supersensitivity psychosis, the 'Hump Course', and tardive dyskinesia.*Journal of Clinical Psychopharmacology* 2, 143–44

Coleman, R. (1999) Hearing voices and the politics of oppression. In: C. Newnes, G. Holmes, and C. Dunn (eds) *This is Madness: A critical look at psychiatry and the future of mental health services*. Ross on Wye: PCCS Books

Davey, B. (1999) Green approaches to occupational and income needs in preventing chronic dependency. In: C. Newnes, G. Holmes, and C. Dunn (eds) *This is Madness: A critical look at psychiatry and the future of mental health services*. Ross on Wye: PCCS Books

Degkwitz, R. and Luxenburger, O. (1965) Das terminale extrapyramidale Insuffizienz- bzw. Defektsyndrom infolge chronischer Anwendung von Neurolepticis. *Nervenarzt* 36, 173–75

Ekblom, B., Eriksson, K. and Lindstroem, L.H. (1984) Supersensitivity psychosis in schizophrenic patients after sudden clozapine withdrawal. *Psychopharmacology* 83, 293–94

Gilbert, P.L., Harris, M.J., McAdams, L.A. and Jeste, D.V. (1995) Neuroleptic withdrawal in schizophrenic patients: a review of the literature. *Archives of General Psychiatry* 52, 173–88

Halbreich, U., Shen, J. and Panaro, V. (1996) Are chronic psychiatric patients at increased risk for developing breast cancer? *American Journal of Psychiatry* 153, 559–60

Hoelling, I. (1999) The Berlin Runaway-House — Three Years of Antipsychiatric Practice. *Changes, 17*, 278–88

Jenner, P. and Marsden, C. D. (1983) Neuroleptics and tardive dyskinesia. In: S. J. Enna and J. T. Coyle (eds) *Neuroleptics*. New York: CNS Psychopharmacology Reprints

Jensen, K.B. (1998) Entgiftung — im großen wie im kleinen. Fuer eine Kultur des Respekts. In P. Lehmann (ed.) *Psychopharmaka absetzen — Erfolgreiches Absetzen von Neuroleptika, Antidepressiva, Lithium, Carbamazepin und Tranquilizern.* Berlin: Antipsychiatrieverlag

Kempker, K. (1998) Erfolg in Zahlen? In: K. Kempker (ed.) *Flucht in die Wirklichkeit — Das Berliner Weglaufhaus.* Berlin: Antipsychiatrieverlag

Kempker, K. (2000) *Mitgift — Notizen vom Verschwinden.* Berlin: Antipsychiatrieverlag

Lehmann, P. (1996a) *Schoene neue Psychiatrie, Vol. 1: Wie Chemie und Strom auf Geist und Psyche wirken.* Berlin: Antipsychiatrieverlag

Lehmann, P. (1996b) *Schoene neue Psychiatrie, Vol. 2: Wie Psychopharmaka den Koerper veraendern.* Berlin: Antipsychiatrieverlag

Lehmann, P. (ed.) (1998a) *Psychopharmaka absetzen — Erfolgreiches Absetzen von Neuroleptika, Antidepressiva, Lithium, Carbamazepin und Tranquilizern.* Berlin: Antipsychiatrieverlag

Lehmann, P. (1998b) Perspectives of (ex-)users and survivors of psychiatry. In: E. Lahtinen (ed.) *Mental health promotion on the European agenda* (Themes from Finland, No. 4/1998). Helsinki: STAKES Publications

Lehmann, P. (1999) Forum — the Declaration of Madrid and current psychiatric practice: users' and advocates' views. *Current Opinion of Psychiatry 12*, 6–7

Lehtinen V., Riikonen E., and Lahtinen E. (1997) *Promotion of mental health on the European agenda.* Helsinki: STAKES Publications

Lindow, V. (1999) Survivor controlled alternatives to psychiatric services. In: C. Newnes, G. Holmes and C. Dunn (eds) *This is Madness: A critical look at psychiatry and the future of mental health services.* Ross on Wye: PCCS Books

Ochsenknecht, A. (1993) Die seelische Balance — Pflanzenheilkundliche Unterstuetzung bei psychischen Problemen und beim Entzug von Psychopharmaka. In K. Kempker and P. Lehmann (eds.) *Statt Psychiatrie.* Berlin: Antipsychiatrieverlag

Ungerstedt, U. and Ljungberg, T. (1977) Behavioral patterns related to dopamine neurotransmission. *Advances in Biochemical Psychopharmacology* 16 193–99

Wehde, U. (1992) The Runaway-House: human support instead of inhuman psychiatric treatment. *Changes 10*, 154–60

Woggon, B. (1979) Neuroleptika-Absetzversuche bei chronisch schizophrenen Patienten: 1. Literaturzusammenfassung. *International Pharmacopsychiatry, 14* 34–56

World Health Organization / European Commission (1999): *Balancing mental health promotion and mental health care: a joint World Health Organization / European Commission meeting.* Broschure MNH/NAM/99.2. Brussels: World Health Organization

CHAPTER 9

Surviving social inclusion

PETER CAMPBELL

Health and Social Services should promote mental health for all, work with individuals and communities, combat discrimination against groups with mental health problems and promote their social inclusion.
Standard One of the National Service Framework.

NAPSBURY HOSPITAL CLOSED in the summer of 1999. Not an event of huge importance in the scale of things but of personal significance for me. I had been using Napsbury regularly since 1984. It was 'my bin'. Its closure meant the destruction of a familiar if not much-loved place of refuge.

But Napsbury Hospital was never my home. Nor were any of the other units and asylums I ended up in over the last thirty years. Like many of my generation of long-term service users, I never spent years in any one hospital. Although I have spent four or five years in asylums of one kind or another, I have never belonged to the asylum.

In many senses, North West London has been my home over the last twenty years. Settling where I now live after a long period on the bed-sit circuit was one of the most significant developments in my life. But on what terms do I, the holder of a mental illness ticket, belong in my 'home' community? On terms of self-imposed secrecy to be honest. I once shared a house with three others, got admitted twice in two years and mental illness was never mentioned. That was in the 1970s, but even now, while I am open and confident with fellow survivors, I keep a plausible story up my sleeve for the football terraces or the cafe.

And we have good reason to be cautious. A few years ago, I had an argument with the couple who lived downstairs. At its climax, the man shouted out: 'We all know about you. You're a nutter. You've got no rights round here.' I have friends who were driven out of their homes because they were seen to be 'nutters'. It isn't just a thing of the past. In the mid-1980s, when service user action was just starting, I agreed to be photographed in my flat by the local newspaper to publicise a new group. For all the activity and the brave rhetoric of the last fifteen years, there is no way I would stand up for that job today.

I have been fortunate in that at the point when I was running out of ideas as to how to fit into a conventional career and lifestyle and be a 'serial lunatic' at the same time, the identity of mental patient began to open out and — through the service user/survivor movement — I found some positive places where I belonged. Nevertheless, it is easy to overestimate what is going on inside and on the fringes of the mental health services and to believe that the fact that people with a diagnosis of psychotic illness are being jetted out to conferences in Frankfurt or Japan has a wider significance.

Society's response to the 'community mental patient' is quite uncertain (Barham, 1997). Our acceptance, along with other disabled people, is provisional, not definite. We may not be returning to crude measures to exclude us — 'euthanasia' programmes, compulsory sterilisation, although we know all about that now. But how far society is prepared to go to really include us? That is a different matter.

Social inclusion: a controlling contract?

The promise of social inclusion is not a new one. General or specific, spoken or implied, it has drifted over the field of mental health services for the best part of the last forty years. The gap between the promise and the reality, for people who had since the 1960s been present in the community but not part of it, was one of the basic if less emphasised reasons for the growth in service user/survivor action. But the image and reality of inclusion does not only have resonance for service users. At a certain point in the last twenty years — and the NHS and Community Care Act 1990 may be some kind of a marker — large parts of society woke up to the fact that 'the mentally-ill' were indeed no longer 'there' but 'here'. The house on the hill with its long boundary walls, gatehouse and tower could no longer continue to be the symbolic or actual container for this group. It was the street corners and public libraries now. And, while at one level, *de facto* inclusion was sanctioned by society, at another, what society was really interested in was not inclusion but control.

It is certainly welcome to see the social and political context of mental health services acknowledged in the National Service Framework (NSF) Standard One[1]. The commitments to combat discrimination and promote social inclusion are helpful. But on what basis is inclusion to be offered to people with a mental illness diagnosis? To what extent do we remain a special group in society, whose full participation is conditional on particular behaviour?

These difficulties may not be unique to people with a mental illness diagnosis. Disabled people and other groups share them to some extent. But we face the particular difficulty that, of all disabled people, we are the ones most likely to be thought both unaware of our best interests and a direct threat to society. These two perceptions make it particularly easy for unusual interventions to be applied to our lifestyles and our participation kept out on the margins.

Service users/survivors have probably never been in a strong position

---

[1] In 1999 the Department of Health in Britain produced the National Service Framework, a set of standards that all mental health services have to attain. One section (National Service Framework Standard 1) is devoted to mental health promotion.

to negotiate with society. This has not been helped by a deepening gulf that has grown in recent years between who service users think they are and might become, and what the government, the media and society think. While many mental health workers clearly believe that people with a mental illness diagnosis have a positive contribution to make, in reality they have had to witness a government approach focused in an essentially negative vision.

In Britain New Labour's early prioritisation of public (and service user) safety in their 'safe, sound and supportive' services may not have inspired service user/survivor activists seeking a positive basis for participation, but it could be argued that it is a necessary prerequisite for more encouraging approaches. Unfortunately, the government's attitude has become further tarnished, in the view of many service users, both by its enthusiasm for compliance and its use of terms like 'nuisance' to describe certain people with a mental illness diagnosis (Department of Health, 1999). In such a context, officially dangerous, unreliable and a nuisance, it is hard to see how people with a mental illness diagnosis can be negotiating their passage to social inclusion at anything but a severe disadvantage.

Continually returning to the long-standing negative perceptions about mad persons must jeopardise the chances of meaningful inclusion, even if you add on at the end that only a small percentage actually fulfil the stereotypes. Social inclusion needs to be based on a positive vision, a belief that the newly-included will bring something valuable, not that if we watch them closely enough then they probably won't mess up.

There are positive foundations for social inclusion and some of these have been indicated by service user/survivor organisations: equal value, equal opportunities, inclusive diversity, the chance to contribute, the chance to opt out, rights, tolerance of difference (Craine, 1998). But they co-exist with equally compelling factors like concepts of risk and dangerousness, compliance with treatment and careplans. The challenge for service user/ survivor organisations is to ensure that social inclusion remains an opportunity for us and not a chance to patch the fences because we made it back to town.

The idea of citizenship as a type of contract where rights are linked to, and grounded in, responsibilities is currently influential. This development may be of uncertain benefit to a conspicuously powerless group like mental health service users, particularly if it starts to impinge on aspects of their service use. Marjorie Wallace of SANE has written: '. . . essentially care in the community is a 'contract' agreed with mentally ill people, balancing their rights against their responsibilities to live within certain rules necessary for the well-being and peace of mind of others' (Wallace, 1999). Although give and take is necessary for any community inclusion, one must wonder, in the current climate, how many and what kind of rules, 'mentally-ill people' would have to satisfy to establish 'the well-being and peace of mind of others'. More than observing the law of the land, one imagines.

In the above scenario, it does not seem too fanciful to suggest that the written care plan may play an increasingly significant role. And not just for those on compulsory orders. Society, learning from mental health workers, invests tremendous significance in people with a mental illness diagnosis *taking their treatments*. What better symbol of that than when the individual *signs up*, showing their willingness to be *controlled*, their capacity to be *in control.* It would not take very much — indeed it is probably already happening — for the care plan (introduced 1991) to slide from being an outline of desired interventions to an agreement to comply. With the latter emphasis it could become a reliable passport to inclusion, carrying the mental health services' dual imperatives — to care for and control — out into society.

The terms for people's inclusion in mental health services, for their inclusion in society and the links between the two, need open discussion. It may be unrealistic to expect that long-disadvantaged groups can be included into society on an equal basis. But it seems self-defeating to reinforce or extend inequalities in the mechanics of inclusion. The current contract available to people with a mental illness diagnosis — both as citizens and as service users — appears to be linked to a vision of our essentially anti-social contribution and to the need for compliance. This sort of deal may reassure society and keep the mental health system ticking over. Whether it is a suitable basis for the liberation of community mental patients remains to be seen.

Changing attitudes: the survivor contribution
Securing rights

Whatever special promises service users may have to make, the success of inclusion/community care depends largely on changing attitudes in society. This can be attempted in a number of ways, for example through legislation, education and effective use of mass media. We now live in a society awakening to the existence of the Disability Discrimination Act 1995, an act that includes, albeit imperfectly, people with a mental illness diagnosis. The Human Rights Act came into effect in October 2000. Imperceptibly, debates in service user/ survivor groups are beginning to include civil rights talk in a way they never did before. Some writers have begun urging survivors to spend more time debating rights than treatments (Perkins, 2000). For the truth is that civil rights have never been a top priority for the service user/survivor movement. While changes to the Mental Health Act have always focused the energies of the movement and provided one of the main areas where national campaigning could be guaranteed, very few activists ever attended the Rights Now rallies leading to the Disability Discrimination Act. Regular participation by service users/survivors in the Rights Now consortium only began after the passing of the Act.

Whatever else this shows, it does illustrate the fact that service user/ survivor activists have concentrated much of their work within mental health services. And not for idle reasons. Efforts to build consensus around the National Service Framework should not conceal that a great deal that is controversial has gone on, and continues to go on, in services. In considering rights, it is understandable if service users are lukewarm about equal access to work when competent people with a mental illness diagnosis can be detained and treated against their will. But, while the divergence between greater civil rights for disabled people and the same or fewer defences against care and treatment interventions for 'the mentally ill' is bound to attract comment, the issue is not whether service user/ survivor groups can see the point of wider civil rights. Rather, it is the problem of how to respond to a whole new agenda that is opening up without deserting the 'brothers and sisters on the back wards'.

The service user/survivor movement is not well resourced, particularly at regional and national level. There are dangers in taking on even more commitments and practical arguments for doing what is already being done better rather than entering new territory. Whatever the movement does in relation to discrimination and civil rights will have to be done in alliance with other groups and organisations. Even in work on the Mental Health Act, our own 'speciality', activists swim in the wake of organisations like MIND. It is hard to see how we could pursue any radical agenda on civil rights (whatever that might be) without forming alliances with other groups of disabled people.

But consideration of such an agenda may be premature. What may be more realistic at this stage is the further development of a discussion on priorities. What is the survivor contribution here? How important is civil rights campaigning? At the same time, there is a strong argument for establishing links between service user/survivor groups and the new Disability Rights Commission, both to explore the possibilities for future co-operation and to present the movement's perspective as currently defined.

The long-term impact of a civil rights agenda on the lives of mental health service users may be great or small. But there is something to be said for being on the inside track at the beginning rather than looking in from the outside later on while others represent your interests.

Public education

An optimistic scenario based on National Service Framework Standard One can anticipate the direction of useful amounts of money and resources into mental health promotion and education — even if it is less clear who is actually going to be doing the work. Already, a new national charity, Mentality, has been established, dedicated to promoting mental health and with a special emphasis on supporting health and social care professionals in relation to Standard One. In its early publicity, Mentality makes it clear it is looking for people with direct experience of mental health problems/service use to do freelance work for them. Once again, a new agenda is being rolled out. Once again, the service user/survivor movement needs to consider its response. How much work do we do? Who do we work with? How do we work together?

Most of the work that service user/survivor organisations have done with mental health professionals since the 1997 Election has been carried out under the banner of partnership. In the immediate future it is likely that the rhetoric of partnership will envelop any collaboration on mental health education between service users and providers. Whether this is a desirable state of affairs should now be a matter for debate. The rhetoric of partnership, implying as it does a large measure of equality and a close identity of interests and objectives, is usually much more comfortable for those with the power, those handing out the invitations, than it is for those on the outside. By agreeing to set their actions within a partnership framework, service user/ survivor groups could be making it more difficult to examine and confront the power imbalances which still haunt their work with civil servants, front-line workers, mental health promotion experts or those conducting research (see Vivien Lindow, this volume).

It could be possible to move beyond the rhetoric of partnership and begin to address the practical challenges of working with mental health workers. The basic necessities for consultation have been agreed and written about by activists since the mid-1980s (e.g. payment of expenses for representatives, no jargon, time to read documents). But somehow the idea of doing things differently has lost out to the need to get results, and having to keep one eye on your funders may not have helped. Nevertheless, at this stage in the history of the service user/survivor movement, groups may have less to lose by insisting on a detailed discussion of the basis for partnership than by being quiet stakeholders in the project. However insecure activists may be, and it is worth remembering that most groups are small and badly-resourced, the contribution of service users/survivors has been significant. In the last two years, the term 'experts by experience' has been increasingly used to describe service users. This is a reminder that, however it might feel, government is not just doing us a favour when it invites us into partnerships. It may be a dream, but it should not be impossible that service users and survivors could be seen to have special expertise in mental health education and that mental health promotion experts set out to facilitate our contribution.

The service user/survivor movement has a long record of action in training and education. The first co-ordinating group of Survivors Speak Out in 1987 had an (unpaid) training officer. Training service users to be trainers has been a regular concern for network groups like Survivors Speak Out, Mindlink and the United Kingdom Advocacy Network. Local groups and individuals have been involved in educating many mental health workers. More recently, a small number of activists have become full-time freelance trainers. Although the level of expertise could be debated, the reservoir of experience held by the movement cannot be dismissed.

Unfortunately, even fifteen years after the emergence of service users/survivors as educators, their real impact is not clear. Although there is much anecdotal evidence in appreciation of their contribution, hard evidence is more difficult to find. How are survivor trainers being used? What is the particular value of their work? What do they feel about the way they are working? How could their input be made more effective? In many respects, these and other relevant questions do not appear to be asked, or certainly not in a way that other educational bodies and the service user/survivor movement itself can learn from the answers.

It is difficult to avoid the general feeling that, although service users/survivors are involved as educators, we are not really involved in the process of education. In many places, we may not have moved very far from being a 'guest spot' in the curriculum. Perhaps that is where we are best suited — but it still feels like a missed opportunity. In September 1996, The English National Board issued 'Learning from Each Other' (ENB, 1996), promoting the involvement of people who use services and their carers in the education and training of nurses. Three years later, a report on mental health nursing 'Addressing Acute Concerns' (SNMAC, 1999), admitted that ' . . . users have no real role in designing and implementing professional education and training'. One wonders how many other professions could make the same admission.

If service users/survivors are to work with mental health professionals on mental health education — and they are certainly going to be asked — they should not repeat the mistakes of the recent past. At the very least, they should ensure that evaluation and opportunities for ongoing development of effective training is part of the relationship. Whether working together is to occur within the partnership framework or not, groups and individuals should have the courage to insist on drawing up terms and conditions and turn down involvement if a favourable basis for action is not on offer. The structure of the service user/survivor movement — many and varied local groups, a few hard-pressed regional and national network organisations, limited resources overall — work in favour of a piecemeal response to any new area of activity, and the arrival of freelance trainers may have accentuated this trend in education. As a result, the impact of the service user/survivor movement is fragmented and its contribution marginalised. There are good reasons for suggesting that the movement should attempt a more co-ordinated approach to the mental health promotion agenda.

We should not assume that service user/survivor activists will primarily work with mental health professionals, although this has been the dominant pattern of activity in the last 15 years. There has always been an argument in favour of doing more work with the disability movement — the possibility of alliances with disabled people can look more attractive than partnerships with professionals — and the emergence of disability discrimination legislation and a rights-based agenda may increase the chances of successful co-operation. While there is no great history of close contact between the two movements, there are now some indications of a willingness to work together, for example the Common Agenda project at Greater London Action on Disability and the Service User Involvement in Social Work and Social Care Education and Training (SUET) initiative. When service user/survivor groups consider their response to public education initiatives they need to decide whether their messages will be best conveyed by staying within the traditional mental health/illness frameworks or by moving to approaches that emphasise common elements in the experiences of people with a mental illness diagnosis, disabled people and other disadvantaged groups. Such judgements may not be easy. Presenting the particular differences of mental health service users to the public to secure constructive valuation is by no means a fool-proof science. But it would be a wasted opportunity if service user/survivor groups decided that the underlying basis of mental health education was beyond scrutiny and debate.

In her book, *From Psychiatric Patient to Citizen* (Sayce, 1999), Liz Sayce has argued strongly for a disability inclusion model, based around the social model of disability, as the most effective basis for educational and other initiatives to secure civil rights and social inclusion for people with a mental illness diagnosis. It is too soon to say whether this model will gain wide acceptance, but it is clear that some service user/survivor activists have identified the need for a workable model to place against the medical model and that discussions towards articulating a social model of distress are continuing. With or without a fully-assembled alternative model, the service user/survivor movement, although not necessarily service users in general, would be unlikely to be happy with public education campaigns based predominantly in the medical model, even if experts were to say that this was the best way to get results.

Having said that, one must remember the relative inaction by service user/survivor groups over the way mental health education messages have been transmitted in the last decade. While the portrayal of people with a mental illness diagnosis in the mass media has attracted action and concern, a movement that has created an extensive literature of booklets, chapters, articles etc. for specialist audiences has produced relatively little aimed at the general public. Meanwhile, a great deal of the basic information material produced by large non-governmental organisations like MIND and the Mental Health Foundation has been problem-oriented and based on a medical framework (eg. Understanding Schizophrenia, Understanding Depression). This has not been substantially challenged by the service user/survivor movement (or by anyone else) and may indeed be a legitimate and valuable contribution to public education. Nevertheless, the balance of basic mental health education information deserves as much scrutiny as tabloid coverage of community care 'scandals'. Such booklets provide the fundamental grammar to set alongside the slang of the mass media and public misunderstanding. Even more important, therefore, for people with a mental illness diagnosis to say whether the grammar is good. Is it accurate? Do the underlying messages help to include or exclude? Would it be helpful to hear more about living in the community and making a contribution and less about suffering from a long-term psychotic disorder?

The call for consensus, like the call for partnership, is an attractive one and it is easy to see the problems that may arise for public education if the educators are conveying antagonistic messages. At the same time, the controversies of the last century do not simply disappear because a government puts a priority on mental health promotion.

The invidious position of people with a mental illness diagnosis in contemporary British society is not just to do with mass media exploitation of madness and violence, but is also a result of an accumulation of messages, attitudes and disempowering practices that have emanated from health and social care professionals over a long period. Furst and Davis (1997), at the end of a literature review on stigma in mental health services, concluded: 'Unless mental health professionals can model a more accepting and positive attitude, users of mental health services will remain stigmatised and unlikely to be integrated within the community.'

The danger for service user/survivor organisations in mental health education, as in other areas of action, is that they become the sauce on someone else's sandwich. In the mass media, it is common for service users to provide the anecdotal material, the 'local colour', and to find the analytical material from their interviews cut out. Such in-put is then provided by the traditional experts. While it is probably true that the first-person narrative has great impact in the mental health arena, the service user/survivor movement should not forego the opportunity to challenge the context of mental health education and present analyses that address the exercise of power and prejudice within the mental health system. As a greater quantity of messages about people with a mental illness diagnosis start reaching the public, the need for scrutiny and the presentation of alternatives may become even more important. While a good number of service users/survivors insist that their well-being was more damaged by the system set up to help them than by their intrinsic problems, that perception deserves proper representation on the mental health promotion/education agenda.

I have argued elsewhere that the service user/survivor movement has positive beliefs and practical suggestions as well as critical analyses (Campbell, 1999). I still think that is true. But what is necessary, if service user/survivor organisations are to have a creative impact on public education, is that the agendas and objectives are clarified. Not in terms of an agreed platform or programme — it is likely that educational work will be carried out by numerous small and disparate groups — but of an overall vision and the beliefs and practices that contribute to its fulfilment. At present, most members of the public have never heard of the movement, do not know what it does or what it is in favour of or against. Yet it provides one of the clearest examples of the positive contribution of people with a mental illness diagnosis in the last twenty years. It would not take a revolution for service users/survivor groups to sharpen up their brief and start getting the word out a bit more. A coherent message does not need to be invented. Yet, without something coherent, it will be difficult for a movement of small, local groups to influence the overall direction of change.

Conclusion

This chapter has not taken a detailed look at the practical difficulties service user/survivor groups face in effectively communicating with the public. The public are an unfamiliar audience and groups may have to learn different languages and techniques to those that have proved successful within mental health services. But the greater difficulties may lie in a struggle over the terms of inclusion, the balance of rights and responsibilities and who controls the messages that go out concerning people with a mental illness diagnosis. If groups are to take serious action to change public behaviour (and there is evidence that direct experience can be effective in altering attitudes), they must create and contribute to a debate on what mental health education is about rather than be illustrative material in a pre-packaged enterprise.They must consider setting up specialist public education groups. They must hold to their own vision of social inclusion.

Equal access to work opportunities, civil rights legislation, a more accurate and sensitive mass media are all desirable aspects of the enthusiasm for social inclusion. But they do not automatically lead to a feeling of belonging. Whatever happens in the next few years, people with a mental illness diagnosis will be hiding their psychiatric histories in their left shoe for some time yet. In the meantime, service user/survivor activists and others should bear in mind that while inclusion on the right basis could be liberating, inclusion on the wrong basis could prove just as painful as exclusion in the old asylums.

References

Barham, P. (1997) *Closing the Asylum*. London: Penguin Books

Campbell, P. (1999) The service user/survivor movement. In: C. Newnes, G. Holmes and C. Dunn (eds), *This is Madness: A Critical Look at Psychiatry and the Future of Mental Health Services*. Ross-on-Wye: PCCS Books

Craine, S. (1998) *Shrink Resistant: The Survivor Movement and the Survivor Perspective*. US Network Working Papers. Exchange and Change

Department of Health (1999) *National Service Framework for Mental Health — Modern Standards and Service Models*. London: DOH

English National Board (1996) *Learning from each other: the involvement of people who use services and their carers in education and training*. London: ENB

Furst, M. and Davis F. (1997) Addressing Stigma in Mental Health Services. Positive Futures Development Group. Bromley. Unpublished literature review

Perkins, R. (2000) 'I have a vision'. *Openmind, 104,* 6

Sayce, L. (2000) *From Psychiatric Patient to Citizen. Overcoming Discrimination and Social Exclusion.* London: Macmillan Press Ltd

Standing Nursing and Midwifery Advisory Committee (1999) *Mental Health Nursing: Addressing Acute Concerns.* London: Department of Health

Wallace, M. (1999) in Risk Factor: Treading a Fine Line. *Community Care, 1274,* 27 May – 2 June, 30–31

CHAPTER 10

When 'No' means 'Yes': informed consent themes with children and teenagers

STEVE BALDWIN

> *. . . The administering of drugs is a chastisement no less than a beating . . .*
> (Aristotle)

IN THE CONTEMPORARY mental health arena, a wide range of treatments is potentially available for children and teenagers. As well as traditional medicine such as drugs and surgery, other high-technology interventions have been developed: these include scanning and related technologies that can substantially improve health outcomes. Nonetheless, children and teenagers require special consideration in mental health service provision. Special procedures are required to help ensure that minors are perceived as autonomous agents in their own world.

Rights perspective

Despite the establishment of a 'full democracy' in Britain, at the beginning of the twenty-first century, human rights agendas are still incomplete. Many citizen subgroups continue to experience a diminished set of rights, based on disenfranchisement from legal and political systems. Minority ethnic groups, prisoners and children frequently experience a very restricted set of rights in the UK. In contrast in the USA, social policy is based on legislation drawn up from the Bill of Rights (enshrined in legal statutes). Unfortunately in the UK few rights exist in law, and attempts to invoke services based on related statutes can prove futile. For children and teenagers, even fewer rights exist, except the statutory obligation of the state to provide education to children until age 15.

Alternative perspectives have been developed in the domain of children's rights. *Liberationists* have maintained that denial of adult rights to children is unjust. These liberationists also propose that only *instrumental reasoning* is relevant to decision-making (i.e. they believe that minors *can* make such informed judgements). Liberationists propose that chronological age is not morally relevant, and that children should not be viewed as 'unfinished adults'. In contrast to liberationists, *protectionists* believe that children are qualitatively different to adults and therefore require special consideration (i.e. a more restricted and less emancipated set of rights).

Consent themes therefore should be viewed in the context of social control forces that are exerted on children by powerful adult authority figures (i.e. parents or legal guardians). In western European societies there has been a strong contemporary tradition of 'family sovereignty'. In this context, nuclear family values have been promoted as normal, desirable and healthy. As an alternative to family values, some European countries have developed a stronger set of state controls. Unfortunately, however, state controls can be at least as pernicious for children as adult control.

Special protection

The final determination about the nature of children's rights has yet to be resolved. Clearly, however, children require protection from exploitation and oppression by parents and other adults. Such oppression can include exploitation for labour or sex, lack of physical or psychological care, mutilation, or use as brides/slaves. Some religious groups also aim to withhold from children physical treatments such as vaccinations or immunisation. At the state level, children and teenagers need to be enfranchised for goods and services, and treatment for physical and psychological well-being.

Even in the 2000s, in the UK there is a clear lack of coherence about themes of consent and other child rights. The absence of case law or judicial review in this area has slowed progress in child emancipation. The tendency toward adversarial and legalistic relationships has created an unfortunate system of 'winners and losers' rather than a co-operative framework of compromise. The climate for children and teenagers in many contemporary mental health services is devoid of core rights-based mechanisms such as individual programme planning (i.e. case management), client advocacy and informed consent.

Rights-based client services

Most contemporary mental health provision has been designed around 'problem-based' services (i.e. delivering interventions that attempt to 'fix' clients' pathologies). During the 1980s and early 1990s there was a shift in the UK, North America and Australia to 'needs based' or 'needs led' services (Baldwin, 1998). Nonetheless, many critics have proposed that human services should be based on rights (Baldwin, 1987). Rights-based services are less likely to infringe the principles of basic human existence (e.g. personal freedom, liberty, justice).

In human services, the invocation of policies and procedures such as informed consent are necessary to avoid coercion of clients. In particular, psychiatric services, techniques and medications have been criticised for application for purposes of political and social control (Szasz, 1994). Children and teenagers, due to their age and social disempowerment, are especially at-risk from adult exploitation in both clinical and research settings (Spece *et al.*, 1996). Minors have often been at-risk both from a breach of their *right to treatment*, as well as a breach of their *right to refuse treatment*.

History of coercive treatments

Historically, people with mental health problems have been subjected to a range of treatments. These have included highly ritualistic and suspect procedures (e.g. exorcism) as well as obscure psychiatric treatments such as the spinning chair, leeches, hydrotherapy, insulin coma therapy and electric shock (Jones and Baldwin, 1992). Much psychiatric treatment has been criticised as a form of social control, rather than as alleviation of personal distress. Since its early origins in psychological science (sic) psychiatry has been criticised for operating against individual freedoms, instead acting in favour of state control.

Much of the contemporary interest in rights and consent originates in the medical experimentation that occurred in the twentieth century. Especially in the 1900s, much of medicine was experimental and 'kill or cure'. As people were likely to die anyway, public expectations were low about medical competence and effectiveness. Psychiatry in particular was viewed as devoid of scientific rigour, lacking in ethical definition and liable to corrupted practice.

The general ethos of medical and psychiatric experimentation was typified by the experiments completed in Nazi concentration camps during the Second World War. The horrific, often gratuitous, 'experiments' included freezing, grafting, poisoning , blinding and acts of sexual sadism. Subsequent reflection on the collusion between German psychiatrists and the Nazis has prompted the observation '. . . the Nazis didn't exploit the psychiatrists – it was the other way around . . .' (Pinka, 2000). These acts of torture were performed on unwilling incarcerated subjects (including minors). As these inmates were unwilling, imprisoned victims, the 'principle of consent' was inapplicable. Nonetheless, the aftermath from these hideous acts eventually set the conditions for a more enlightened world of scientific investigation.

The establishment of the Nuremburg Code in 1946 helped generate a climate of rights and responsibilities for subsequent medical experimentation. Extension of the human rights identified in the Nuremburg Code led to the World Medical Association 'Declaration of Helsinki' (1964). This declaration included specific direction about client consent. A distinction was also made between 'therapeutic' and 'non-therapeutic' research. Therapeutic research was considered to be of direct benefit to the client group. Non-therapeutic research was considered to be purely investigative.

Coercive treatments

There are eight ways of gaining control: proper compulsion, compulsive pressure, proper coercion, coercive pressure, manipulation, persuasion, enticement and request. These are based on the three core themes of rational persuasion, manipulation and coercion. These control agendas are particularly important in the context of child and adolescent services, where adults routinely seek to gain social and political control over the actions of minors. Especially in the mental health field, children and teenagers are at-risk from coercive treatments such as shock or drugs. When the social behaviour of minors appears to be out-of-control, adult authority figures may act to impose sanctions or implement coercive treatments. In such situations, themes such as consent and advocacy can seem irrelevant. For minors, coercion can be a threat to the moral view of a person as an autonomous and responsible social agent.

Coercive treatments and technologies are sometimes justified for children and teenagers by recourse to the principle of harm prevention. Simply put, the minors may be at-risk of harm to themselves or to other persons. Liberty-limiting interventions (e.g. drugs, physical restraints) may be invoked to exert social control over the minor. A paternalistic principle of harm prevention may be used to justify treatments to prevent the minor from harming him/herself. In this context, children often are not considered as fully autonomous beings, and therefore incapable of making rational decisions.

Children and teenagers are considered to have different levels of competence to adults with regard to standards for decision-making. The capacity for rational decision-making requires that children can (i) express a preference (ii) understand and appreciate the situation (iii) reach a reasonable decision and positive outcome. Psychiatric states however are considered to affect decision-making (because they may influence the outcome). In the case of so called psychiatric conditions, disease or illness processes are considered to influence the rational decision-making process.

In the case of Attention Deficit Hyperactivity-Disorder (ADHD) however there is major controversy about the underlying nature of the disorder (Baldwin and Cooper, 2000; Degrandpre and Hinshaw, 2000; also see Breggin, this volume). For more severe (and possibly life-threatening) conditions that require neurosurgery (e.g. brain tumour, epilepsy) the theme of consent may be illusory. In these instances the severity of the condition may effectively prohibit rational decision-making. Children or teenagers with such severe conditions are doubly disadvantaged (by their youth and because of impairment).

Hence minors may be susceptible to coercive treatments such as shock and medication imposed by powerful adult authority figures. Such adults often endorse coercive treatments for minors on the grounds that these young people may be a danger to themselves (or others). Paradoxically so-called outpatient treatment may be the *most coercive of all interventions*. These community programmes (e.g. Program of Assertive Community Treatment) can infringe the fundamental *right not to be treated*. The early intervention psychosis projects in Australia and the USA aim to medicate normal, undiagnosed teenagers with powerful neuroleptics who *might become psychotic later* (Gosden, 1999).

Consent: abuse, misuse and neglect

Physical or psychological damage can occur when children/teenagers are exposed to abusive practices by adults (or other children). Such abuse is considered doubly damaging for child victims, who may subsequently experience related problems when they are adults. The subordinated oppression of children in private familial space can be perpetuated by social control methods such as psychiatric medication. For example, when methylphenidate (MPH) has been prescribed after a diagnosis of ADHD, the medication exerts a powerful social control force on the behaviour of the youngster (see Breggin, this volume). The resultant behaviour of children and teenagers is similar to that of caged animals fed a diet of amphetamines: constriction of affect, blunted expression, narrowing of focus and stereotyped behaviour (Anderson and Baldwin, 2000).

It is only recently that the needs and rights of children have been the subject of considerable attention. Traditional views have associated childhood with innocence, dependence and vulnerability. In contrast, adulthood has been associated with knowledge, independence and strength. Twenty-first century views should include a moral and political discourse that promotes the special interests of the child, so that their needs and rights are enshrined. The genital mutilation of pre-pubescent young girls for example is no doubt *intended* as a positive cultural act of ritual, but has irreversible, profoundly negative psychological and health sequelae on the child, which often permeate into adulthood.

In the context of outright child abuse, consent is not relevant; in this situation the youngster is a victim of adult exploitation, and consent themes are redundant. 'Misuse' is less easily defined. One example of misuse might include the involvement of children in adult (public) entertainment. In this case, the child is an apparently willing participant giving consent, but may be subject to considerable coercion or pressure from adults in authority (e.g. parents or teachers). In the case of child neglect, adult care falls short of the minimum desirable standards. Physical cruelty involves the infliction of deliberate harm to children in the form of punishment, or torture for adult pleasure. The 'Wonderland' sex ring typifies such harm.

Psychiatric treatment

In the case of psychiatric treatment, many interventions may contribute to (or detract from) the optimal psychological and physical development of the child. In the case of ADHD for example, proponents of amphetamine medication have reversed the standard health education proposition that 'drugs are harmful'. Instead they have inverted the argument to propose that 'not medicating your child is unethical'. Psychiatric treatments such as shock and drugs can be viewed as exemplars of 'collective abuse' by society. In these instances, social control is exerted on youthful behaviour by social, economic and political agencies. In this context, the adult exploitation of children can become a means to its own ends (i.e. drugging a child in guise of psychiatric treatment for a supposed medical condition to achieve the real, hidden agenda of social control). This type of 'triple damage' is particularly pernicious, as the future adult may be deeply damaged by the childhood trauma.

This subversion of therapy into 'harmful helping' is one of the most disturbing aspects of contemporary psychiatric provision for children and teenagers. The selling of DSM as a supposed scientific enterprise (Kutchins and Kirk, 1997), the marketing of ECT as a 'life saving treatment' for troubled children (Baldwin and Oxlad, 2000) and the purposeful misdiagnosis and maltreatment of ADHD-labelled infants and children with amphetamines (Baldwin, 2000; Breggin, 1998; McCubbin and Cohen, 1999; Stein, 1999a;b) all represent a cynical abnegation of human rights of the most vulnerable section of the human population. In these contexts it is meaningless to discuss consent themes. In these instances, the proposition of *volenti non fit injuria* ('to one who has consented, no wrong is done') simply does not apply. The 'control as care' agenda of modern psychiatry is the *ultimate social injustice* (i.e. the so-called treatment of non-existent conditions with unproven medications that have harmful side-effects to maximise economic profit) and a total perversion of adult morality.

Legal themes

The intersection of medical and legal domains has always been problematic from a human rights perspective. In particular the medical expansionist agendas (Barker, Baldwin and Ulas, 1989) within psychiatry have promoted social control themes at the expense of individual liberty and freedom. The consideration of social justice for children and teenagers has been vexatious for rights activists. In the UK, implementation of the Children Act (1989) was an attempt to establish and defend minor rights, including the legal maxim that society should '. . . have regard to the ascertainable rights and feelings of the child concerned [considered in the light of his age and understanding] . . .' (Children Act, 1989 part 1, 13). These statutes were established to promote adult respect for the child's expressed wishes. In this framework, children would be treated as if they could make their own choices.

Informed, implied or presumed consent?

Minor consent is a complex domain with unclear boundaries. Rival factions that represent different interest groups dispute much of the territory. Medical researchers, legal advocates and NGO agencies (e.g. NSPCC, National Early Years Network) have adopted different positions in the negotiated territory of minor rights. The theme of 'consent' is not clear-cut and involves several aspects. For example, *implied consent* is assumed when adult clients voluntarily attend the outpatient clinic/surgery. The collection of 'routine' test material from adults (e.g. blood/urine samples, blood pressure readings) is considered acceptable and normal practice by medical personnel. These medical privileges are usually extended when minor clients attend clinics or hospitals (although such children may be unwilling and non-compliant attendees, who have *not* given their consent even to attend).

In contrast, *informed consent* is considered to have occurred when the person has given their voluntary permission to a procedure or intervention, based on appropriate information and knowledge. This permission should accord with the person's personal values and preferences. With minor clients, the determination of consent is more complex, as the process of personal decision-making may be less transparent to adult observers. (Some children for example show an 'assent bias' in their personal style, which may reflect not real agreement, but rather a 'desire to please adults'.) A third category, *presumed consent*, is inferred under the special conditions of health or medical emergency. In this special category, admission to an accident and emergency unit would set the conditions whereby life-saving treatments (e.g. resuscitation, transfusion) are essential to preserve the life of the individual. This category is considered equally applicable to adults and children.

Aspects of informed consent

There are multiple aspects to the principle of informed consent. First, the client should have access to all the necessary information to make an appropriate determination of the situation. Second, the client should be able to understand this information and then form a reasonable conclusion. (Children and people with an intellectual disability are typically excluded on these grounds.) Third, the person should give their unequivocal consent. Fourth, authorisation is required (usually a written, signed statement testifying to consent).

The client should also be given full information about the risks and benefits of alternative treatments (including the option of 'no-treatment'). Client 'understanding' requires that the necessary information has been given to the client in functional not technical terms (i.e. 'you may lose your memory' not 'transient cerebral dysfunction may produce temporary anterograde amnesia'). 'Informed consent' therefore means a non-coerced and voluntary choice by the client. This choice would favour a specific treatment option, having considered (and rejected) other equivalent interventions, based on a free, unfettered decision. 'Authorisation' should mean more than a signed consent form (this is the minimum requirement) but a reasoned decision based on an agreement to proceed.

The most benign explanation for the exclusion of young people ('minors' as defined by legal statute) from giving consent is that they are considered too young to have yet formulated a set of personal values. There are however less benign explanations: critics maintain that many adults in authority refuse to grant minors the power of consent so that they can be better controlled. Sceptics have observed that in the modern 'adultocentric' social world, it is easier to withhold than to establish juvenile rights. Other social and cultural obstacles to the enshrinement of juvenile rights include the difficulties with comprehension of statistics and the probability of (un)successful intervention.

The contemporary service preoccupation with avoiding lawsuits means that many clinicians and researchers are obsessed with obtaining a signature on the consent form, rather than using the document as a vehicle to uphold client rights. Medical personnel and hospital psychologists, moreover are often trapped in the dual role of 'clinician-researcher'. These staff function as 'double agents' who have to operate in a conflicted capacity to determine 'what works' in an environment that protects societal, not personal interests. Often, adult expediency will determine the experience of minor clients.

Exceptions to informed consent

There are five situations where informed consent is considered inapplicable (where normal client rights can be waived). These include: a physical emergency (e.g. wartime conditions), medical emergency (i.e. real life-threatening conditions), patient incompetence (by virtue of limited intelligence, or disability), patient waiver (i.e. voluntary abnegation of rights) and therapeutic privilege (i.e. 'doctor knows best'). Unfortunately in law, minors are not considered legally competent (although this proposition has been challenged in some courts in the USA and the UK). Therefore in law, consent reverts to the parents (or legal guardians *in loco parentis*). For institutionalised minors, the state assumes legal custody *in parens patriae* (as 'parent of the nation'). Such 'wards of the state', institutionalised in welfare agencies, are often considerably at-risk for experimentation and unwarranted interference.

Historically, so-called medical experimentation has subjected vulnerable groups to the most horrific exploitation and abuse, sometimes amounting to torture. In the infamous Tuskagee Syphillis Study conducted between 1932 and the 1970s, black males with venereal disease were *left untreated* (despite the availability of an effective remedy) to determine the natural progression of the disease. Other more recent examples include the continued prescription of the thalidomide drug to pregnant women, despite known genetic risks to neonates. Other vulnerable groups have been injected with live cancer cells and the hepatitis virus to 'promote medical knowledge'.

Even institutionalised minor clients have been forced into experimentation at the very margins of acceptable practice. Orphaned infants in religious institutions have been subjected to the most horrific experiments. For example, 200 Australian infants in Victoria were infected with a live influenza virus to test new vaccines, where Catholic nuns claimed they 'gave consent' (sic) on behalf of the orphans. During the 1980s in UK social services residential homes, so-called 'pindown' techniques were used to physically restrain hundreds of minor clients (Baldwin and Barker, 1995). In the UK during the 1990s, many general hospitals removed organs from thousands of deceased infants for supposed research, without the consent of the parents. The UK serial killer Harold Shipman continued to be licensed as a general practitioner whilst detained in custody (unrestricted by General Medical Council regulation) until his eventual imprisonment many months later. The abject failure to act by the medical establishment has been viewed as a major impediment to the establishment of a rights agenda in health services.

Medical negligence/malpractice

Sometimes medical treatment does not achieve the minimum standard required for safe and effective practice. Physician failure to disclose full information about a treatment is one example of medical negligence. In this case, the physician may have omitted important information about side-effects, risks or adverse consequences of a treatment. Equally, the physician may have omitted to inform the client about alternative treatments. These behaviours constitute *medical negligence* and are actionable in law. The personal injury sustained to the client can be financially calculated, with respect to lost earnings/education, or reduced life quality. Decisions about compensation are based on the judgement that a reasonable person with all the facts would not have consented to the treatment. In law, 'un-consented touching' is considered as a tort of battery and therefore legally actionable. Children are especially vulnerable to unconsented adult touching.

Amphetamine prescription and ADHD

In the USA in the 1990s, between 3 and 4 million children were prescribed methylphenidate (MPH) after a diagnosis of ADHD (Breggin, 1998). In the UK, MPH prescription rates increased by a factor of twenty-five between 1991 and 1998 (Baldwin and Anderson, 2000; Anderson and Baldwin, 2000). The medical rationale for MPH prescription is presumably based on some variant of deficit theory, although the exact mechanism has never been clarified (Baldwin and Cooper, 2000). Proponents of MPH maintain that hyperactive behaviour can be controlled with amphetamines, so that learning can take place in educational settings. Nonetheless even this proposition has been discounted by the highest federal health authority in the USA (NIMH, 1998).

In the UK the Department of Health has provided an overview of MPH prescription for 'severe ADHD' via the NHS publication from the National Institute for Clinical Excellence (NICE, 2000). The report delimits the prescription of MPH to children aged 6 and older, in the context of a 'multidisciplinary approach' to treatment. The report also makes specific recommendations about desisting with MPH treatment if clinical improvement cannot be demonstrated.

Unfortunately the theme of consent is largely ignored in advice to UK physicians in the NICE report. Mostly, parents of children labelled with an ADHD diagnosis are not given the facts about methylphenidate. A recent report (Baldwin, 2001) has confirmed that in a sample of 100 families with children labelled ADHD, parents were not informed even that MPH is a member of the amphetamine family. Moreover, parents were not informed about drug side effects (DSEs) or the possible adverse drug reactions (ADRs) from taking the medication. Many parents reported they were told the drug was 'safe, effective and non-addictive'. None of these is true. Parents also reported they were never offered an alternative to MPH treatment. Most were informed the treatment choice was 'methylphenidate or nothing'. Such a forced choice is an obvious breach of consent procedures.

Electric shock treatment with minors

Electric shock therapy (EST, commonly called electro-convulsive therapy, ECT) has been used with minors since the late 1930s. The application of shock to children and teenagers was documented after the Second World War in the USA (Bender, 1947) and Europe (Heuyer *et al.*, 1947). In contemporary psychiatric services, the extent of electroshock with minors is difficult to determine, as prevalence rates are obscured by methods of counting. In the USA it has been estimated that between 500 and 3500 minors are given electric shock treatment every year (Thompson and Blaine, 1987). UK figures as reported by the Department of Health for EST administration unfortunately do not break down prevalence rates into age groups.

When minors are given EST, consent is virtually never obtained. The only survey of consent with minors given shock reported that less than 1% of 217 cases even mentioned consent in the published account (Baldwin and Oxlad, 1996). Neither was parental consent used as a substitute for minor consent. Moreover the authors of the survey reported many cases where the minor had refused to agree to EST, yet the treatment had been given anyway (Baldwin and Oxlad, 1996). Shock treatment was not used as a life-saving treatment, but rather as a means to control unwanted social behaviour (e.g. aggression, withdrawal).

In contemporary mental health services, there is no justification for the use of shock with minor clients. There are more than 230 alternatives to shock treatment. Children with mental health problems require the most sensitive approach by adults. The use of shock and drugs to control the unwanted social behaviour of children and teenagers is a clear example of health fascism.

Summary

Children and teenagers are at-risk of adult exploitation and abuse in human services. The absence of rights-based service provision in human services means that minors are often in jeopardy from staff employed to protect them. Successive public enquiries in both health and social services settings have failed to prevent serial abuse of children and teenagers in adult care. Procedures such as 'informed consent' are designed to protect clients from exploitation and abuse. Informed consent procedures should be modified and extended to child and teenage clients.

References

Anderson, R. and Baldwin, S. (2000) What's in a name? Amphetamine and methylphenidate. *Journal of Substance Use, 5* 89–91

Baldwin, S. (1987) From communities to neighbourhoods. *Disability Handicap and Society, 2(1)*, 41-59

Baldwin, S. (1998) *Needs Assessment and Community Care.* Oxford: Butterworth Heinemann

Baldwin, S. (2001) Audit survey of 100 families with children diagnosed ADHD/ADD. *International Journal of Risk and Safety in Medicine* (in press)

Baldwin, S. and Anderson, R. (2000) The cult of methlyphenidate: clinical update. *Critical Public Health, 19(1)*, 81–6

Baldwin, S. and Barker, P. (1995) Uncivil liberties: The politics of care for younger people. *Journal of Mental Health, 1*, 41–50

Baldwin, S. and Cooper, P. (2000) How should ADHD be treated? *The Psychologist* December, 13(12), 598–602

Baldwin, S. and Oxlad, M. (1996) Multiple case sampling of ECT administration to 217 minors: Review and meta-analysis. *Journal of Mental Health, 5(5)*, 451–63

Baldwin, S. and Oxlad, M. (2000) *Electroshock and Minors: A fifty year review.* Westport CT: Greenwood

Barker, P., Baldwin, S., and Ulas, M. (1989) Medical expansionism: some implications for psychiatric nursing practice. *Nurse Education Today, 9*, 192–202

Bender, L. (1947) One hundred cases of childhood schizophrenia treated with electric shock. *Transactions of the American Neurological Association, 72*, 165–9

Breggin, P. (1998) *Talking Back to Ritalin.* Monroe, MA: Common Courage Press.

DeGrandpre, R.J. and Hinshaw, S.P. (2000) ADHD: Serious psychiatric problems or all-American cop-out? A debate between Richard J. DeGrandpre PhD and Stephen P. Hinshaw PhD, *Cerebrum: the Dana Forum on Brain Science 2(3)*, 12–38

Department of Health (1989) *The Children Act.* London: HMSO

Gosden, R. (1999) Prepsychotic treatment for schizophrenia: Perventive medicine, social control, or drug marketing strategy? *Ethical Human Sciences and Services, 1(2)*, 165–77

Heuyer, P.G., Dauphin, M. and Lebovici, S. (1947) La pratique de l'electrochoc chez l'enfant. *Acta Paedopsyiatrica, 14*, 60–4

Jones, Y. and Baldwin, S. (1992) Shock lies and psychiatry. *Changes: An International Journal of Psychology and Psychotherapy, 10(2)*, 126–35

Kutchins, H. and Kirk, S. (1997) *Making Us Crazy: The psychiatric bible and the creation of mental disorders.* New York: The Free Press

McCubbin, M. and Cohen, D. (1999) Empirical, ethical, and political perspectives on the use of methylphenidate. *Ethical Human Sciences and Services, 1(1)*, 81–101

NICE (2000) *Guidelines for the use of methylphenidate (ritalin, equasym) with children with ADHD.* London: NHS Executive

NIMH (1998) *Diagnosis and treatment of attention deficit hyperactivity-disorder.* NIH Consensus Development Conference. Rockville, MD: NIMH

Pinka, A. (2000) Personal communication.

Spece, R., Shimm, D. and Buchanan, A. (1996) *Conflicts in Clinical and Research Settings.* New York:

Stein, D.B. (1999a) A medication-free parent management program for children diagnosed as ADHD. *Ethical Human Sciences and Services, 1(1)*, 61–79

Stein, D.B. (1999b) *Ritalin is Not the Answer.* San Francisco: Jossey Bass

Szsaz, T. (1994) *Cruel Compassion.* New York: Wiley

Thompson, J.W. and Blaine, J.D. (1987) Use of ECT in the United States in 1975 and 1980. *American Journal of Psychiatry, 144,* 557–6

CHAPTER 11

Controlled bodies, controlled eating: the treatment of eating distress

VIVIEN J. LEWIS AND SARA CURETON

Women are told from their infancy, and taught by the example of their mothers, that a little knowledge of human weakness, justly termed cunning softness of temper, outward obedience, and a scrupulous attention to a puerile kind of propriety will obtain for them the protection of man; and should they be beautiful, every-thing else is needless, for, at least, twenty years of their lives.

I once knew a weak woman of fashion, who was more than commonly proud of her delicacy and sensibility. She thought a distinguishing taste and puny appetite the height of all human perfection, and acted accordingly. I have seen this weak sophisticated being neglect all the duties of life, yet recline with self-complacency on a sofa, and boast of her want of appetite as a proof of delicacy that extended to, or perhaps, arose from her exquisite sensibility . . .
(Mary Wollstonecraft, *A Vindication of the Rights of Women* 2nd Edition, 1792)

SINCE THE LABELLING of 'anorexia nervosa' in the late nineteenth century by William Withy Gull and E. C. Lasegue, experiences of distressed eating have been constantly misunderstood and hence maltreated. This chapter will present an historical and cultural perspective on the social construction and control of the experiences labelled 'eating disorders' in the context of a wider view of the oppression of women. Present day therapies and regimes will be examined, in many cases little changed from Gull's nineteenth century moral therapeutic approach, and in others more punitive and depersonalising than the incarceration of criminals. Finally, alternative perspectives on these predominantly female experiences will be offered alongside suggestions for future approaches.

Women are told
In May 2000, the British Medical Association released a report on 'Eating Disorders, Body Image and The Media' (BMA Board of Science and Education,

2000). In the Foreword, Ian Bogle states, 'The report considers the role of the media in perpetuating body dissatisfaction, especially in young women, and triggering eating disorders in vulnerable individuals.' In the Discussion, the authors state, 'The media, if they adopt responsible attitudes, can provide valuable health information to young people, and aid the development of high self-esteem and sense of achievement which is not tied to body size.' On 21st June 2000 the UK Government held a summit addressing 'body image and the links between media imagery and eating disorders'. Tessa Jowell, Minister for Women, was quoted on the front cover of The Eating Disorders Association's *Signpost* magazine for June 2000 as saying, 'Young women are tired of feeling second rate because they can't match the thin ideal that they so often see in the media.' Older women as well as younger ones are tired of feeling second rate. In addition to the shame of not having perfect bodies themselves, they carry guilt that their daughters also subscribe to these ridiculous ideals and search for somewhere to place the guilt they feel at not having protected them. Hence mothers of young females with diagnoses of 'eating disorders' are sending samples of their saliva to a medical institute as part of a research project looking at genetic factors in eating disorders, desperately seeking some means by which they can assuage the guilt and the blame they feel.

About halfway between Mary Wollstonecraft's attempt to vindicate the rights of women and the present day, William Withy Gull in England and E. C. Lasegue in France independently claimed the apparently voluntary experience of partial self-starvation as a medical or mental condition and gave it the label 'anorexia nervosa'. Gull did not ascribe the cause to the media or genetic predispositions but almost simply to the fact of being female, and he may have been right, although not for the reasons he described: 'That mental states may destroy appetite is notorious and it will be admitted that young women at the ages named are specially obnoxious to mental perversity' (Gull, 1874).

In depicting the experience of eating distress in this way, it seems to be understood that it is the woman's mental state that is the cause of the experience and thus the experience from then on is deemed to be an illness, the focus of which lies within the individual herself. Such thinking gives credence to treatment regimes which plunder the depths of the individual in order to root out what is believed to be the cause, barely pausing to consider that it may lie outside the place being plundered. There has been now more than a century of putative causes of eating distressed experiences, including: being female, decreased potassium levels, unresolved grief, biological factors, genetic factors, the family, media, zinc deficiency, childhood sexual abuse, phobic avoidance, a variety of sociocultural factors, and so forth. We suggest that these putative factors have served to divert attention away from a more insidious and covert factor in eating distress, namely an oppression of women that has continued since before Mary Wollstonecraft's time (Lewis, 1996). The result of this diversion has been to stymie an examination of the role society plays in the development and perpetuation of eating distress, specifically the role women have, or maybe more to the point have not, within that society. Women *are* their bodies in a way that a man is not. Little wonder then that women choose to mutilate this body as a very visible means of expressing themselves within society.

The Concise Oxford Dictionary (1934) defined 'oppress' as 'overwhelm with superior weight or numbers or irresistible power; lie heavy and weigh down'. Perhaps, when overwhelmed with 'superior *weight*' or '*weigh*(ed) down', the choice to diminish one's own body weight, or increase it as in other experiences of eating distress, may seem like the only option. Indeed it may be that the individual experiencing eating distress is in some way making a rational choice when she chooses to speak with her body in a society which overvalues the size and shape of women's physical form but fails to hear the female voice within it. She is trying to make herself heard by speaking in a language valued by society, literally 'body talk'. Thus we argue that one of the main causes of eating distress lies in the oppression of women. Furthermore because the examination of the role of society in this experience goes unexplored, so-called treatments focus on the individual, thus the oppression not only continues but is perpetuated.

Should they be beautiful?
The importance, for females, to conform to the current cultural construction of beauty has been in place since long before Mary Wollstonecraft wrote *A Vindication of the Rights of Women* and remains in place to this day. It seems that no pain is too much if it results in transforming the body so that it meets with current societal ideals for the female shape and form. The mutilation of females in the name of beauty has moved on from foot-binding, neck-stretching and the voluntary ingestion of tapeworms, but only in form, for now we have surgical means by which to construct beauty. Modern technology enables females to choose (though 'choose' is the operative word) to be mutilated in a variety of ways. A plethora of techniques exists: the removal of back teeth to create hollowing of the cheeks, the removal of ribs to make the waist smaller, breast reduction, breast enlargement, liposuction, and many forms of plastic surgery.

Certain breeds of dogs and cats have been so inbred for particular show-winning beautiful characteristics that they cannot breathe properly or cannot give birth except by Caesarean section, or are otherwise physically impaired. These are animals that are owned. They are registered as the property of human beings who have complete control over their destinies and, as such, their importance lies in the extent to which one animal's humanly constructed beauty wins in competition with another. Control by human beings renders these creatures objects and powerless — like females within our society who win or lose on their success or failure in matching a socially constructed ideal of beauty. This is, however, not the cause of eating distress but rather the medium within which the experience of eating distress can flourish, a medium within which women are judged, and indeed in many cases judge themselves, primarily on their physical shape and qualities. This is a medium in which their intellectual abilities are neglected, a medium within which feeding one's female form, having and responding to one's own needs induces guilt. This is not merely a cultural context of fitness, but also a cultural context of competition.

Puny appetites
The experience of partial self-starvation arises in this frame of competition and the ideal for females of extreme thinness — the female child grows up

and is socialised within this frame, where a starved body is thought something worth having while a well-fed one is something to be ashamed of. For the young female some thing or things happen. She experiences some failures or shames, abuses or guilts that create an overwhelming threat to the self. Panic eventually sets in as the self fears disintegration. The natural physical consequence of this panic is in the activity of the suprarenal glands, and hence some weight loss. Thus a means of how to hold the fragile, battered self in one piece is discovered as the individual is protected through her semi-starved state from the emotional tidal wave she would otherwise be engulfed by. It has the added bonus that it is, at first, rewarded by society because society admires the diminishing frame, the semi-starved look. She has found something she is good at, can apparently win at, and as she goes on winning, this becomes her raison d'être. And society goes on rewarding even when she has fallen into the trap of more complete self-starvation, because the fragile death-inducing physical frame screams and is heard in a way that the voice is not. Thus she finds a way to speak from within. But the sad irony is that though the scream is heard, the message is not, because treatment revolves around the sharp point of the scream and fails to hear the message contained within it. The message is also not heard because the medium also induces panic and confusion in the potential listener.

Mental perversity

In William Withy Gull's time, the treatment of choice for what was known as mental perversity was moral therapy, hence this was applied to young females who had won at losing weight and developing puny appetites: 'The treatment required is obviously that which is fitted for persons of unsound mind. The patients should be fed at regular intervals, and surrounded by persons who would have moral control over them; relations and friends being generally the worst attendants' (Gull, 1874). The recommendation therefore was that the young woman was removed from her family and friends, restricted to bed-rest, fed large quantities of food and not listened to: 'Food should be administered at intervals varying inversely with the exhaustion and emaciation . . . The inclination of the patient must be in no way consulted.' Barbaric? Perhaps, but this particular therapeutic approach is still widely practised today in the 21st century.

Incarceration is sure eventually to be the fate of any female whose body weight falls to a level which exceeds the threshold for anxiety of her family and professional helpers, whether or not her body weight *is* actually critically low for her health. If there is a specialist placement available or there is money to fund such a placement, she will go to a specialised unit for 'eating disorders', voluntarily or otherwise. Where such a place is not available or funding is denied she will find herself in a state psychiatric ward where staff have no specialist knowledge, though she may feel this to be no particular disadvantage in terms of her eating distress given the so-called treatment she would receive in the former. She may be restricted to her room, often without visitors or stimulation, and with her levels of activity limited. Her privacy is likely to be totally violated for fear that she will vomit the food she has been forced to eat. The window may have restricted opening to prevent her from vomiting outside. Initially she is likely to be able to wash and to go to the toilet only when accompanied, and she will probably be expected to ingest as many as 3000 kilocalories a day of food and highly nutritious drinks. Restoration of normal activities, if not liberty, will depend upon her gaining a required amount of weight. She will have to behave herself and be a 'good girl' if she is going to escape. Many females subjected to this form of so-called treatment view it in these terms. They are serving a sentence under an oppressive regime for having committed a crime, which ironically was in the beginning not only condoned but applauded by society. When they have reached the required standard they escape. Unsurprisingly having escaped, like felons who have had no treatment, they will re-offend, take off all the weight, go back to the weight they started from or worse: 'just a little bit lower . . . just to make sure'.

The treatment method

A striking example of this kind of so-called treatment was given by Rosalind Caplin at a conference organised by Survivors Speak Out (Pembroke, 1992):

> Though my stomach had shrunk with lack of food I was presented with dinner plates piled high with stodgy potato, tough lumps of over-cooked liver and boiled cabbage. When I just could not, would not eat I was force fed. It became the norm that every mealtime I would be held down by two members of staff, one pinning my arms behind the chair whilst the other mechanically shovelled food into my mouth. The more this occurred the more I struggled until each meal became a literal battleground, and I was left at the end with scratches all around my mouth and face and bruises upon my arms. On one occasion I fell off the chair, and still struggling a third nurse came in, held me to the floor and held my nose, whilst simultaneously continuing to force whole chips down my throat. I could not breathe, the food went into my windpipe and my fighting became one for lack of oxygen.

At the same conference, in her introduction, Louise Pembroke stated:

> Through my own experience and contact with others I have seen ridiculous and cruel treatments employed. From force-feeding to hormones, E.C.T., to sensory deprivation. Even brain surgery has been offered. Some people have entered psychiatric units without eating difficulties but have left with them. For example, being made to eat food forbidden by your religion or being given major tranquillisers which increase weight dramatically.

In 1999, the 'brain surgery' Louise Pembroke referred to was offered to Lena Zavaroni, a one-time popular child singing star, who was alleged to have died as a result of a chest infection in hospital three weeks after such surgery.

People who have experienced partial self-starvation often try to tell their stories, verbally or in writing, but are seldom listened to by those who would have control over them. The tragedy is that their dominant story is one of not having a voice. So professional helpers may at best offer service users token representation, but seldom really listen to what they do not want to hear. In a book written by those who have experienced eating distress, stories are told which should teach such helpers something about how to help as opposed to how to hinder (Shelley, 1997). For example, drug treatments frequently cause more harm than good. 'Hospitalisation was one of the worst experiences of my life . . . They put me on a high-calorie diet and large doses of Largactil.' 'Alison' gained sufficient weight to be released, then lost it all and more in total confusion. Frequently individuals felt like the guinea pigs they were. In the same book, 'Cherry' writes: 'I soon got to know the names of the masses of chemicals they forced into me without my permission: sleeping pills, Largactil, amitriptyline, insulin, iron, vitamins. Then came the ones they would not tell me the names of nor would they tell me what they were for. I now believe they were being tested on me.' 'Derine' writes: '. . . I was put on bed-rest 24 hours a day for six weeks in total. I was given increased doses of Largactil to stimulate my appetite and induce constant sleep.' 'Jean' writes: 'I was given an injection of insulin, then left without any food . . . where were the ethics in such a sadistic form of treatment?' Anne writes:' I attended all their self-help groups and took part in their research, often finding this detrimental to my health as in the case of a drug study.'

The problem is that the voices of service users go unheard or unheeded if they are heard, and hence what might be termed bad treatment continues. Such treatment may be worse than none at all, when females who partially self-starve are incarcerated like criminals and punished far more than if they had committed an offence in law; the effect upon them can be life-threatening. We do not for one moment wish to understate the seriousness of the experience of eating distress nor the necessity for help. However it feels as though such barbaric oppressive treatments are condoned by society because they stem from an implicit societal law that expects females to conform to the current ideal, whatever that is, and, when they fail to do so, such failure *is* an offence for which the offender can be punished. It is almost as if by virtue of their apparently voluntary self-starvation anything can be resorted to. Again, 'Cherry' writes: 'When I reached about four stone and I had become too exhausted to eat let alone vomit, I was threatened with Electric Shock Treatment and a lobotomy if I did not eat. I was so scared that I really tried.' For 'Jean', ECT became a reality. 'I was given ECT on three occasions. I did not want the treatment but was forced to go through with it . . . When I came round from the anaesthetic . . . I was confused, disorientated, did not know who I was, where I was, what had happened in the past or what I was going to do next . . . some memories were lost forever.'

Even so-called non-invasive treatments can be oppressive, abusive and also ineffective for all forms of psychological distress (Masson, 1992). Indeed some psychological therapies can invade parts of the individual that physical so-called treatments cannot reach. 'Derine', for example, describes her experience of behaviour therapy: 'I was put on complete bed-rest; all my possessions were taken away on a punishment/reward system where if you did something "good" such as eat a meal, you were rewarded by being given back one of your possessions. If you did something "bad" it was taken away again. I put on four stone in eight weeks under that regime. I then returned home to lose it all again' (Shelley, 1997). 'Helen' had experienced years of sexual abuse from her father, but never disclosed it to anyone, until: 'The college counsellor was called — I talked to her. My words were full of intense pain and anger. For the first time I spoke about the abuse. I was in a terrible state afterwards. She couldn't calm me down; I wanted to be alone so I left and went home. Meanwhile the counsellor called my parents and told them everything I had told her in confidence. I couldn't believe it. My mother beat me when I got home. Later when I was alone my father came in and said that no matter what I said about him and no matter to whom I said it he would always deny it. Then he beat me.' Helen's secondary abuse was subtle: the betrayal of confidentiality by her counsellor.

Others have experienced more flagrant sexual abuse, as in the case of the Clinical Psychologist, Peter Slade. Although he was prevented from practising clinically again his professional body, the British Psychological Society, allowed him to retain his membership and Fellowship of the Society (*The Psychologist*, 1998). As Pilgrim (1999) notes in reference to Peter Slade: 'If a paedophile is arrested they are denied access to new potential victims forthwith. In contrast, an abusive therapist under investigation may continue to practise and may re-abuse during the investigatory period.' The case of Peter Slade is not an isolated incident. Garrett and Davis (1994) reported that 3.4% of clinical psychologists responding to a postal survey had engaged in sexual contact with current or discharged patients. The punishment for some psychological therapists identified as having sexually abused their clients might be merely to sideline them into another area of work.

Immoral control

The dominant story of the young female who partially starves herself within her family is of having no voice, so she speaks in body speak, the language of the body that she expects a society which values the physical form to hear. Unfortunately the message goes unheeded as her voice is ignored even with regards to her own treatment, and the abuse and oppression of a larger society are replicated within the confines of the specialist treatment she receives. She feels powerless, worthless, helpless and hopeless. She does not starve herself because some supermodel appears to — the culture of thinness does not cause eating distress, it provides the milieu. Indeed the pressure on females to mutilate themselves in the name of beauty is simply another example of their oppression. The control of females to silence their voices happens not only to those who partially starve themselves, but also to those who try to make a difference.

Throughout Britain the nature and quality of treatment that females experiencing eating distress might receive is purely serendipitous. In some areas there is no specialist service, and here individuals are likely to receive ad hoc interventions from hopefully well-meaning but have-a-go, half-trained mental health workers. Indeed even within the specialist units, both National Health service and private, they are likely to be supposedly cared for by such people. There are instances when individuals receive so-called treatment from someone who wants to use them as a case history for their training, with no consideration for their level of expertise in the area. In extreme circumstances they might be referred out of county to so-called specialist units where they could receive the treatment described by Rosalind Caplin and 'Derine' previously, at the same time as being separated from their family and social supports. Where specialist services do exist the likelihood is that they will have been designed almost exclusively with financial considerations in mind, because the Health Authority concerned was alarmed by the ever-increasing budget for sending individuals out of county. Rarely are clinicians paid any attention, and even more rare are the occasions when purchasers genuinely listen to and heed service user representation. In many areas there are lone clinicians who do try to make a difference, but frequently at personal cost.

Jones and Schreiber-Kounine (2001) describe two years so far of attempting to establish a specialist service for eating distress in Avon and Western Wiltshire which made sense to current ways of thinking, ways which have been demonstrated to be successful by other specialist units. Their plan, in line with thinking nation-wide, was to have a Day Therapy/ Community Mental Health Team Service developed initially, followed much later by in-patient services. Their experience was one of constantly changing rules and expectations — even the Trust within which they worked changed shape. It was decided to incorporate the in-patient service plans into the first development, significantly reducing the monies available for the Day Therapy Service. Increasingly, Jones and Schreiber-Kounine found themselves being presented with decisions that had been made elsewhere. Thus they experienced a lack of information and impoverished communication. Eventually user representation at planning meetings was 'no longer sought'.

The 'immoral control' experiences of Jones and Schreiber-Kounine, as they argue, can be likened to the experience of the individual who is partially self-starved within the family. The rules constantly change, and the young female has no voice in their formation. More broadly she has no voice in the wider society, where the rules are clear but impossible to adhere to, such as win, work, earn, be thin (but not *too* thin), be mother, be lover, be more things than it is possible for one person to be and survive. Nobody told Jones and Schreiber-Kounine what the rules were in their organisation, and they had to try to keep up with them as they were constantly shifting. They found themselves feeling de-skilled and hopeless, despite knowing that they were 'innovative, creative and hard working clinicians'. The breakdown of communication they experienced led to them feeling 'demoralised, helpless and powerless', much like the young female within this insane society. Initially they felt powerful and in control because of their expert knowledge and skills, as the young female feels when she begins to control and restrict her food intake, but eventually felt that their knowledge was 'increasingly perceived as a nuisance and marginalised', a state roughly equivalent to the out of control phase of eating distress. They also experienced an eventual feeling of worthlessness, as initially their service had seemed to generate considerable interest and energy, but later seemed to rest exclusively on financial considerations. This they likened to the experience of the young female in therapy, initially 'interesting and glamorous' but when failing to progress, 'frustrating, draining and less interesting'.

Our experience in our local area has been similar to that of Jones and Schreiber-Kounine. The first author used to start training sessions for health professionals on eating distress by giving participants a fantasy-type exercise — they were to imagine that they were in their place of work and were suddenly told that a young woman had come in, body weight 5 stones, urgently asking for help, and would they see this woman right away. VJL then asked them how they imagined they would feel at this point and what their thoughts would be. Typically participants would come up with exactly what was expected: anxious, powerless, angry and so on. Eventually VJL would say, 'well, that's just how the young woman would feel too'. In some way feeling herself separate from that experience then, VJL now no longer feels so separate. We have campaigned for a specialist eating disorders service in our local area, and have found that our enthusiasm and goodwill, our very sense of ourselves, has been eaten away as the goal posts and rules shift and sway. Trusts have divided and merged again, managers have come and gone, money has been here and then not. Finally, after seven years of submissions and hope, there is some money for a very limited service, but not for a service initially designed by professional expertise or service user representation — rather a service initially designed by out of county funding and purchasers' and managers' considerations. More than this, whether or not innovative services are funded is also likely to depend on current Government policies and electoral influences.

We would argue that the female in our society is undermined and oppressed, her voice is not heard, neither in her experience of eating distress nor in the treatment of it. Service users state that it is no longer acceptable, if indeed it ever were, for individuals experiencing eating distress to be taken from their families and social supports, fed huge quantities of food like calves being fattened for market, doped, drugged and shocked, and then returned to those supports heavier but no wiser. Such treatments perpetuate the oppression of women and will continue to do so while the voices of service users are ignored and those professionals in agreement with them are marginalised and pathologised in a macabre re-enactment of the factors that drove their 'patients' to the experience of eating distress in the first place, namely the silencing of women's voices. It may be of interest to ponder on the values of a society that allows lamentably little money for the establishment of services for eating distress for a predominantly female population while at the same time allocating a 'substantial amount' of money from Sports England Lottery Funding to the Football Foundation for the development of football at grass roots level, which is of course predominantly male oriented (Government announcement 25.7.2000; spokesperson Department of Culture, Media and Sport, 12.10.2000).

A vindication of the rights of women

Society is competitive, oppressive and adversarial. Until the time when there is a genuinely anti-oppressive culture of co-operation within which women can speak and be heard, the experience of eating distress will continue to exist. The dilemma for someone wishing to help individuals experiencing partial self-starvation as well as other forms of eating distress is that it is probably impossible to promote anti-oppressive practices within an organisation such as the National Health Service. Each system mirrors the oppression of the larger system it lies within. At the Survivors Speak Out conference in 1992 there was a debate between Louise Pembroke and a National Health Service psychologist in the audience about whether or not the system could be changed from within. Perhaps we so-called professionals are merely protecting our mortgages and pensions and, as Louise Pembroke stated, 'dancing with the devil'. But maybe on the other hand we are opting out and protecting ourselves from the abuses of a system that is structurally oppressive and which ultimately defeats the courage, bravery, innovation and creativity of the professionals within it and the service users outside, silenced by oppression.

There is a need for females to have spaces where their justified anger is not pathologised, but rather channelled creatively. Medusa had been a beautiful maiden but was made hideous and literally mortifying after being raped by a male god and betrayed by a female goddess. All that is usually remembered about Medusa is that men who looked at her hideous rage were turned to stone, not that her rage was justified. Nor is it often remembered that, after she was beheaded by Perseus, out of her serpent hair was believed to have come the art of music (Valentis and Devane, 1994). Female anger is frequently viewed as monstrous, without considering what might have led to that anger. There is a depressing and oppressive circularity operating within society with which we all collude: women are denied a voice, and appropriately enraged they turn their anger in on themselves by, amongst other things, denying themselves food and drink. When they thus inadvertently find a voice, they are once again silenced by a society which at worst condones and at best ignores abusive treatment regimes, perhaps in fear of the power behind women's voices.

Louise Pembroke believed that the only option was to abolish the National Health Service (and, in particular, mental health services) and start again. Masson (1992) suggests that all forms of so-called therapy are potentially abusive, and that what most people in distress need is friends. However the experience of eating distress is life-threatening — *something* has to be offered. Perhaps the only way forward is outside the National Health Service with women's therapy centres specialising in experiences which are predominantly, if not exclusively, female, and with co-operative communities utilising, for example, developments in systems and social action psychotherapy (e.g. Holland, 1989). Women need to be able to select from a range of psychological therapies, free from the constraints of a male, medical-model-dominated system. They need to be educated and empowered to be able to make fully informed choices. They need to have opportunities to collect together and combine their energies creatively for positive and constructive action. They also need to feel enabled to claim time and space for themselves to reflect on their own particular journeys. Finally, they need to develop a voice that is truly listened to without them having to shout literally or metaphorically. Women have to rediscover their power and be enabled to develop constructive means of *ex*pression in order to be able to denounce and oppose the manifold means of their *op*pression.

References

British Medical Association, Board of Science and Education (2000) *Eating Disorders, Body Image and the Media.* London: Chameleon Press.

British Psychological Society (1998) Notices from the Disciplinary Board. *The Psychologist, 11(11),* 555

Concise Oxford Dictionary of Current English (1932) Third Edition. Oxford: The Clarendon Press

Garrett, T. and Davis, J. (1994) Epidemiology in the U.K. In: *Patients as Victims: Sexual Abuse in Psychotherapy and Counselling,* Chichester: John Wiley

Gull, W. W. (1874) Anorexia Nervosa (Apepsia Hysterica. Anorexia Hysterica). *Transactions of the Clinical Society of London, 7,* 22–28

Holland, S. (1989) Women and urban community mental health: twenty years on. *Clinical Psychology Forum, 22,* 35–37

Jones, A. and Schreiber-Kounine, C. (2001) Developing a Specialist Eating Disorder Service: the Trials and Tribulations. *Clinical Psychology Forum, 147*, 39–42

Lewis, V. J. (1996) A glutton for punishment: the 'greed' of starved women? *Clinical Psychology Forum, 92*, 14–18

Masson, J. (1992) *Against Therapy.* (2nd edition) London: Harper Collins

Pembroke, L. R. (1992) *Eating Distress. Perspectives from Personal Experience.* Chesham: Survivors Speak Out

Pilgrim, D. (1999) On keeping a disorderly house. *Clinical Psychology Forum, 124*, 47

Shelley, R. Ed. (1997) *Anorexics on Anorexia.* London: Jessica Kingsley

Valentis, M. and Devane, A. (1994) *Female Rage.* London: Piatkus

Wollstonecraft, M. (1792) *A Vindication of the Rights of Women.* (2nd edition) Poston, C. H. Ed. (1988) London: Norton

Recommended Reading

MacSween, M. (1993) *Anorexic Bodies. A Feminist and Sociological Perspective on Anorexia Nervosa.* London: Routledge

Malson, H. (1998) *The Thin Woman. Feminism, post-structuralism and the social psychology of anorexia nervosa.* London: Routledge

CHAPTER 12

Relatives and carers

OLIVE BUCKNALL AND GUY HOLMES

THIS CHAPTER IS ABOUT CARERS. The British Government's document *Caring about Carers* states that 90% of carers are relatives. Talking about carers rather than relatives changes the ways these people are conceptualised and channels the way that we think about certain issues. For example, if there is a group of people called *carers* then there must also be a corresponding group who need care (the *cared for*). The carers become a homogenous group — all the dynamics that might exist between, for example, a mother and daughter or a husband and wife, are lost. Also lost is the idea of reciprocity — in a group of people living under the same roof, roles such as the needy person, the caring person, and the ill person are fluid and interchangeable, especially in the area of mental health. Classifying people as carers and the cared for sets these roles in concrete. There are also practical and political implications to describing people as carers. It is carers, not relatives, who have entitlements to services. Some of the socio-political implications of these issues are discussed later, but the interested reader is referred to Pilgrim and Rogers (1999) as a good text on this general area. In this chapter we have used the term carer and relative interchangeably as the chapter is based on the first author's experiences and she describes herself as a relative and carer.

What happened to Olive and her family

Our family life had been pretty much like anyone else's. My son Terry was a quiet and reserved boy who spent a lot of time in his room dismantling wireless sets and then putting them back together. He seemed intelligent, passed his 11+, and after leaving school became a scout leader, joined the RAF Cadets and was an apprentice electrical engineer. He was an excellent driver but his three-wheeler was involved in a bad accident. The other driver was fined. Terry refused to go in the ambulance. Two weeks later, although I have never found out exactly what happened, he had an accident where he suffered a head injury caused by a fall from the roof of a building where he was working. Around this time he went to his GP. This was very unusual as he was never doctor orientated. I was informed that Terry should go into the local psychiatric hospital for 'two weeks rest'.

'Doctors know best' was a strong belief in our family. I also thought that when someone was admitted to hospital under medical supervision they would eventually be discharged either well or at least improved. However, every time I saw Terry, either in the hospital or during home visits with a social worker, he was obviously worse. He seemed to be a completely changed person. It was almost unbelievable and absolutely shocking to see the difference in him. It is only subsequently that I have come to realise that many of the changes in him were a direct result of the treatments he was given.

Visiting a psychiatric hospital is an unnerving experience. Nurses look at you from behind the glass of the nurses' station. You get the same experience as the patients — of being in a zoo, of being watched and observed. I needed people to help me feel welcome, to listen to me, and to explain what was happening to my son. No-one ever talked to me about what they felt was the cause of Terry's difficulties. No-one ever explained that many of the disturbing changes I was witnessing in Terry were a direct result of the medication he was being given. I was kept completely in the dark as to what went on in the hospital and was unable to talk to Terry's consultant psychiatrist.

In time Terry must have come to realise that the hospital was a bad place for him because, without informing anyone, he left. Why do so many people try to run away from a psychiatric hospital when it is unheard of to run away from a general hospital? Doesn't this lead the people who work there to question what they are doing? It was a terrible time. For months I did not know whether Terry was alive or dead. This is every mother's worst nightmare. Eventually, after I organised a newspaper appeal, someone let me know that Terry was in a hospital in Southern England. I went to see him and was met by the matron who showed no appreciation of what I had been going through. She ended the conversation by saying 'Don't you know that your son has schizophrenia?' Despite all the years Terry had been involved in psychiatric services, this was the first mention of this word.

Terry was readmitted to the local psychiatric hospital. On more than one occasion that I visited him there he had burn marks on both sides of his head after being given Electro-Convulsive Therapy (ECT). Once I asked where he was and was told that he was on a mattress after being put into insulin coma[1]. At that point I collapsed and awoke four days later (after obviously being drugged). It was all too much. I was subsequently given ECT and on one occasion I clearly remember having my hand held as I signed the consent form. Having experienced what a hospital and psychiatric treatment is like from the inside I have learned much that is kept hidden from relatives or carers.

Over the years there has been a reluctance to reduce Terry's medication despite many requests to many different psychiatrists. I have never been given an explanation as to the root of Terry's problems or proper information about the adverse effects of the treatments he has been given — just told that they are 'needed'. I cannot recall having a proper conversation with a psychiatrist during a clinical consultation. You are left to feel so guilty. Without help to think and talk about the possible cause of the initial problem, you feel you are to blame, especially when you hear or read in a report or book that it might be genetic, due to a virus, or to do with the way your child was brought up, and especially when you believe that you had just been trying to do the best for your child.

Largely as a result of his treatments and of being institutionalised, my son has lost much of his memory, practically all motivation for anything beyond smoking, and appears to need 24 hour care. In the past he has repetitively dialled the phone and when asked what he is doing has immediately said 'I'm doing it in order to cancel the ECT'. He talks to himself and continually asks for cigarettes. He once said: 'I've got psychiatric angina. They have taken my soul away'. Experts talk about high expressed emotion: how can you not be emotional when your family suffers such a tragedy?

How relatives/carers might be helped

Relatives would be helped the most by good services being available for people with mental health problems. For example, places of real asylum (such as the Wokingham MIND Crisis House — see Jenkinson, 1999) rather than psychiatric institutions where people tend to be only monitored and drugged; access to mental health professionals who smile, are thoughtful and kind, and who listen and offer guidance rather than treatments like ECT and medication; services that welcome relatives rather than treat them with suspicion. Visiting someone in a psychiatric institution makes you realise that there is nothing that is normal about these places. Many of them do not have an area where you can talk in private, make tea, and feel relaxed. Relatives need to know about the adverse effects of medication so that when their loved one is dribbling, pacing up and down, ballooning in weight, staring at them with a cold expression, or shaking uncontrollably they know that this is a direct result of the treatment rather than part of their 'illness'. Relatives should not have to be driven mad and become patients themselves in order to find out what goes on behind the closed doors of the institution. Ideally, patients would have access to independent advocates, but when relatives advocate on behalf of patients too incapacitated by their experiences or treatments to speak out for themselves, they need to be listened to by staff. Services could improve by giving thoughtful consideration to comments on the service made by relatives. As John O'Brien, North American Service Development Trainer, has said: 'When people who are not used to listening hear people not used to speaking out then real change is possible.'

The National Service Framework[2] (HMSO, 1999a) makes some good recommendations about how carers might be helped. It remains to be seen however whether this latest in a long line of government directed initiatives will have any effect on the ways services are actually delivered and the ways in which recipients actually experience the services. It is not clear whether it will change the types of conversations mental health professionals have with service users and relatives. Although it states that relatives should be given information about 'treatments', it remains to be seen whether they will be given an information leaflet like the one by Arscott (1999) or will just be told that their relative 'needs ECT' and it will 'work' and 'make them better'. The National Service Framework also states that carers should be given information on what to do in a crisis, but it is unclear whether professionals have very much to pass on to relatives about how to help people in crisis. Mental Health Support Lines often just tell people to take their medication (as if they had not considered that); admission to psychiatric units is invariably accompanied by heavy sedation with tranquillising drugs. Some professionals have a long history of helping people in crisis states, for example members of the Philadelphia Association[3]. But despite forty years of experience in helping people go through and come out of psychotic states, and helping the people that they live with to remain calm, supportive and firm with the person in crisis, their work is now marginalised, not widely known, and not recommended as the 'treatment of choice'. Just as with help for people who hear voices (e.g. Coleman and Smith, 1997), it may be that service users and relatives know more about helping people in a mental health crisis than the majority of professionals (see Wallcraft and Michaelson, this volume).

Relatives want to know what is the core problem of the person they care about. The closest they tend to get to this is being given a diagnosis. This sometimes provides initial relief ('At last they know what the problem is . . . Now they will be able to sort things out . . . We're finally getting somewhere'). However, in the longer term, a psychiatric diagnosis invariably leads to more heartache and fear. The stigma associated with a diagnosis of schizophrenia is massive. Not only that but, unlike medical diagnosis of physical health problems, a diagnosis of schizophrenia rarely leads to successful treatment and cure. A diagnosis is the way a mental health professional conceptualises a person's problem, but once given it sticks to the person, creating social disadvantage and identity problems of its own. It would be better if professionals kept their labels to themselves, and just concentrated on the things that might help the person.

The Government, in its policy document 'Caring about Carers: A National strategy for Carers' (HMSO, 1999b), emphasised respite care. It pledged £50 million for respite care in the year 2000/2001. By its own figures in this document, this worked out at just £10 per carer. Decades ago R.D. Laing suggested that every street should have a house at the end of it that people living in the street could use whenever they needed respite, asylum, a bit of distance or time out from the people they lived with. In comparison the Government's plans seem meagre. The executive summary of their plan is full of platitudes; for example: 'Carers care for those in need of care. We now need to care about carers'. Rather than spending society's tax revenues on practical things that would assist service users and carers alike, they seem more interested in social engineering. The document states 'Caring forms a vital part of the fabric and character of Britain'. They want free care or the cheapest care (care assistants are rarely paid salaries above a minimum wage that the government has set at poverty inducing levels).

The Government says it cares about carers and cares about patients, but it distinguishes between the unfortunate mentally ill who need care and the dangerous mentally ill who need monitoring and treating or locking up against their will. It fails to realise that its stigmatising and inaccurate descriptions of people with mental health problems needlessly frighten relatives and a wide range of people who might provide support and help to both service users and relatives alike. Ordinary ways of helping people in distress are not tried because the person is seen as having a special disorder that requires specialist treatment which is outside the remit of carers/ relatives/friends. In a series of workshops over the last five years, the second author and Craig Newnes have brought current and ex-service users, relatives and mental health professionals together to talk about what has helped them to cope during a 'mental health crisis', what helps them 'to maintain their mental health', and what sort of help they would want if they had a 'breakdown' or 'mental illness'. At every workshop the participants have emphasised the ordinary rather than the technological: a safe place to stay; the chance to be alone but know someone is nearby; to be able to walk in a beautiful place; to stay in a really nice hotel; the chance to be with people who are wise, calm and reassuring; to be with pets. Hardly anyone has referred to medication, psychotherapy or hospitalisation. No-one has wanted ECT.

National Service Framework Standard 6 states that anyone providing regular and substantial care for a person on CPA (the Care Programme Approach) should have an assessment of their needs and a written care plan. However it says nothing about being entitled to have those needs met. Since the 1980s people have been given increasing entitlements to assessments without adequate or appropriate funding to ensure decent NHS and Social Services. The focus has been on assessment rather than assistance (a notable exception to this in Shropshire has been the employment of a benefits expert who has been instrumental in getting people their benefits, not just by assessing and advising them, but by helping them to fill in the bewildering application forms). The whole concept of assessment has become mythologised and professionalised. This has meant that the money goes into the pockets of a burgeoning group of 'experts' from all mental health professions who spend increasing amounts of their time doing assessments rather than helping people. Giving the money directly to the carers would be better. Some, in the eyes of the professionals, might misuse it, but more of the money would end up helping the people it is supposed to help.

Everyone needs practical and emotional support at times, and if relatives are unable to get help from their own circle of family and friends then professionals could help, by providing a sympathetic ear and practical assistance. Someone who calls to see how you are coping and give some support; someone who helps to prevent feelings of isolation; someone to turn to in times of crisis. Carers groups can also provide this type of help, as well as tips and guidance and a forum for discussion about how to respond to people in distress and how to cope with and 'work' the psychiatric system. 'When X is not sleeping should we encourage him to try and sleep or let him wander about all night?' 'When Y is talking to her voices should we encourage her, join in, or tell her to stop it?' 'Z has bought a large bottle of paracetemol and has it in his room — what should we do?' No-one pretends that such dilemmas can easily be resolved, but relatives ought at least to be able to meet with people who could help them think through these dilemmas and have some suggestions to make. Relatives do not want professionals to blame them for creating mental health problems in the people they live with. However, they do want to know what role they might play in any recovery process. Facing up to the fact that they might be part of the problem might help them become part of the solution. If the vast literature on families and mental health problems (see Johnstone, 1999) is right, there might be vital roles that relatives can play in helping someone recover. That might involve them caring in different ways from the way they have traditionally cared.

If the person has problems of the type that often leads to a diagnosis of schizophrenia, how might relatives help them with their difficulties? They might be able to help them cope with or live with experiences that they find problematic — for example cruel voices or bizarre beliefs. They could help them go through a workbook like *Working with Voices: Victim to Victor* (Coleman and Smith, 1997) or help the person with cognitive challenges to their beliefs (Chadwick, Birchwood and Trower, 1996). But they may be able to do much more than this, and help the person to resolve some of the underlying problems that he or she may be struggling with (see Johnstone, 1999). Relatives are in a key position to help family members who are experiencing difficulties centring around dependence and independence, identity confusion, and blurred boundaries in relationships, because these are not solely individual problems but problems in relationships. Relatives are in a key position to do this because they are bound up in these difficulties as they interact on a daily basis with the person identified as having the mental health problem. For example, relatives may be able to make the ways they communicate clearer, less confused and less contradictory; or may be able to change the ways they interact so that each family member can be both dependent on each other and independent from each other. In order to do this, all members of a family may have to face up to some of their own difficulties with these issues. Whatever might be the core difficulties of the person identified as having the mental health problem, it is clear that relatives can hold some of the keys to recovery.

However, such change does not occur easily. Bringing about any change in the ways family members talk and behave to each other is often very difficult. Within families there may be little or no agreement about what the problems are let alone what the solutions might be. Scapegoating appears to be an almost universal phenomenon within human groups. There has to be a willingness within the family to do things differently. Of course, some people called carers might not care, and cruelty and physical and emotional abuse are inevitably disturbing. However, whenever a group of people wish to think about the dynamics between them and how these might affect someone diagnosed with a mental health problem, they should have the opportunity to meet with someone outside the family who is good at (and perhaps well trained in) helping people talk through the difficulties they have in living together (or living apart). A third person who can see things from a different point of view. This type of help (e.g. systemic family therapy) has only tended to be available in specialist units where families are observed from behind a one-way mirror whilst engaging in this process — something that is much too unnerving for most people. In contrast, psycho-educational family programmes are available in many parts of the country. These teach carers that the person they live with has a mental illness (e.g. schizophrenia), what that means according to a narrow interpretation of the medical model (e.g. that their brain chemicals cause them to speak or act in a bizarre way), and how to monitor their symptoms and contact services in order to prevent relapse (services would usually increase or change a person's medication). However, what happens to families who do not believe such a model fits their situation? Just as a good therapist providing individual help will try and help a person develop their own ways of understanding and alleviating their problems (see Hulme, 1999), someone providing carers or families with help ought to be able to work with the family's models. There has to be alternatives to both relatives and patients getting compliance therapy and relatives becoming unpaid community nurses whose job it is to monitor mad people and inform services of any possible relapse. As services are reliant on relatives, surely they have a right to have their opinions heard and respected, as well as help to find ways of alleviating problems that all members of the family might be experiencing.

Final thoughts

Whilst the Government and mental health professionals talk of care — care plans, care program approach and caring for carers — the user movement increasingly focuses on recovery (see Coleman, 1999). For many relatives this might be a helpful shift of focus — from one of being carers to people who need care to one of being part of a range of things that might help someone recover. There are many blocks on this; for example families dependent on benefits have to use medical language and emphasise the chronicity of the identified patient in order to get benefits such as Disability Living Allowance. Many things a person might need to recover may be outside the remit of the family, and people in families find it terribly difficult to change the ways they interact with each other, but as this chapter hopefully shows there are lessons to be learned from the experiences of relatives that could benefit mental health services and the people who use them.

References

Arscott, K. (1999) ECT: The facts psychiatry declines to mention. In: C. Newnes, G. Holmes, and C. Dunn (eds) *This is Madness: A critical look at psychiatry and the future of mental health services.* Ross-on-Wye: PCCS Books

Chadwick, P., Birchwood, M. and Trower, P. (1996) *Cognitive Therapy for Delusions, Voices and Paranoia.* London: Wiley

Coleman, R. (1999) *Recovery: An alien concept.* Runcorn: Handsell

Coleman, R. and Smith, M. (1997) *Working with Voices — Victim to Victor.* Runcorn: Handsell

H.M. Government (1999a) *A National Service Framework for Mental Health.* London: HMSO

H.M. Government (1999b) *Caring about Carers: A National Strategy for Carers.* London: HMSO

Hulme, P. (1999) Collaborative Conversation. In: C. Newnes, G. Holmes, and C. Dunn (eds) *This is Madness: A critical look at psychiatry and the future of mental health services.* Ross-on-Wye: PCCS Books

Jenkinson, P. (1999) The duty of community care: the Wokingham MIND crisis house. In Newnes, C., Holmes, G. and Dunn, C. *This is Madness: A Critical Look at Psychiatry and the Future of Mental Health Services.* Ross: PCCS Books.

Johnstone, L. (1999) Do families cause 'schizophrenia'? revisiting a taboo subject. In: C. Newnes, G. Holmes, and C. Dunn (eds) *This is Madness: A critical look at psychiatry and the future of mental health services.* Ross-on-Wye: PCCS Books

Pilgrim, D. and Rogers A. (1999) *A Sociology of Mental Illness.* London: Open University Press

Acknowledgment

We would like to thank Barbara Gibb, Shropshire's Carers' Link Officer (Mental Health), for her comments on carers' needs and help in obtaining information for this chapter.

Notes

[1] From the 1930s onwards, in European Psychiatric Hospitals, insulin was administered to people with a variety of diagnoses in order to induce coma. It was believed that, on coming out of the coma, patients would experience fewer 'symptoms', in particular delusions, lethargy and depression.

[2] In 1999 the Department of Health in Britain produced the National Service Framework, a set of standards that all mental health services have to attain. One section (National Service Framework Standard 6) is devoted to carers.

[3] The Philadelphia Association, based in London, was originally formed by R.D. Laing and colleagues in the 1960s. It owns several houses in which people with mental health problems live. With the help of their house mates and visiting therapists, people in these houses are supported whilst in crisis states or having psychotic experiences.

CHAPTER 13

Survivor research

VIVIEN LINDOW

NOW THAT WE PSYCHIATRIC system survivors[1] have begun to escape from our system-imposed boxes, we are not going back. Researchers belonging to some oppressed groups do emancipatory and anti-discriminatory research in order to bring about fundamental changes in the support offered to their members. This is now beginning to happen in the field of mental and emotional distress.

The psychiatric patients' liberation movement is under way, under a variety of names (Campbell, 1999). Those with power, especially the government and professional leaders in psychiatry, are doing their best to ignore what we say. In an increasing number of countries they coerce us to take poisonous drugs outside hospital. In the UK the government threatens to keep some people imprisoned for life by psychiatric diagnosis and tabloid scare-mongering when they have committed no offence recognised by the legal system.

This chapter covers issues of importance to survivors of the psychiatric system who do research: research topics, difficulties in gaining funding, outcomes and what counts as evidence, different levels of survivor participation in research, a little about methods and more about ethical issues. The chapter finishes with the importance of using research to influence people. The more survivors who research, the more evidence we will have to bring about change.

Why do survivor research?
Research is one of the main justifications that the groups who currently control mental health resources use to continue their hold and funnel money their way. To make a case to move resources away from mind and spirit destroying methods, strong research is needed (Perkins, 2000). (For a discussion of spirit-breaking, a term used in the USA psychiatric consumer

---

[1] I use the term psychiatric system survivor (or survivor for short) to refer to anyone who has used, or still uses, specialist psychiatric or mental health services. Where there is life, there is hope: for those who have lost hope, we burn the light.

movement, see Deegan, 1990.) To find out what works for people currently badly served by existing medical and social services, we need research from our perspectives. To counter research that judges outcomes of traditional services by criteria acceptable to workers rather than recipients, a new set of questions is being formulated.

Here is a personal anecdote. Correction, anecdotes are not acceptable evidence to powerful people: re-frame this as personal testimony.

When, with great difficulty, I had got free of psychiatry after eleven hospitalisations, sexual exploitation by mental health workers, electric shocks to my head and prescribed zombiedom, I looked around. It was before the survivor/service user movement had hit the UK, and I was angry and wanting to do something about the psychiatric system. As a madwoman no-one would listen — and in those days I was scared to express an opinion. So I decided: 'If I can't beat them, I'll join them'.

Night school and most of a psychology degree later, I wanted to do research. I approached one of my degree teachers, Andy Treacher, as a possible supervisor. He looked sceptical that a well-meaning undergraduate had anything to offer: 'Have you ever even been inside a mental hospital?' This was is my moment, I must come out of the closet. 'Yes, I spent my twenties going in and out of hospital.' He leaned forward and said 'Oh, fantastic. You are exactly the sort of person who should be doing research. We academics hardly know what questions to ask. Yes of course, I'll be your supervisor.' And he got me a scholarship to do my PhD.

We do know what questions to ask. People with vested interests as researchers and professionals often cast aspersions on our objectivity, but research is never a neutral act (Campbell and Oliver, 1996). Scientific researchers, like kings and queens with their subjects, still pretend objectivity although it is generally recognised now that their research methods, and the questions they ask, are mediated by both individual and social culture. The position of survivor researchers is the same as psychiatrists who research psychiatric treatment, mental health nurses who research mental health nursing and social workers who research social work. Except that, since these professional endeavours are meant to benefit service recipients, we might be said to have an exceptionally valid perspective in looking at the effectiveness and outcome of mental health interventions.

There is also the issue of trust. It is a well-established phenomenon that research into health services tends to elicit favourable replies. Trust between peers, though not guaranteed, is more favourable to honesty about shortcomings of services. Also, as disabled people's and survivor organisations create new rights-based theories (see Campbell, this volume), survivor researchers are well placed to test these theories.

Getting started

If research questions are biased by the prevailing culture and power structure, so is access to funding sources. Like most oppressed groups, psychiatric system survivors are interested in their hidden history. But in the UK most research funding for medical history comes from the Wellcome Foundation — money from a drug company. This presents a difficult ethical dilemma, as many survivor researchers are unwilling to use money that has come from damaging our own and fellow survivors' central nervous systems and emotional life.

This example of how hard it is to find the resources to do our own research is symbolic of many of the difficulties that survivor researchers can encounter. It points up the enormous amounts of money that traditional researchers have at their disposal compared with those who are ploughing this newer furrow. Committees that make research grants and their referees are usually dominated by medical model defenders or accepters. This includes many social scientists.

It is important to note how helpful some traditional researchers have been, and can be in the future, to survivor researchers. Championing such as I received and the hands-off support and technical assistance to survivor researchers that many of us have encountered are essential in re-shaping the research scene to create equal opportunities for us.

Research topics

One of the complaints of people who receive services is that the research does not address the issues they consider important (AWWT, 2000). Considerable thinking about alternative models of mental and emotional distress has already been done by survivors, often informed by the work of other oppressed groups such as black women and men (hooks, 1993), and people disabled by societies' barriers (Morris,1993; Campbell and Oliver, 1996). Here I will outline some sources of thinking about what users/ survivors of psychiatry consider important issues for research today. An international group of survivors who communicate on the Internet, PeopleWhoNet, based in the USA, have posted a short research agenda developed by The Madness Group (1998). This embraces existing services and treatments plus new, survivor-developed initiatives. The first item, of ten, is about forced treatment and compliance:

> *What are the longer-term effects of forced interventions and coercive treatments? How does coercion affect compliance? Is there an increase in non-compliance after patients have been coerced? Is there an increase in treatment avoidance among people who have been coerced? Does coercion interrupt the personal process to the detriment of recovery and the increase in rebellion? Is a diagnosis of PTSD* [post traumatic stress disorder] *being missed?*

The document also includes theories of causation (research into childhood abuse in adult survivors); the value of mutuality and connection with fellow survivors; issues related to the long-term effects of medication and withdrawal; stigma; and ethical considerations. Topics are not considered in detail, but this is an excellent guide to survivor research interests.

Another agenda is that of a UK survivor research project, *Strategies for Living*, funded by the National Lotteries Charities Board. The *Strategies for Living* project's primary aim was to find out what strategies people use who live with mental distress. Because it was a three year programme, issues raised by the first phase (Faulkner, 1997) informed the agenda for later pieces of work, for example into complementary therapies (Wallcraft, 1998) and into spirituality and mental distress (Strategies for Living, 1999). Much more detailed interviews were conducted on these main themes, which also included talking treatments (Faulkner and Layzell, 2000). Some funds were allocated to six individual survivors, each to carry out a small piece of research using their personal agendas (Nicholls, 1999) which included an investigation of the role of the Mosque in the well-being of men attending worship.

Two more major themes that emerged from the *Strategies for Living* research were of mutuality and peer support, and of stigma. Jean Campbell (1994) writes that the whole area of self-help is under-researched. There are many exciting developments, such as what in the USA is usually referred to as the recovery movement and in the UK more often as self-management. The National Self-Harm Network has produced the *Hurt Yourself Less Workbook* (Dace *et al.*, 1998) and the Manic Depression Fellowship has developed a regime of self-management (Campbell, 1997). Bell hooks' (1993) work about Sisters of the Yam groups might be taken up by black women survivor researchers. Sassoon (1999) has started survivor research with Asian women in the UK. The work of survivors who experience self-harm makes a clear link with childhood sexual abuse (Pembroke, 1994; Harrison, 1995). Many other user/survivor-run projects are suitable for survivor research (Lindow, 1999). Research agendas of survivors from ethnic minority communities are long overdue for further investigation and implementation by survivor researchers from those communities.

Outcomes and evidence

As part of their research agenda The Madness Group (1998) ask: 'Whose frame of reference defines success, recovery, rehabilitation?' In current jargon, resources will go to services that show success using outcome measures, or clinical effectiveness. Practice will be 'evidence based'. So a critical research issue for survivors is to define what are good outcomes, and to state what they count as effective mental health treatments and services. With the various forms of discrimination with which mental health services are riddled (Fernando,1995; Coppock and Hopton, 2000), one measure of effective services might be equality of survivor-defined outcomes for members of every sector of society (Sayce, 2000).

In a focus group with people who use forensic psychiatric services one man, baffled by our questions about the quality of care in the medium secure (i.e. locked) psychiatric unit, said: 'Well, the main point was to get out'. This echoes so many comments of people who use mental health services. The main point is not what the food is like or the respect with which people are treated (though these are important) — for many, the main user-defined good outcome is to get out of psychiatric control as quickly as possible.

Jean Campbell (1994) discusses how powerful outcome research has become in shaping change in mental health services. It is something we can seize to our own advantage. Among many ideas of how survivor orientated researchers might use outcome research, Campbell notes:

> *The concept of chronicity is embedded in mental health practice leaving indicators to measure recovery unexplored as an outcome of service, although consumer groups are adopting a recovery orientation in their advocacy and self-help groups.*

The UK Department of Health has published *Severe Mental Illness Outcome*

Indicators (Charlwood *et al.*, 1999). While one may look in vain, for example, for specific anti-racism or anti-sexism indicators there is some scope for survivor research related to these indicators. Look at indicator 9: 'User-assessed health-related quality of life for a service-provider population of people with severe mental illness' (sorry about the language); indicators 12 and 13 about financial and accommodation status; or indicator 18 about the 'use of non-psychiatric health care services by people with severe mental illness'. Lack of physical health care is an issue that frequently arises in survivor groups. Using such documents as a basis for funding applications is one way to fund research that fits with our agendas.

Research partnerships

This chapter is primarily about people who have experienced psychiatry doing their own research, and not about other researchers finding the views of survivors/service users. This is not to suggest that research by non-survivors is not valuable: in the light of consumerism in health and social care it is essential. But it is important to clarify different levels of survivor participation in research (see Table 1).

It will be evident that from a psychiatric system survivor viewpoint, partnership, user-focussed and survivor controlled research are the most satisfactory ways of measuring mental health interventions and service outcomes. Care must be taken, especially in partnership and user-focussed research, that the process is not wittingly or unwittingly highjacked by the more powerful partners (Moore *et al.*, 1998).

Like all academic-invented taxonomies, it is likely that these categories do not cover every scenario: they are presented here to illustrate some boundaries. It is difficult sometimes for outsiders to judge whether a research project is truly survivor-controlled or user-focussed. The only test of this is if the survivors/service users themselves say so, perhaps in a foreword or endorsement note, as researchers often claim a greater role for survivors than actually exists.

With these distinctions in mind, as well as warnings about hijacking by non-survivors, there are two interesting developments in partnership working to mention here. First is the Sainsbury Centre for Mental Health user monitoring scheme (Muijen, 1998). The Centre has facilitated survivors to devise interview schedules for use by local service users to monitor various mental health settings. These are adapted locally. Local service users are trained as interviewers.

This has potential for good survivor-controlled work, though resulting local projects may vary in terms of ultimate control of the research. It is also hoped that pre-existing questions do not limit the thinking of local survivor researchers and interviewers when considering topics for research when monitoring local services. Also, before adopting this method, managers providing funds for service user monitoring might consider putting the work out to tender locally, so that survivor-controlled organisations and individual survivor researchers have the opportunity to compete with the well-resourced Sainsbury Centre.

The other project noted here is an initiative to involve 'consumers' in mainstream NHS Research and Development (see Hanley *et al.*, 2000) for a source book with excellent cartoons). Here, the categorisation lies between

Table 1: Levels of survivor participation in research

Absent-survivor research	Most traditional research was (and sometimes still is) like this. Professionals devise the questions and decide what is a good outcome of treatment or service. Service users play no part in the research except to be observed, and are not asked their opinion about whether an intervention has helped or not.
Lip service research	Service users/survivors are asked their views as research 'subjects' but professional opinion remains dominant.
Partnership research	Survivor and non-survivor researchers work together as equals — including equal pay scales — with the perspectives of each made explicit.
User-focused research	Survivors/service users are given important roles in the research, and their views are respected, but the project is managed, and usually written up, by non-survivor researchers.
User-led research	A vague term that is used to describe both user-focussed research and survivor controlled research.
Survivor controlled research	This indicates that service users/survivors have control of all parts of the research from writing the funding proposal to disseminating findings. It also usually indicates participatory ways of researching. Non-survivor researchers may give technical assistance.

lip service and user-focussed research, although the Consumers in NHS Research Support Unit use the categories 'comment', 'consultation' and 'collaboration' as well as 'control'.

Methods and procedures
An aspect of the *Strategies for Living* project was the Research Support Network. They produced an invaluable resource, *The DIY Guide to Survivor Research* (Faulkner and Nicholls, 1999). Other useful materials, in print and audiotape, have been produced by The Monitoring Team (1997) in East Yorkshire.

In the classical method of natural science there is a period of observation before formulating research questions, and much survivor research is in that period. It is well accepted that the scientific method developed to study stones and atoms is too simplistic for an holistic view of individual humans or for the complexities of human societies. The social science methods that survivor researchers most often use are qualitative.

Survivor researchers, usually working from a rights-based theoretical stance, try to ensure inclusiveness and to centralise marginalised groups throughout the research process. Much has been written about research empowering all participants, and the method and processes are important factors in this (Franklin, 1994; Bowes, 1996; Moore *et al.*, 1998).

The *Strategies for Living* funding application was written by survivor researchers, and the project started with a consultation and outreach stage to form a national steering group of people who have received psychiatric services (Wallcraft, 1999; Faulkner and Layzell, 2000). Managed by qualified and experienced survivor researchers, other survivors/service users were trained as interviewers to conduct the fieldwork. The range of people included as interviewers and those interviewed were considered: this meant including women and men, plus members of ethnic minority groups in sufficient numbers to be heard. Other factors researchers should consider are age, sexuality and all the factors that cause people to be discriminated against in mental health services and in wider society.

As well as a range of people taking part in research, relevance of experience is important. For example, *Strategies for Living* wanted to ensure that people living with long-term mental and emotional distress were included, which they monitored by self-reported diagnosis. It is relevant when researching in-patient services to focus on advisors and interviewers who have had that experience, likewise with forensic psychiatric services and other special situations. If one claims expertise by experience, then the experience needs to relate to the research topic as closely as possible.

Methods of collecting data are of course varied in survivor research. Unstructured or semi-structured interviews (using topic guides rather than interview schedules) are popular, as people can respond in their own words and in the order that is natural to them. Focus groups are also widely used as they allow people to spark off ideas from each other. Survivor researchers are likely to decide the questions used in individual and group interviews with people with the experience being studied. Action research, in which researchers take part in the project being evaluated and feed back findings during the research process, is another method that lends itself to including participants in the research. Critical incident analysis (studying particular incidents by getting the viewpoint of all participants and witnesses), plus follow-up interviews for long-term effects, might be an excellent method for survivor researchers to look at coercive interventions by mental health professionals.

It may be useful here to make a distinction between survivor researchers and survivor interviewers. As with other professions, research involves qualifications — usually by a first degree and then training and practice in research, including research methods, leading to a research qualification, often a Masters degree or PhD. Survivors who want to become acupuncturists or mental health nurses get training and qualifications, and it is the same for researchers. This is for two reasons: one is that survivor research cannot expect the same respect as other research if it is undertaken by untrained people. Minimum standards of knowledge, communication skills and writing skills are essential. Survivor interviewers have a much shorter training in interviewing and any other role they take. The second reason why I believe that survivor researchers should be well trained is that research involves important and complex ethical issues, some of which are discussed in the next section.

Ethical and personal issues

Survivor research often seems challenging to mental health and research professionals. This is one reason why funding is difficult to obtain, and it can also be a threat to the integrity of a research project: how far do researchers submitting proposals to funders 'fit in' with what they know will be funded, and use more conventional-looking methods in order to gain funds? Sometimes it might be worthwhile to do a conventional piece of research if there is no alternative, but such decisions need to be made thoughtfully within an ethical framework.

All research in the NHS must be passed by a research ethical committee. Quite rightly, these committees protect patients in the NHS, but they often consist of traditional researchers who do not understand perspectives different from their own, or who may be contemptuous of them. The paperwork for ethical committee consent is often more suitable for drug trials than for an investigation of a community service. I know of no research ethical committee that contains representatives of local mental health system user/survivor groups. This is not the same as including people who happen to have used services, but do not talk from the perspective of 'service user' informed by fellow members of a user-controlled organisation. This is an area for campaigning by survivor researchers.

Many ethical issues are the same for survivor researchers as other researchers, but there are some differences. One is limits to confidentiality. Within services, these limits are usually that, if a worker considers the person to be an immediate threat to others or to themselves, they may breach confidentiality. Some survivor researchers might consider it unethical in the latter case, if someone is suicidal, to report them against their will to a service that they have previously experienced as harmful. Researchers have no duty of care, and so the legal position with suicide risk is different both from a situation of potential harm to others and from the position of a mental health professional [2]. In the case of potential harm to others, there is a legal (and ethical) duty to act to protect others, and this will include breach of confidentiality if necessary. Mental health workers who fail to take action in the case of potential danger to self can be disciplined and sued because of their duty of care — this is not so for researchers.

These difficult issues of confidentiality should be discussed in any research project, though they seldom are (Monahan *et al.*, 1993). Whatever is decided, it is essential to inform the people taking part in research as to the limits to confidentiality during the consent process. It is also important to have in place procedures for when these situations arise, for example to

---

[2] The legal position of researchers in relation to potential harm to self has been checked with two lawyers in the UK, both University-based.

try to get the research participant's permission to get acceptable help, to give immediate support to the person and to have other forms of support in mind (advocacy services, alternatives to psychiatry). Policies are also needed about offering or obtaining help or information for people who have obvious unmet needs. Support arrangements for all researchers and interviewers are also an ethical requirement: everyone should be empowered in survivor research (Bowes, 1996).

Payment of research informants is another ethical issue. People are often expected to take part in research for altruistic reasons. Survivor researchers may take the view that people who receive psychiatric services may not feel that they want to contribute out of the kindness of their hearts. A payment that recognises this contribution but does not endanger benefits is becoming usual. The counter-argument, that a person might be induced by money to take part in a harmful drug or other medical trial is less pertinent in this situation (Neuberger, 1993; Harries and Edwards, 1994).

Most qualitative research, particularly if it has a high degree of participation, is based on relationships between researchers and the people being researched. The issue of ending the research needs to be sensitively handled, and the end-point made clear from the beginning. Control of the ending is one aspect of the power the researcher has in relation to the researched, and survivor researchers need to keep all aspects of power relations to the forefront, and out in the open.

Another issue is feeding back research findings to participants. This might be by accessible written (or audible) research findings, or might include group events, in which case travel expenses are needed. Part of the deal with research participants is that their contribution will make a difference. Lack of publication and dissemination of research findings is a breach of that deal.

An ethical issue related to the situation of working with one's fellow survivors is that of self-disclosure. If it is important to the research that people know that they are being studied by their peers, then self-disclosure is essential. Research projects need to develop policies about how disclosure takes place, and how far it might go. A quotation from a non-survivor researcher in Canada, who works in a participatory way, is interesting in this context:

> *The changes evoked by this approach were profound. Perhaps of most significance was the blurring or outright deletion of the line I had previously established between my personal and professional selves.... I learned that becoming an ally meant bringing more of myself to the table.* (Church, 1997)

It is difficult not to sound pious when writing about ethical issues. The ones mentioned here are presented as discussion points, though my personal views are clear. They represent aspirations, and I certainly cannot claim always to have reached all these standards all the time: we learn as we go along. A comprehensive ethical code for survivor researchers needs to be developed.

Using research to influence people

While I am not enamoured by the cult of the personality, it has to be faced that in human societies little happens if no-one takes the lead. As already mentioned, everyone's time and money is wasted if research does not inform mental health services and/or the wider community. Part of this influence can be the creation of a survivor research 'scene'. Professor Peter Beresford (pioneering and continuing user participation researcher, among other research interests) and the Strategies for Living group led by Alison Faulkner, with Jan Wallcraft (programme director at the Mental Health Foundation) are making waves reaching out from London. Rachel Perkins, an influential writer, psychologist, mental health service manager and survivor, writes (not specifically about research):

> *While I am under no illusions about the limits of my influence, I think it is equally important not to underestimate the power of such a position. There are people who read what I write, listen to what I say. Even when they disagree, many take it seriously in a way that they might not but for my privileged status.* (Perkins, 1999)

It may not be to the taste of some researchers, or within the reach of others, to be part of this scene, but it is important in ensuring that our research findings have influence that there are those leaders, and they can help make sure that survivor research results get heard where needed.

Jean Campbell (1994) discusses the difficulty of survivor research getting published in peer reviewed journals, which might influence other academics, because of our different perspectives and methods. Much survivor research appears outside the academic scope, in newsletters and reports rather than books and journals, and so is not found in mainstream libraries and indexes. This is a problem to overcome: one idea is always to send a copy of findings, with a one-page summary, to key government policy makers and academic policy writers. To influence them, we probably do need to use some of their language in reports aimed at the professional communities: clinical excellence, outcome measures, evidence-based practice and so on.

Most of us do our best to avoid the impenetrable language and writing style that seems to bestow academic respectability on research findings. Academic belittling of 'popularising' is part of the game by which they attempt to protect their position of power. A few research funders (for example, the Joseph Rowntree Foundation) do expect and support researchers to produce research findings in an accessible form that is useful to people receiving and working in services. The newsletters and reports of survivor research reach parts of the mental health system that conventional academic reports do not.

There are many efforts by psychiatry to educate service users into the bio-medical model. There is a version of what used to be called brainwashing called 'compliance therapy', psychiatric workers attempting to ensure that people take drugs whether they produce personally desired outcomes or not. Findings from survivor research could provide evidence to policy makers of effective alternatives to such coercive methods. Some people would say this is the most important group of people to reach with research findings, but some would say that dissemination to individual survivors and survivor groups who can use research findings for personal empowerment, and as campaigning tools, is equally important. Dissemination methods here demand imagination and a good grasp of accessibility.

Research has its part to play in developing solidarity among psychiatric system survivors, and helping to raise the expectations of those who have been 'educated' to live with an unacceptable quality of life. Survivor research can be a small but key part in the move to seize freedom within an oppressive and excluding society.

References

AWWT (2000) *Service User Empowerment and Involvement Strategy.* Bath: Avon and Western Wiltshire Mental Health Care NHS Trust

Bowes, A. (1996) Evaluating an Empowering Research Strategy: Reflections on Action-Research with South Asian Women. *Sociological Research Online, 1,1,* 1–18

Campbell, Jane and Oliver, M. (1996) *Disability Politics.* London: Routledge

Campbell, Jean (1994) *Consumerism, Outcomes and Satisfaction: A Review of the Literature.* Missouri Institute of Mental Health, on the MadNation website (www.madnation.org/citations/consumerism/.htm), which also contains lists of survivor-friendly research citations

Campbell, K. (1997) Avoiding a Crisis: The Role of Self-Management. *Crisis Point, 3,* 6–7

Campbell, P. (1999) The service user/survivor movement. In: C. Newnes, G. Holmes and C. Dunn (eds.)*This is Madness: A critical look at psychiatry and the future of mental health services.* Ross-on-Wye: PCCS Books

Charlwood, P., Mason, A., Goldacre, M., Cleary, R. and Wilkinson, E. (eds.) (1999) *Health Outcome Indicators: Severe Mental Illness. Report of a working group to the Department of Health.* Oxford: National Centre for Health Outcomes Development

Church, K. (1997) Madness in her method: creating a 'survivor frame' for mental health research. *Journal of Psychiatric and Mental Health Nursing, 4,* 307–308

Coppock, V. and Hopton, J. (2000) *Critical Perspectives on Mental Health.* Routledge: London

Dace, E., Faulkner, A., Frost, M., Parker, K., Pembroke, L. & Smith, A. (1998) *The Hurt Yourself Less Workbook.* London: The National Self-Harm Network, PO Box 16190, London NW1 3WW

Deegan, P.E. (1990) Spirit Breaking: When the Helping Professions Hurt. *The Humanistic Psychologist, 18, 3,* 301–313.

Faulkner, A. (1997) *Knowing Our Own Minds: a survey of how people in emotional distress take control of their lives.* London: The Mental Health Foundation

Faulkner, A. and Layzell, S. (2000) *Strategies for Living: A report of user-led research into people's strategies for living with mental distress.* London: The Mental Health Foundation

Faulkner, A. and Nicholls, V. (1999) *The DIY Guide to Survivor Research.* London: The Mental Health Foundation

Fernando, S. (ed.) (1995) *Mental Health in a Multi-ethnic Society: A Multi-disciplinary Handbook.* London: Routledge

Franklin, A. (1994) Anti-Racist Research Guidelines. *Research Policy and Planning, 12, 2,* 18–19

Hanley, B., Bradburn, J., Gorin, S., Barnes, M., Evans, C., Goodacre, H., Kelson, M., Kent, A., Oliver, S. and Wallcraft, J. (2000) *Involving Consumers in Research and Development in the NHS: Briefing Notes for Researchers.* Winchester: Consumers in NHS Research Support Unit (conres@hfht.org)

Harries, U. and Edwards, J. (1994) Gift or Gain. *Health Service Journal,* 27 October, 26–27

Harrison, D. (1995) *Vicious Circles: An Exploration of Women and Self-Harm in Society.* London: Good Practices in Mental Health

hooks, b. (1993) *Sisters of the Yam: black women and self-recovery.* London: Turnaround

Lindow, V. (1999) Survivor controlled alternatives to psychiatric services. In: C. Newnes, G. Holmes and C. Dunn (eds.) (1999) *This is Madness: A critical look at psychiatry and the future of mental health services.* Ross-on-Wye: PCCS Books

Monahan, J., Appelbaum, P., Mulvey, E., Robbins, P. and Lidz, C. (1993) Ethical and Legal Duties in Conducting Research on Violence: Lessons From the MacArthur Risk Assessment Study. *Violence and Victims, 8, 4,* 387.

Moore, M., Beazley, S. and Maelzer, J. (1998) *Researching Disability Issues.* Buckingham: Open University Press

Morris, J. (1993) *Pride Against Prejudice: Transforming Attitudes to Disability.* London: The Women's Press

Muijen, M. (1998) Users Monitoring Mental Health Services. *Q-Net, 6,* 1

Neuberger, J. (1993) An abuse of altruism. *Health Service Journal,* 3 December, 17

Nicholls, V. (1999) Supporting User-led Research: The Realities. In: Strategies for Living report *The Big Alternative Conference II.* London: The Mental Health Foundation

Pembroke, L. (ed.) (1994) *Self-Harm: Perspectives form Personal Experience.* London: Survivors Speak Out

Perkins, R.E. (1999) My Three Psychiatric Careers. In Barker, P., Campbell, P. and Davidson, B. *From the Ashes of Experience: Reflections on Madness, Survival and Growth.* London: Whurr Publishers

Perkins, R. (2000) Solid evidence? *Openmind, 101,* 6

Sassoon, M. (1999) Issues for Asian Women. In: Strategies for Living report *The Big Alternative Conference II.* London: The Mental Health Foundation

Sayce, L. (2000) *From Psychiatric Patient to Citizen: Overcoming Discrimination and Social Exclusion.* Basingstoke: Macmillan Press

Strategies for Living (1999) *The Courage to Bear Our Souls.* London: The Mental Health Foundation.

The Madness Group (1998) *The Research Agenda.* http:/www.peoplewho.org/Projects/Research.htm

The Monitoring Team (1997) *Monitoring our services ourselves: A practical manual and audiotape for mental health user groups and mental health services.* Yorkshire: East Yorkshire Community Healthcare

Wallcraft, J. (1998) *Healing Minds.* London: The Mental Health Foundation.

Wallcraft, J. (1999) Strategies for Living Research. In: Strategies for Living report *The Big Alternative Conference II.* London: The Mental Health Foundation

The Mental Health Foundation, 20–21 Cornwall Terrace, London NW14QL – www.mentalhealth.org.uk

CHAPTER 14

This is therapy: a person-centred critique of the contemporary psychiatric system

PETE SANDERS AND KEITH TUDOR

USERS AND SURVIVORS of the psychiatric system in Britain, as elsewhere in the world, are understandably suspicious of many professionals and disciplines involved in the field of 'mental health'.[1] There is, nevertheless, a long and strong history of support for service users and critical thinking and practice in the field of psychiatry and the related fields of politics, the law and social policy, social work, nursing, and occupational health. In this chapter we argue that *therapy* (psychotherapy, counselling and counselling psychology), which promises much and often delivers little to people labelled mentally ill, must also be subject to critical attention. We are proponents of the person-centred approach but are not uncritical of therapy in general or of the person-centred approach[2] itself: indeed, as we argue, we *must* be critical and take a reflexive stance.

In this chapter we consider why and where therapy has failed the users of psychiatric services and review what difference therapy could and should make. In doing so, we review the person-centred approach to the politics and psychology of diagnosis, treatment and cure, briefly reflecting on the nature of mental health and illness. We seek to address three audiences with three purposes: those involved in the mental health field — with the purpose of presenting a radical and person-centred approach to psychology which emphasises the phenomenology of 'madness'; those involved in psychology and related fields — with the purpose of presenting a view of the radical psychology of the person-centred approach; and those practitioners (counsellors, psychotherapists, counselling psychologists, etc.) who identify with the person-centred approach — with the purpose of reclaiming it as an

---

[1] Although we use the term 'mental health' in this chapter we consider it a disputed term which confuses mental *health* with mental *illness* (see Tudor, 1996).
[2] Specifically meaning the psychotherapeutic theory and method originated by Carl R. Rogers (see Rogers 1951 and 1959). Contemporary definitions and positioning of this approach are reviewed by Sanders (2000).

approach which is both necessary and sufficient in working in the field of mental health, including those who have been diagnosed with severe mental illnesses and personality disorders. Indeed, we are proponents of the person-centred approach precisely because it offers a radical view of psychology and psychotherapy and a crucial contribution to contemporary concerns about mental health. Specifically, it offers:

- An emphasis on the constructive view of the changing person (the person *in process*) — and, therefore a more integrated understanding of health and illness.
- A radical subjectivism in which the focus is on *the subject's* construction of themselves, others and the world — and, therefore, the possibility of value being derived from an internal rather than external process, and power (and politics) being personal.
- A view of the person as *intersubjective* being — pro-social and responsible — pursuing *both* autonomy and connectedness through the innate ability and need to empathise with fellow humans.
- A specific view of the role of the therapist as provider of conditions of change and as *facilitator*, not director, of personal change — and, therefore, of the desirability of collaborative therapeutic relationships.

Why has psychotherapy failed to improve the lives of the users of mental health services in Britain?

Problems with the theories

The theories that drive the various schools of psychotherapy were, like all scientific theories, conceived in particular contexts: personal contexts (to do with the personality of the originator) and social contexts (i.e. the family, cultural, religious and scientific mores of the time). These theories are products not of the truth about unhappiness and distress, but of the distillation of these contexts through life experience and, at times, social and political expediency. The theories, and the founding fathers and mothers of psychoanalysis and psychotherapy, were also deeply embedded in the medical model and medical establishment, thus therapy came to be viewed as a medical treatment. Given this, we might reasonably ask whether these theories and therapies are sufficiently in touch with the lives and concerns of 21st century users of the mental health system since the theories, almost without exception, were formulated by white, educated, middle-class, Euro-American, heterosexual, able-bodied men. Can such ethnocentric theories be credible intermediaries in the healing of black, female, gay, lesbian, disabled, working class people? Was systematised, institutional and societal oppression ever high up in the list of causes of mental distress in these theories? We think not. Regarding racism and psychiatry, for instance, Patel and Fatimilehin (1999) have critiqued psychological models which are limited in relation to socio-political processes, and the Black Health Workers and Patients Group (1983) have described the repressive role of psychiatry in supporting the corporate state.

We also suggest that theories of therapy are largely out of touch with the psychologies of 21st century users. All attempts to understand human psychology are models, or metaphorical maps, rather than the territory itself. Not so long ago, great thinkers believed that human psychology could be best represented by legends and myths, or that mental life might be understood if we imagined little homunculi dashing around in our heads carrying messages, or that the brain should be seen as a telephone exchange or latterly a computer. Of course, the brain, mental life or human psychology are none of these things. The metaphorical frameworks of models of therapy are influenced by the *zeitgeist*: Freud used classical mythology as the main vehicle for his theories; behavioural therapists have shifted from crude telephony to equally crude computer technology in their image of the programming of learning; and cognitive therapists' metaphors simply reflect a more up-to-date computer technology. Do these metaphors mean anything to ordinary people or are they simply a way of facilitating esoteric communication between therapists? One of the features of the second half of the 20th century was how free-market capitalism tended to champion the individual; 'the customer is always right' became the catchphrase of this *zeitgeist*. This was, we remind ourselves, a grotesque confidence trick: the customer is only 'right' if they submit to being swindled into consuming a physically and psychologically toxic lifestyle for the sake of increased profits. This distorted pop-phenomenology, however, carried the potentially liberating message that everyone's version of reality is valid and with it the idea that each of us is an expert in our own lives. It wasn't always like this. Not so long ago knowledge ('truth') about our bodies, souls and psyches was held by others: the priest knew when we were good or bad, the judge told us when we were right or wrong, the doctor pronounced us well or ill. The shifting sands of popular culture now find us caught uncomfortably between an old need for the reassurance of the expert, and a new need to claim our own experience, find our own truth, demand to be received as valued equals and treated like unique human beings. Models of therapy that cling to a process wherein experts and expertise are valued, or that treat people like computers requiring re-programming or machines in need of a manualised service, run the risk of being out of touch with the needs and understandings of people in the 21st century.

As person-centred practitioners, we prefer to think of human psychology in terms of a different, more enduring — and, for us, a more satisfactory — metaphor, namely an ecological one. The person-as-biological-system is best understood as a complex micro-system within and connected to a complex macro-system. Psycho-technology, then, is of no more use in human healing than technology has been in taming the forces of nature. Interfere with one part of a complex ecosystem and the whole system becomes critically unbalanced. The person-in-context is best observed, understood without judgement and *related to* without intrusion or interference (the skills of the ecologist and person-centred therapist) rather than stopped, dissected, treated with chemicals, reprogrammed and normalised (skills of the psycho-technologist and psychiatrist). It follows that we would prefer so see humans flourish in their individual, social and species contexts, rather than be (more) normal, efficient units of a larger machine.

Theories of therapy are, to say the least, politic-lite. The context in which the individual develops and lives usually appears in the theories in terms of the family. Family is the structure through which society delivers its important messages and, as such, is accorded a position of some importance in the shaping of the psychology of the individual. However, in many theories the psychology of the family is presented as the *only* mediator of social processes.

What about an awareness of the effects of mass-media, of peer-groups, of poverty, of the institutionalised lack of opportunity — and of ideology itself (see Szasz, 1974)? The person-centred approach is not immune to such criticism. In his own reflexive critique based on an analysis of the self concept of the theorist (i.e. Carl Rogers), Holland (1977) suggests that:

> *There is a clear direction of retreat from external and religious principles into the self . . . the theme of retreat is a constant one . . . it seems that nothing external or social has ever seriously interfered with this privileged retreat into a beautiful and natural environment or with the psychological goal of remaining in process of self-discovery.* (p. 71)

The unwavering focus on the individual and the self means that therapists' vision is limited to an understanding of the individual in virtual isolation (or retreat), rather than understanding individuals in relationship, connected, interconnected or in context. In the worst cases, therapists, limited by theory, eschew common sense and act on the notion that the individual is responsible for everything and that the individual alone can change their own lives through their intrapsychic and interpersonal processes. Psychotherapy has to help people struggle to develop a fulfilling and sustainable individual and *relational* self in the midst of a culture determined to socialise and regulate its members into obedient, conforming individuals dedicated to the maintenance and promotion of society at the expense of the physical and psychological health of the individual (Williams, 1999). In focusing on the understanding of the individual, many therapy training courses do not encourage exploration of the social and contextual, let alone the political or the economic, or even acknowledge that these have any relevance in helping heal psychological (social, contextual, political, economic) damage.

Problems with practitioners
In the 1940s Carl Rogers adopted the term counselling because professional protectionism at the time prevented anyone from calling their work psychotherapy unless they were medical doctors. Psychologists also were an inferior, separate breed, allowed to measure things, but not to treat patients, since treatment was limited to restraint by chemical or physical means, surgery or shock. The die was cast, then, for talking cures to be second best, inferior, the lay and, therefore, unprofessional activity. This view seems to have become internalised into the psyche of therapists to the extent that the vast majority are still in awe of medical practitioners, and even those who are theoretically critical of the medical model often adopt it uncritically for their own personal use. Counselling training courses reinforce this feeling of inferiority by encouraging uncritical acceptance of the medical model and the psychiatric system. At the same time, some courses also promote an artificial superiority in taking an *uncritical* stance against psychiatry and its tools with the result that many therapists lack a necessary and sufficient understanding of psychiatric terminology and treatment or the effects of psychoactive medication. This is particularly important since most clients presenting for therapy in a mental health setting will be taking such medication. As a result, therapists do not understand the psychiatric system well enough to debate on equal terms or challenge the authority of the medical

model, psychiatrists or the psychiatric system itself, and thus are unable to best serve clients who may be users of these systems. Thus tamed by compliance or excluded by their own arrogance, therapists are incapable of adequately representing their clients either as individuals in case discussions or as a constituency of users of the system when policy reviews are conducted. Therapists and therapists-in-training are often unaware of historical or current critiques of the psychiatric system and do not realise that there is a place for talking cures in the care of clients with severe and enduring mental health problems.

Just as we have claimed that many theories of therapy fail to contextualise human psychology, we also believe that therapists, in general, are politically naïve and, espousing a bourgeois psycho-meritocracy, help perpetuate the myth that not only should we all pull ourselves up by our own bootstraps but also, if we really try hard in therapy, we can be happy or free from distress. If we cannot, and are not, then we must be resistant and only have ourselves to blame. Notwithstanding the efforts of the organisation *Psychotherapists and Counsellors for Social Responsibility* and critical authors in this field (e.g. Kearney, 1996; Samuels, 2001), the majority of therapists naively believe that therapy as an activity is politically neutral: *'by remaining "neutral" in an oppressive situation psychiatry, especially in the public sector, has become an enforcer of established values and laws'* (Steiner, 1971a: p.281 original italics). In our opinion, the vast majority of therapists fail to see that therapy is driven by middle-class values, have no awareness of ideology, and, increasingly, subscribe to short-term solutions that deliver 'stress-fit work addicts' (Thorne, 1996) back to the fast food joint or the telephone call centre — workplaces which institutionalise the forever smiling face of incongruence ('Have a nice day!') and discourage genuineness. Many are too frightened to question the emperor's lack of clothing. As Thorne (1996: p.10) states: 'There are too many vested interests not least . . . among those counsellors and psychotherapists who are desperate to make a living at all costs' — a critique which applies to all mental health professionals.

Problems with the system
By the system we mean 'the psy-complex, more often referred to as the mental health system . . . we have simply called it psychiatry' (Holmes and Dunn, 1999: p.1). Problems with the system could be summarised in the words professionalisation, protectionism, snobbery, vested interests, endorsements, registration and accreditation. There is a library of papers, chapters and books that detail the way the system serves itself rather than the users of the system. When multi-national drug companies and psychiatrists take a well-deserved pasting (e.g. Breggin, 1991) it feels safe and all can join in the name-calling. However, we are more interested when the finger points uncomfortably close to home in the shape of the continued professionalisation of therapy, from the chartership of psychologists through to the registration of psychotherapists and counsellors (see Mowbray, 1995; House and Totton, 1997; Bates, 2000), moves supported, in large measure, by spurious arguments based on unproven assumptions. Therapists seem wilfully oblivious to the obvious: that the professionalisation of therapy and psychology is a political, ideological and organisational issue more than an issue about good and bad therapeutic practice. Professions exist to keep people out,

corner the market, engage in pyramid selling, push up wages and divert attention from the truth – that what heals people is good human relationships (Rogers, 1957, 1959) and what prevents us getting ill in the first place is secure income, good housing, accessible health care and inspiring education.

A system which supports the cult of the expert fits neatly into the personal psychology of a number of practitioners. Much has been written in the last decade exposing the power relationships in therapy (e.g. Masson, 1993) and some on power relationships in training (see Robertson, 1993), although in the psychiatric system, therapists actually wield a fraction of the statutory and professional power of psychiatrists, doctors, social workers and psychiatric nurses. Nevertheless, therapists frequently employ methods that verge on the tactics of the bully (Masson, 1993) and it is ironic that some therapists continue act on the principle that a vulnerable person may be empowered by being duped into believing that the therapist is the expert and knows best. It is crucial that therapists do not ape the medical profession in its celebration of expertise to the exclusion of other qualities.

Therapists are undervalued in psychiatric settings and, indeed, often refused access to psychiatric wards. Within the field of psychotherapy, the NHS favours traditional approaches more in line with the medical model and short-term, brief and supposedly cost-effective, therapies (e.g cognitive-behaviour therapy), whilst humanistic therapies are largely ignored or discounted. With evidence-based research all the rage (see Holmes, Newnes and Dunn, this volume), person-centred practitioners, amongst others, are required to complete research schedules which make no sense in terms of the therapy they offer. Although Bates (2000) chastises therapists for relying on research evidence, we believe talking therapies must do battle with physical therapies whenever and wherever the occasion arises. If this means slugging it out on the home ground of positivist, experimental evidence so be it; after all, the evidence is actually on our side (e.g. King *et al.*, 2000). So although we may use scientific evidence if the occasion requires us to, we understand that at heart this is an ideological battle: we want there to be a choice of humane talking therapies readily available for every patient rather than a limited list of enforceable physical treatments — a strategy for emancipation rather than containment.

Therapy: helping, hindering or healing?

As has been indicated in the first part of the chapter, one of the problems of therapy is that, historically and institutionally, most approaches to or 'schools' of therapy derive from the allopathic medical model of diagnosis > treatment > cure. In this part, we briefly review diagnosis, treatment and cure, particularly from a person-centred perspective.

Diagnosis

At best, diagnosis, which derives from the Greek words meaning distinguish or discern and perceive, is an attempt to know something about a state or condition. However, there are a number of problems with the process, content and outcome of diagnosis.

Rogers (1951) was opposed to the use of diagnostic labels applied to psychological dynamics, calling it unnecessary, unwise and in some ways detrimental. He advanced two main reasons for taking this attitude. First, he viewed the process of diagnosis as one which situated *the locus of evaluation* in the hands of experts which encouraged dependency in the client: 'there is a degree of loss of personhood as the individual acquires the belief that only the expert can accurately evaluate him, and that therefore the measure of his personal worth lies in the hands of another' (p.224). This loss of personal worth is exacerbated in the context of a diagnosis of mental illness or disorder, as often concomitant with it is a loss of liberty, rights and control over treatment. Also there is a bitter irony in that very often, these external experts (doctor, psychiatrist, approved social worker, therapist, etc.) do not *know*, and do not — and are not required to — *discern*.

Rogers' second objection was that diagnosis has undesirable social and philosophical implications. The responsibility for making decisions about another person's needs, conflicts, and motives etc. is likely to be accompanied by a degree of control over the person concerned, however well-intentioned: 'the management of the lives of the many by the self-selected few would appear to be the natural consequence' (Rogers, 1951: p. 225). This objection is not unique to the person-centred approach. Steiner (1971b), an early transactional analyst involved in developing what he and others referred to as radical psychiatry and radical therapy (of which more later), argued that *'alienation is the essence of all psychiatric conditions . . .* everything diagnosed psychiatrically, unless *clearly* organic in origin, is a form of alienation' (p.5, original italics) (see also Tudor, 1997). Steiner (1971a) also argued that 'psychological tests and the diagnostic labels they generate, especially schizophrenia, must be disavowed as meaningless mystifications the real function of which is to distance psychiatrists from people and to insult people into conformity' (p.281). Another undesirable implication centres on the meaning attached by all involved in a particular diagnosis as well the wider society to the distinctions, discernments and perceptions which derive from the process and action of diagnosis. Diagnosis is not value-free and, in fact, is value-laden and can be politically motivated. For example, one might question the value of the diagnostic category, personality disorder, currently viewed by the psychiatric establishment as untreatable, except as a way for psychiatrists (and society) to consign certain people — and a certain class of people — to a hopeless and helpless existence. Add to this the tabloid press which perpetuates the conflation of 'mad' and 'bad' 'dangerous people' and a Home Secretary, Jack Straw, who, despite the fact that 'dangerousness' as a criterion for assessment, present in the 1959 Mental Health Act, was removed in the 1983 Act, opines: 'there is a group of dangerous and severely personality disordered individuals from whom the public are not properly protected' (Hansard, 15 February 1999). The person-centred approach has a specific contribution to this debate in viewing personalty as a *process* rather than as a structure which may be ordered and disorderd.

Given the current predominance of the medical model in mental health services and in therapy and its influence on — even determination of — resources, including people's access to therapy, even the most die-hard anti-diagnostic therapist (person-centred or otherwise) has to define their position and relation to diagnosis. There is, within person-centred therapy, a debate between those who eschew diagnosis completely, represented by Shlien (1989), and others, such as Schneider and Stiles (1995), who see advantages in developing a systematic person-centred diagnostic frame of reference. Of the latter, there appear two related strategies: first, to understand other systems of psychology and psychiatry and their approaches to diagnosis, assessment and treatment and to translate them in person-centred terms and, second, to develop the person-centred approach to 'illness', principally in elaborating the concept of incongruence in terms of a person's *process* (rather than hypothesised and, by implication, fixed *disorder*). Within the person-centred approach, this strategy is represented by the work of Fischer (1989), Bohart (1990), Schneider and Stiles (1995), Warner (1991; 1998) and Biermann-Ratjen (1998).

Rogers (1951) did concede one point on diagnosis in suggesting that making evaluations and diagnoses of clients may be useful only insofar as it provides therapists with a sense of security, and thereby enables them to be more empathic and acceptant of their clients. However, in our view, this end does not justify the means: empathy and acceptance based on false security is no true empathic understanding and no genuine acceptance; moreover, at worst, it encourages a dependency on diagnosis on the part of the therapist.

Treatment

One of the problems of the medical diagnosis > treatment > cure model is its linear nature; thus, one of the problems of 'treatment' is that it is dependent on diagnosis. Of course, in practice, we know this breaks down, especially when there is no precision about discerning a particular mental illness. In working on psychiatric wards and attending ward rounds, one of us regularly came across the situation where, in the absence of a diagnosis, a treatment would be tried (e.g. lithium) and, if it worked, the diagnosis applied by implication or indication and retrospectively (manic depression) — a process which would be laughable if it were not so serious and the practice so widespread.

Many therapies ape the medical model by defining treatment and treatment strategies. A somewhat radical alternative is suggested by Shlien (1989), who argues that since the primary purpose of diagnosis is to determine treatment and since client-centred therapy has only one treatment for all clients, then diagnosis is irrelevant. In this case, the treatment is the helping or therapeutic relationship, characterised by certain (necessary and sufficient) conditions which, if provided, lead to therapeutic change (see Rogers, 1957, 1959). Traditionally, the person-centred approach has emphasised the therapist-provided core conditions of congruence or genuineness, unconditional positive regard and empathic understanding. This limited understanding, even by proponents of the approach, has led to the person-centred approach being viewed as somewhat lightweight in its psychology. We prefer a more complete (and accurate) understanding of the necessity and sufficiency of all six conditions and a more dynamic and dialogic perspective on the relationship *between* therapist and client (see Tudor, 2000). Considerable work has been developed within the approach on the necessity of and strategies for making psychological *contact* (the first of Rogers' six conditions) (see Prouty, 1976; Van Werde, 1998). In a similar vein (though from a different perspective), in discussing a response to the element of psychosis which is expressed as a 'fixity', Hulme (1999) suggests and elaborates three 'transformative core processes': 'in the end, true insight cannot simply lie in getting a better fix on reality . . .[it] must lie instead largely in improving our capacity to reflect, to relate, and to be relativist' (p. 168). These qualities are, for Hulme, essential in working with those who find reflection in and of itself particularly difficult.

Therapists also need to consider the *form* or modality of treatment or therapy. Individual therapy may only confirm the individualisation of the client and should not be viewed as the therapy of choice or 'default setting' for therapy. As Steiner (1971a) puts it:

> *extended individual psychotherapy is an elitist, outmoded, as well as nonproductive form of psychiatric help . . . It silently colludes with the notion that people's difficulties have their source within them while implying that everything is well with the world . . . It further mystifies by attempting to pass as an ideal human relationship when it is, in fact, artificial in the extreme* (pp.280–1, original italics).

Group therapy has many advantages over individual therapy, not least as it offers 'universality' (the notion and sense that we are not alone in our distress) as an important therapeutic factor (see Yalom, 1995). Reversing the usual logic then, *group* therapy may be viewed as the therapy of choice, especially for clients for whom madness and its diagnosis and treatment further exacerbate their sense of alienation, marginalisation, exclusion and segregation. Moving beyond the group raises the issue of wider organisation. After all, if the diagnosis is alienation, then the treatment must be not only the restructuring of the individual personality: 'genuine disalientation is . . . impossible without a total restructuring of society' (Bulhan, 1980, p.260).

Cure

The third element in the linear sequence of the medical model, cure, carries all our assumptions about human nature, mental health and mental illness. In a sense it is implicated in the beginning of the sequence as diagnosis is construed as being about distinguishing 'what's wrong' *in relation to* 'what's right' or 'cured'. Indeed, amongst the nuances of meanings of the word is the *restoration* to health through successful treatment; it is also interesting to note that curing (as in meat) carries a sense of cleaning; thus the notion of cure has tones of health fascism and even eugenics. In this sense, therapy, like psychiatry, may be viewed as about social adjustment — adjustment, that is, to prevailing conditions and dominant ideologies (for a case study of which, the history and role of psychotherapy in the Third Reich is well documented by Cocks, 1997). Again, each school of therapy has, explicitly or implicitly, some notion/s about cure, illness, health, well-being, etc. which underlie and inform the aims of the therapy. The problem in focusing on mental *illness* and *disorder* is that this focus frames the understanding of it and casts it in the light (or shadow) of *health* and *order* (and hence the need for adjustment to the social order). This is reflected in the usual and widespread conflation of the terms 'mental health' as (and meaning) 'mental illness'. In our view, this focus and frame does dis-service both to our understanding of illness and dis-ease as well as to any notions and concepts of health and well-being (see Tudor, 1996). If psychotherapy is not to remain stuck in a medical (mental) illness/pathology paradigm, it needs to develop a view about the healing *process* (as distinct from a fixed cure) and to concern itself with health and a vision of human beings and society.

One of Rogers' principal contributions was to focus attention more on the *process* than outcomes of therapy. He referred to process as the fluid and changing nature of organisms and viewed 'being process' as a direction which describes 'that self which one truly is' (Rogers, 1961), a phrase he borrowed from the existential philosopher, Kierkegaard. In his process conception of psychotherapy, Rogers (1961) describes a movement from *fixity* — characterised by a remoteness of experiencing, an unwillingness to communicate, a lack of recognition of feelings, personal meanings, or problems, rigid personal constructs and a lack of desire to change — to *fluidity* — characterised by a continually changing flow of feelings, living freely in a fluid process of experiencing (and using this as a reference for behaviour, ready communication and relationships), congruence, a changing construing of meaning in experience, and a subjective living of problems for which the person is responsible. As may be seen, this is a deeply experiential and phenomenological view, one which is construed and co-created *in relationship*. As a direction of process, fluidity is clearly a value, but one which not everyone shares: 'this will be one of the social value judgements which individuals and cultures will have to make' (Rogers, 1961: p.155). Being fluid and in process does not mean that the person is cured (ordered, adjusted, salted and cleaned). It does mean that we are open to experience, to existential and phenomenal living including the difficult, the distressing, the dis-eased and the dis-ordered as ways of making sense of our immediate and wider worlds. It does mean that therapy, as a relationship in which we can create and experience 'collaborative conversation' to use Hulme's (1999) phrase, helps us to be increasingly open to this process, the characteristics of which are observable and easily described (Rogers, 1959).

In several subsequent contributions, Rogers describes the person — and, importantly, the culture — which emerges from this process. The person is characterised by an openness to experience; a trust in one's organism; an internal locus of evaluation; and a willingness *to be a process* (rather than a product or a goal), including the ability to live in the present and be attentive to each moment — and, in another contribution on 'the person of tomorrow', Rogers (1980) interestingly identifies anti-institutional as one of their qualities. This emerging culture has its parallel in the pro-active and pro-social actualising tendency found in all organisms and organic structures, is based on the reclaiming of personal power, and is directional in similar ways to Rogers' process conception of psychotherapy it would have a (r)evolutionary effect on psychiatry and mental health services, based on a movement towards:

- A non-defensive openness in all interpersonal relationships — throughout the psychiatric system, regardless of status.
- A holistic approach and attitude to the individual — for example, complementary health practitioners working in psychiatric services.
- Human-sized, rather than institutional-sized, groupings — reflected in an emphasis on small units at all levels of the psychiatric system (i.e. primary, secondary and tertiary).
- Attention to the quality of personal living — both in the community and in the asylum (crisis house, hospital, etc.).
- A more genuine and *inclusive* caring concern for those who need help —

which would require a radical shift of thinking and practice on community care, more along the lines of the 'Italian experience' of reform (see Tudor 1990/91), and an openness to creative, therapeutic alternatives to institutional care (see Stamatiadis, 1990).

The fixity of 'cure' is thus replaced by the fluidity of a permanent cultural (albeit quiet) (r)evolution in attitude to the person and to society and its services.

Summary
The history of madness is the history of people's fear and society's refusal or exclusion of the unknown, the 'other'. This operates in a number of ways specifically in relation to gender, race and class (for a review of which, see Tudor, 1996). The history of therapy includes disputes between radicals, even some revolutionaries, who essentially view(ed) psychoanalysis and psychotherapy as a liberating force, and reactionaries who, broadly, view therapy as a way (technique) of social adjustment and control. Just as it is dangerous to assume that psychiatry is a benign force in social policy or that Home Secretaries know anything about personality disorder, neither should we accept or assume that therapy is in itself benign, useful or effective. Nevertheless, there is a radical tradition in psychiatry and there are critical voices in mental health, especially from users; similarly, there is a radical tradition in the history, theory and practice of psychotherapy and critical cries heard in the therapeutic field, from some practioners and also (and increasingly) from users (e.g. France, 1988; Sands, 2000). In 1971 the Radical Therapist Collective published a 'radical psychiatry manifesto' (Steiner, 1971a). In the spirit of reflexive, political psychology (and psychopolitics), and by way of presenting an open-ended conclusion which invites both reflection and action, we offer a new manifesto for psychotherapy in general (not only its radical margins):

1. Psychotherapists are therapists that serve the people.
2. Psychotherapists are concerned with change, not adjustment; are explicit about their values and are intentional — socially and culturally.
3. Psychotherapists base their practice on a thorough and critical understanding of psychiatry and psychotherapy *in context*.
4. Psychotherapists strive to facilitate the reclaiming by clients of personal power in therapeutic relationships characterised by collaborative power.
5. Psychotherapists' practice reflects the awareness that the struggle for mental health involves changing society.
6. Psychotherapists organise and challenge oppressive institutions, especially psychiatric hegemony in the organisation of mental health services, professional monopoly on the control of service provision and direction, and the colonisation of the voluntary sector in mental health.
7. Psychotherapists support the service user movement in general and, in particular, service user involvement in mental health service development and service user-controlled alternatives to psychiatric services.
8. Psychotherapists, in their work, account for social inequalities.
9. Psychotherapists are open to alternatives (e.g. as regards 'treatment') and seek to build alliances which emphasise user/survivor perspectives (on, amongst other issues, hearing voices and survivor-controlled

alternatives), and encourage and promote greater public access to information through new technology as challenging the knowledge-based power of professionals.

10. Psychotherapists maintain their independence and integrity by recognising that they are still in a process of learning about human psychology, culture and social systems and, therefore, that we need to be open to new approaches to clinical work, training and learning as well as organisation.

This manifesto describes an *attitude* to therapy which is both political and personal. It is not unique to or the property of any one approach to or school of therapy — although, from our experience and perspective, it is deeply influenced by humanistic psychology and radical psychiatry and is deeply embedded in the work of Carl Rogers and the development of the person-centred approach. Some approaches and certainly some practitioners are more radical than others; it is for us to continue the struggle.

References

Bates, Y. (2000) Still whingeing: The professionalisation of counselling. *Changes, 18*(2), 91–100

Biermann-Ratjen, E-M. (1998) Incongruence and psychopathology. In: B. Thorne and E. Lambers (eds.) *Person-centred Therapy* (pp.119-130). London: Sage

Black Health Workers and Patients Group. (1983) Psychiatry and the corporate state. *Race and Class, XXV*(2), 49–64

Bohart, A.C. (1990) A cognitive client-centered perspective on borderline personality development. In: G. Lietaer, J. Rombauts and R. Van Balen (eds.) *Client-centered and Experiential Psychotherapy in the Nineties* (pp.599–622). Leuven: Leuven University Press

Breggin, P. R. (1991) *Toxic Psychiatry. Drugs and Electroconvulsive Therapy: The truth and the better alternatives.* New York: St Martin's Press

Bulhan, H.A. (1980) Frantz Fanon: The revolutionary psychiatrist. *Race and Class, XXI*, 251–70

Cocks, G. (1997) *Psychotherapy in the Third Reich* (2nd edn.). New Brunswick, NJ: Transaction Publications.

Fischer, C.T. (1989) The life-centered approach to psychodiagnostics: Attending to lifeworld, ambiguity and possibility. *Person-Centered Review, 4*(2), 163–70

France, A. (1988) *Consuming Therapy.* London: Free Association Books

Holland, R. (1977) *Self in Social Context.* London: Macmillan

Holmes, G. and Dunn, C. (1999) Introduction. In: C. Newnes, G. Holmes and C. Dunn (eds.) *This is Madness: A critical look at psychiatry and the future of mental health services.* Ross-on-Wye: PCCS Books

House, R. and Totton, N. (eds.) (1997) *Implausible Professions: Arguments for pluralism and autonomy in psychotherapy and counselling.* Ross-on-Wye: PCCS Books.

Hulme, P. (1999) Collaborative conversation. In: C. Newnes, G. Holmes and C. Dunn (eds.) *This is Madness: A critical look at psychiatry and the future of mental health services* (pp.165–78). Ross-on-Wye: PCCS Books

Kearney, A. (1996) *Counselling, Class and Politics: Undeclared influences in therapy.* Ross-on-Wye: PCCS Books

King, M., Sibbald, B., Ward, E., Bower, P., Lloyd, M., Gabbay, M. and Byford, S. (2000) Randomised controlled trial of non-directive counselling, cognitive behaviour therapy and usual practitioner care in the management of depression as well as mixed anxiety and depression in primary care. *Health Technology Assessment, 4*(19)

Masson, J. (1993) *Against Therapy.* London: HarperCollins

Mowbray, R. (1995) *The Case Against Psychotherapy Registration: A conservation issue for the human potential movement.* London: Transmarginal Press

Newnes, C., Holmes, G. and Dunn, C. (eds.) (1999) *This is Madness: A critical look at psychiatry and the future of mental health services.* Ross-on-Wye: PCCS Books

Patel, N. and Fatimilehin, I.A. (1999) Racism and mental health. In C. Newnes, G. Holmes and C. Dunn (eds.) *This is Madness: A critical look at psychiatry and the future of mental health services* (pp.51–73). Ross-on-Wye: PCCS Books

Prouty, G.F. (1976) Pre-therapy, a method of treating pre-expressive, psychotic and retarded patients. *Psychotherapy: Theory, Research and Practice, 13*(3), 290–95

Robertson, G. (1993) Dysfunction in training organisations. *Self and Society, 21*(4), 31–35

Rogers, C.R. (1951) *Client-centered Therapy.* London: Constable

Rogers, C. R. (1957) The necessary and sufficient conditions of therapeutic personality change. *Journal of Consulting Psychology, 21,* 95–103

Rogers, C.R. (1959) A theory of therapy, personality and interpersonal relationships, as developed in the client-centred framework. In: S. Koch (ed) *Psychology: A study of science, Vol. 3: Formulation of the person and the social context* (pp.184–256). New York: McGraw-Hill

Rogers, C.R. (1961) *On Becoming a Person.* London: Constable

Rogers, C.R. (1980) *A Way of Being.* Boston: Houghton Mifflin

Samuels, A. (2001) *Politics on the Couch.* London: Profile Books

Sanders, P. (2000) Mapping person-centred approaches to counselling and psychotherapy. *Person-Centred Practice, 8*(2), 62–74

Sands, A. (2000) *Falling for Therapy: Psychotherapy from a client's point of view.* Basingstoke: Macmillan

Schneider, C. and Stiles, W. (1995) Women's experience of depression. *The Person-Centered Journal, 2*(1), 67–77

Shlien, J. (1989) Boy's person-centered perspective on psychodiagnosis. *Person-Centered Review, 4*(2), 157–62

Stamatiadis, R. (1990) Sharing life therapy. *Person-Centered Review, 5*(3), 287-307.

Steiner, C. (1971a). Radical psychiatry manifesto. In: J. Agel (ed.) *The Radical Therapist* (pp. 280–82). New York: Ballantine Books

Steiner, C. (1971b) Radical psychiatry: Principles. In: J. Agel (ed.) *The Radical Therapist* (pp.3–7). New York: Ballantine Books

Szasz, T. (1974) *Ideology and Insanity.* Harmondsworth: Penguin

Thorne, B. (1996) The cost of transparency. *Person-Centred Practice, 4*(2), 2–11

Tudor, K. (1990/91).One step back, two steps forward: Community care and mental health. *Critical Social Policy, No 30, 10*(3), 5–22

Tudor, K. (1996) *Mental Health Promotion: Paradigms and practice.* London: Routledge

Tudor, K. (1997) Being at dis-ease with ourselves: Alienation and psychotherapy. *Changes, 22*(2), 143–50

Tudor, K. (2000) The case of the lost conditions. *Counselling, 11*(1), 33–37

Van Werde, D. (1998) 'Anchorage' as a core concept in working with psychotic people. In: B. Thorne and E. Lambers (eds.), *Person-Centred Therapy* (pp.195–205). London: Sage

Warner, M.S. (1991) Fragile process. In: L. Fusek (ed.) *New Directions in Client-centered Therapy: Practice with difficult client populations (Mongraph Series 1)* (pp.41–58). Chicago, IL: Chicago Counseling and Psychotherapy Center

Warner, M.S. (1998) A client-centered approach to therapeutic work with disssociated and fragile process. In: L. Greenberg, J. Watson and G. Lietaer (eds.) *Handbook of Experiential Psychotherapy* (pp.368–87). New York: The Guilford Press

Williams, J. (1999) Social inequalities and mental health. In: C. Newnes, G. Holmes and C. Dunn (eds.) *This is Madness: A critical look at psychiatry and the future of mental health services* (pp.29–50). Ross-on-Wye: PCCS Books

Yalom, I. (1995) *The Basic Theory and Practice of Group Psychotherapy* (4th edn.). New York: Basic Books

CHAPTER 15

The future approach for community mental health

FRAN SILVESTRI AND SUSAN HALLWRIGHT

THE IDEA OF CONSUMER/USER RECOVERY in mental health care is challenging the very foundations of the community mental health system (CMHS)[1] right down to the philosophies that led to its establishment. This concept of recovery is itself still in its formative stages, a somewhat amorphous notion that is shaping up to have a profound impact on the CMHS. The challenge for those of us who work in a community mental health system is to grasp how these emerging principles will change not only the way we think about a community care system, but the way in which that system is structured and the way that it acts.

In this chapter, the contribution of the recovery 'movement' to the evolution of the CMHS is described from an historical perspective, and its future potential to contribute to the ongoing metamorphosis of the CMHS is considered.

The ideas presented in this chapter aim to stimulate the leaders of the key stakeholder groups, including the leaders of the provider organisations and the funders, to think about the ways in which they can shift towards a system design that promotes consumer recovery. The chapter also aims to provide a clear view of the provider role in the proposed future system of community care.

The concepts presented within this chapter are based on the authors' experiences of mental health care delivery not only in the U.S.A., but also in the U.K., Canada, Italy and New Zealand where similar changes have been occurring. Over the last decade, there has been an acceleration of international learning in mental health as concepts emerging from one country are taken, adapted and applied in others. It is hoped that the concepts presented here will contribute to this valuable learning process.

The chapter will be organised into three sections:

---

[1] In this context, the CMHS includes the network of mental health providers. It includes all types of community providers, whether governmental or non-governmental; large or small; multi-service or single service.

- Looking at our history: an historical overview of the community mental health movement.
- Recovery-oriented systems: building recovery and integration into the community care philosophy.
- Funding for recovery: ensuring the funding approach supports recovery-oriented systems.

Looking at our history

Before considering how we might re-focus a community mental health system into a recovery supporting system, we have to first understand the changes that have already taken place within the CMHS movement.

The CMHS movement has achieved a great deal over the years. It has helped some users leave institutions, prevented others from ever experiencing them, and it has assisted many service users to improve their quality of life. The CMHS has proven to be both clinically effective and cost efficient.

The philosophy of community care was built on the idea that it was possible to deliver services in the community rather than delivering those services in an institutional setting. When de-institutionalisation began most providers and leaders held some or all of the following views:

That people could have a better quality of life if services that were historically based in the institutions were to be delivered within the community.

That professionals can minimise people's symptoms of mental illnesses through correctly diagnosing and treating the illnesses and that the use of new medications held the key to people with serious mental health problems living successfully within the community.

That people with serious and persistent mental health problems need active daily supports to live in the community and could never really recover and have 'normal' lives.

Based on these premises, the new community mental health systems that were developed were generally designed as follows: institutional services were transferred to the community, and 'experts' controlled the design and structure of the new CMHS to ensure that that those services would work (i.e. funders or major providers of services).

So this first evolution of a community mental health system relied on moving services out from the institution into the community. Those who designed the systems often sought to change the setting but not the characteristics or nature of the services provided. This was a community concept that was based on some of the same institutional ideas, but without the grounds, corridors and physical restraints. Further, there was an expectation that users would probably need at least brief periods of hospitalisation from time to time.

In the U.S., for example, providers designing new community services were instructed that their the design should focus on the ' five essential services'. Those services were: inpatient, partial hospitalisation, outpatient, emergency services, and community consultation and education.

The underlying principle at the service level was that users would leave the hospital, live under various levels of support in group homes, and come into partial hospitalisation/day programmes and, when they needed intense services, they would return to the hospital.

This re-location of services alone was more successful than most planners anticipated. Not only did service users achieve an improved quality of life as a result of leaving the institutions, many achieved far more than clinicians had predicted they could achieve before they left the institutions. It was only a matter of time before the service design based on an institutional model would be challenged.

In the U.S., as the years passed two pressures began to emerge. The first was that new users were entering the system and were never experiencing institutional care, and the five essential services did not provide the support they wanted or needed. Secondly, those service users who had become more independent after leaving the institutions were demanding an array of services that was quite different from the five essential services they were still being offered.

This launched the next trend in community care. Services in the community now had to evolve, moving on from their institutional origins and from a heavy reliance on psychiatric treatment, and were beginning to shape themselves around what users needed in order to be more independent and live successfully in the community.

The premise that services based in the institutions should be delivered within the community was now being challenged and service user needs were becoming the focus of the new CMHS designs.

The second premise from the de-institutionalisation era, that medications alone held the key to people with serious mental health problems living successfully within the community, was now being challenged. There was a growing recognition that living in an institution actually results in people losing their ability to care properly for themselves, and that to live successfully in the community people leaving an institution will need assistance to re-develop this ability.

In the U.S., as in other parts of the world, in order to cope with the new and different demands, central authorities (usually purchasers or funders) began to re-design the types of services that would be provided. Newly designed services included case management, diverse day programmes, rehabilitation, and then psychosocial rehabilitation, all in an attempt to offer better supports and help users to achieve a quality of life that had not been thought possible in the 1960s.

It would, however, be a long time before the third premise from the de-institutionalisation era, the premise that people with serious and persistent mental health problems could never really recover and have 'normal' lives, was challenged. It would take the voice of the service users, and their word 'recovery', to challenge this last premise.

In the meantime, central authorities continued to design services that were aimed at meeting service users' mental health needs, providing support for living in the community and improving their ability to care for themselves. Designs and structures of CMHS were still controlled by 'experts' in isolation. Increasingly, these experts were the service funders.

This led to the development of a whole new range of community mental health services. Providers were paid on condition that they delivered the type, volume and style of services that purchasers or funders wanted.

While these changes resulted in more improvements to the range and relevance of services, new demands and challenges were emerging and placing pressure on both the CMHS and the purchasers.

In particular, a number of groups were seen as poorly served by the existing system. They included the high number of new users entering the system who were abusing either alcohol or drugs; children and youths; the increasing number of service users who were being diverted to the criminal justice system and been incarcerated in jails; people diagnosed with post traumatic stress disorder, personality disorders and Alzheimer's disease; and some of the service users who were originally in institutions for long periods of time — though they had become a small minority of service users, they continued to require very high levels of service.

Demands for services to better meet the needs of these groups placed pressure on governmental authorities to provide additional local community services. Additional funds were awarded and purchasers began to buy specific services to meet the specific demands of these groups.

Since demands for service were outstripping the resources, legislators demanded accountability for usage of these funds. As a result, funds were 'silo' focused, i.e. specifically targeted to meet a particular unique demand through provision of a separate and often new service designed with its own set of unique protocols. Entry criteria were tightly defined, each user was 'certified' as meeting the correct entry criteria for the services, and services were monitored to ensure appropriate usage. Providers were required to demonstrate that the services they were delivering were those funded through increasingly detailed and time consuming reporting processes.

With a myriad of small services and programmes to meet the needs of specific groups of people, coordination was becoming a growing problem. Furthermore, people with mental health needs often also had a range of other health and welfare needs as well.

The newly designed 'silo' services, and the clear delineation between social services, mental health services, medical services and drug and alcohol services, only served to hamper service users' recovery from the problems they faced. Worse, the confusing array of services involved added to their pre-existing difficulties the burden of keeping track of, and coordinating, the activities of the myriad of services and agencies with whom they were involved.

While the limitations of the centrally designed 'silo' services were becoming evident, other limitations of the CMHS were also emerging. Awareness of these limitations was being raised by a new group of service users: people who were leaving the services having successfully recovered. This group, along with some supportive professionals and family members, were beginning to challenge the final underlying premise that had survived unchallenged since de-institutionalisation began, that people with serious and persistent mental health problems need active daily supports to live in the community and could never really recover and have 'normal' lives.

People who had recovered and re-established their lives without using the services represented incontrovertible evidence that this premise was faulty. This new group of recovered people reviewed the designs of the services.

While acknowledging that the services did help, these people and their families pointed to difficulties accessing services, delays in responses, poor coordination, and a lack of flexibility. They argued that poor service designs were hampering recovery.

The purchasers now responsible for the design of the CMHS found themselves under multi-level attacks: user leaders were saying that the design of services was wrong, access poor, quality ineffective and providers not responsive; communities and pressure groups were seeking explanations about why residents were falling through the large cracks in the system; the legislators were saying 'enough' to the ever-increasing expenditures, and professional staff were arguing that they were overwhelmed by the process and information requirements from funders and no longer had the time to provide support, or to learn the newest trends in care.

The introduction of managed care in the U.S.A. arose out of the growing frustration with the old service designs and the need to contain the escalating costs of health services. Managed care is a process whereby the funders contract with an intermediary (a managed care company) who stands between the funders, users and providers and controls the access and delivery of care to all users. The managed care company has no direct involvement in service delivery. It derives its profits from minimising expenditure on health care. Managed care was seen as a 'quick fix' to the growing problems for purchasers. It failed to help those with long-term support needs and in many ways only exacerbated the service design problems. Managed care became predominantly a mechanism for controlling the costs of service delivery: the companies' best practice guidelines are replete with tightly prescribed amounts and types of service that they would fund for each diagnosis.

As a result of the 'silo' approach to funding and the increasingly tightly prescribed service provision, providers found themselves less and less able to design flexible care programmes tailored to meet individual service user needs.

Today, two problems continue to limit progress in moving toward a CMHS that could better support recovery. These are: the continued widespread belief that someone who is experiencing serious mental health problems cannot recover; and decision making about the spectrum of services that service users could access resting with the funder of those services, far removed from the service users, families, providers and the community in which the users lived.

In order to make further progress towards the achievement of recovery from serious mental health problems, some new changes are required of the CMHS. Fundamental to these changes is the notion that people who have experienced serious mental health problems can and will live in their community and will recovery more rapidly and more fully if they become full citizens of that community, contributing to it and finding ways to meet their day-to-day needs through the resources it has to offer.

This means that the service design needs to be developed, organised and structured within a natural community environment. It must therefore aim to develop community resource, not replace it, and needs to be designed in conjunction with the community, not imposed by a central funder.

Community care should include all of the community. It should be a process whereby the responsibility for supporting a service user to achieve recovery is not the provider's alone. The responsibility for recovery lies with the larger community, with those who use the services and their families and friends. Of course the service provider has a part to play, too, both in supporting the service user and in assisting others to play their part.

The role of the CMHS has been in the past to deliver the services identified by funders. The new role is for CMHS and all providers to facilitate recovery.

To do this the CMHS must promote the following: users can recover, and will not always need professional services; the design of community services should be the responsibility of the community, not imposed from the outside; and funders should promote unique solutions and re-focus more on monitoring the outcomes, and allow communities the flexibility to design the services that best meet their needs.

In the next sections of this chapter, the way in which the CMHS can contribute to recovery and the role of funding are discussed.

Recovery-oriented systems
Recovery
We can define recovery in a narrow sense (the absence of a previously present mental health problem) or we can define it in a more broad sense (the re-establishment of a fulfilling life that has been lost through serious mental health problems and overinvolvement in the psychiatric system). People will measure recovery according to their own values, understanding and beliefs and there never will be a definitive test to see whether recovery has occurred.

The real test for recovery is when the person feels that they have recovered, that is they see themselves as living a quality of life that is not dominated by their past situation or their current difficulties and stresses.

When you interview people with mental health problems who use high levels of support services, they tend to seek outcomes that are quite different from those identified by mental health decision makers. Historically, the CMHS has focused on developing outcome measures that are indicators of mental health status. Users, on the other hand, seek to achieve a wider range of outcomes.

The following areas in which users seek to achieve favourable outcomes have been adapted from the work of the Village in Los Angeles (California Alliance for the Mentally Ill, 1993) — work and home, money, friends and social life, access to services, community involvement, hope and respect.

Consumers care little about the measures of mental health status and care a great deal about the direct impact of their mental health problem on their daily lives. We need to re-focus and give priority to consumer-valued measures of outcome and recovery.

Challenging old beliefs
To help people to achieve recovery, we therefore need to believe that people who have a serious mental health problem *can* recover; recognise that medication plays only a relatively small role in the achievement of recovery; and recognise that consumers do not need controlling supports to live successfully within the community.

Of these the most important is believing that people can recover, and yet it is the most difficult belief for service providers to change. We have been so indoctrinated that we find it hard to genuinely believe that recovery is possible. We transmit our hopelessness to service users and they, too, lose hope. Yet this is the most significant element of recovery. Once people see that others honestly and truthfully believe in them and their ability to recover, then all is possible.

All users can recover no matter how distressed they are.

If we read that sentence and immediately find ourselves asking what is meant by recovery, how to define recovery, how to measure recovery, we know that, deep down, we do not feel it is true. It is belief that matters. People who use the services know whether service providers think they can get better, whether or not it is ever put it in words. Belief alone has the power to have a major influence on the recovery of another person.

A story best illustrates the difficulty we have in believing that others can recover — and how wrong we can be. For many years Fran Silvestri sat on an incident review committee where more than half of the incidents that occurred involved those who had been given the diagnosis 'borderline personality disorder'. He asked, 'Why is this? Isn't there anything we can do?'. The answer he was given was 'This is because they are borderlines. They are very difficult to work with, place excessive demands on us and have a very poor prognosis (very few will ever recover).'

Then a new approach to care called Dialectic Behavioural Therapy (DBT) (Lineman, 1993) became more widely known in the U.S. Though some providers still debate its efficacy, it is clear that many people with the diagnosis borderline personality disorder who receive services based on the DBT principles make an outstanding recovery.

This story illustrates two points. The first is that our beliefs today about recovery may be proved wrong tomorrow, or may be being proved wrong elsewhere right now. The second is the power of the clinician's beliefs in effecting recovery.

It is highly likely that a major contributor to the success of the DBT approach is the effort that goes into staff education and support. Staff are supported to confront their biases about people with the diagnosis of borderline personality disorder and to examine how their own behaviour and usage of language reinforces the sense of helplessness. They have to learn to better understand the reality that the users experience and believe they can recover. Clinicians found it hard to accept that they themselves increased the stigma associated with the diagnosis and that, by not believing these users could recover, they were themselves limiting the potential for users to recover.

To make CMHS recovery oriented, we have to tackle these old beliefs within ourselves and within organisational behaviour. Service users can and do recover.

Systems and services can also recover. The fact that, for so long, few if any service providers have believed in recovery means that major and fundamental change is needed on the part of many clinicians and providers if systems are to become recovery oriented. There are administrators and decision makers who believe it is not possible for people who have worked in institutions and then in early CMHS services to themselves 'recover' and believe that people using their services can get better.

Even communities who have forgotten how to care about people who are less fortunate can recover.

If we are to effect major system change, we need to have faith in the ability of all people who have given up hope to recover: the service users, the staff, family members and even the community at large.

The role of the community mental health system in recovery

Up until this point, we have been defining the CMHS as the network of mental health service providers. However, in the recovery oriented system, this definition must change. If people who have recovered expect to live a full life within the community, then providers of mental health services are not the only ones to support service users to achieve this.

Recovery in this context requires a paradigm shift away from a network of mental health providers delivering services to users to treat their illnesses and provide all the supports and skill training necessary for them to live in the community. The new CMHS is a community, and within it each user, their family and friends, and their services together working to support the service user in achieving recovery.

To achieve this paradigm shift will take a great deal of work. The change needs to begin within the mental health provider organisations and their funders. Here a recovery approach to organisational development is needed. The shift will include: believing in the ability of all people to achieve recovery; learning to work in partnership; supporting people to implement their own plans; recognising the role of family, friends and the community in recovery; moving from fragmented, centrally specified services to services that are well integrated by individual plans driven by consumer outcomes; and moving from 'silo' funding to flexible use of resources to implement individually tailored plans.

When the shift to a recovery orientation has occurred in mental health service funding and provision, it is proposed that, within the new and expanded CMHS, mental health providers play the role of catalyst for the wider changes required.

Within the recovery oriented community mental health system, the role of the provider and its funder expands to include that of facilitator and coordinator, engaging families, friends and the wider community to enhance recovery. This is a shift away from centralised/provider control toward a collaboration and partnership with the three key stakeholders within the community mental health system: the users, the families and the wider community[2]. These three groups are key to the achievement of recovery.

The new roles for the provider and its funder include: designing the recovery focused CMHS; working collaboratively with the local community to design the new CMHS to achieve the outcomes that service users value; building community capacity; working to dispel myths and create opportunities within the local community; achieving recovery through partnerships; and service providers working in partnership with individual service users and their family and friends to develop and implement recovery plans. These roles are now discussed in greater detail.

Designing the recovery focused community mental health system

Funders, providers, service users, families and the wider community all have a role to play in the design of the recovery focused CMHS if we want: users, families and communities all to play a role in the CMHS and therefore contribute to recovery; our CMHS to achieve the outcomes that are desired locally.

---

[2] In this context, the community includes the mental health service provider and other agencies involved.

Implementing a recovery focused CMHS will involve: agreeing to shared values; understanding the outcomes; developing a CMHS design to achieve the outcomes; developing a plan to make the changes necessary; establishing measures to track progress and impact; and continuously reviewing and improving the design.

The key to this strategy is to begin by developing and promoting a strong sense of values. These values will be the foundation for the recovery oriented CMHS design, the plan to achieve the changes necessary to put the system in place, and the actions of every component of the CMHS.

If the recovery oriented CMHS is to be capable of delivering the outcomes that local service users, their families and their communities are seeking, then the design for the CMHS will need to be informed by a good understanding of these desired outcomes. Primary among these are the outcomes that the service users themselves desire.

These outcomes will differ from person to person, and will be influenced by each person's culture and background, so we can expect that systems designed to achieve the outcomes valued by consumers, families and the local community will look different in different parts of the world.

Having designed the recovery oriented CMHS, a plan to implement the changes will need to be developed. In the plan, it will be important to ensure that there are mechanisms for measuring both progress (achievement of milestones) and impact (achievement of pre-defined outcomes).

Periodically, the CMHS will need to measure user satisfaction and family satisfaction with the way in which the wider CMHS is helping them to recover (as distinct from their satisfaction with the individual services that they use).

The impact of the changes to CMHS design (in terms of outcome achievement and user and family satisfaction) will be used to continually review and modify the chosen CMHS design.

Building community capacity
The second role for providers and their funders is to build the capacity for consumers to achieve their recovery by assisting others in the expanded CMHS to recover from old beliefs and lack of understanding about mental health issues. The provider and funder work to build a CMHS environment whereby the key stakeholders integrate their efforts to ensure there is maximum opportunity for recovery. We use the term 'community capacity building' to describe this process. Why is it necessary?

A century ago the idea was to send those who had serious mental health problems away from the community so that they could better be cared for in an institutional setting. When de-institutionalisation began, communities expected that the CMHS and the providers within that system would be the new caregivers.

To illustrate this, Fran Silvestri recalls:

I would often hear the remark 'Is he one of yours?' when a companion would see someone who looked as though they may be suffering from serious mental health problems. It was as if this person who was harmlessly walking the streets was my organization's responsibility or my own personal responsibility. More than that, it was as if I 'owned' the people who used my services. My standard response to the question 'Is he one of yours?' became, 'NO, he is one of us'.'

The message 'this person is yours: he is your responsibility' is a leftover of the institutional era. It reflects the community's beliefs that people who use mental health services cannot be responsible themselves, that the community bears no responsibility for such people and that someone else should assume that responsibility.

Also a leftover from the institutional era are a myriad of myths and unfounded fears about people who experience serious mental health problems. For many years the community had minimal exposure to people with serious mental health problems while the institutions were thriving, and this allowed the myths and fears to go unchallenged and to grow.

This combination of a community that is fearful and ill informed and that feels no responsibility for people with serious mental health problems has resulted in major barriers to recovery. Many users consider that their recovery includes leading a full life, actively participating in community activities rather than relying on their mental health provider to meet their needs. If nobody wants to employ you, have you as a tenant, have you in their shop or see you on their street, then what chance do you have to recover and lead a full life, actively participating in your community?

Providers and funders have to work hard to break the long-held views that someone who has serious mental health issues is not a member of the community and belongs in an institution. They have to challenge the community's tendency to waïve responsibility for these of its members. They have to dispel the myths and fears. The more the community moves away from its old stereotypes, the fewer obstructions service users will encounter on their path to recovery.

Not only do providers and funders have to remove the barriers to recovery within the community, they must also work hard to create a community that actively supports recovery. If a service user is able to re-enter the workforce, then it is important that the 'community' (whether it is the shop floor, foreman or personnel office) understands about mental health care, how people can recover and what they can do to support recovery.

One way to build the capacity of a community to support recovery is to develop a community recovery plan. The plan will be unique, based on the particular characteristics of the community involved.

The diagram following shows some of the components of a community recovery plan.There are two key areas covered in the plan: education and integration. The first area is the education of the wider community. Education aims at dispelling myths and fears and reducing fear, and at educating people about the role they can play in recovery focused mental health care.

Education is delivered through public speaking forums, as well as targeting the media with personal success stories (where users are willing), news about the success of the CMHS and responses to any misinformation included in other stories. More focused training may also be made available to specific groups of influence (e.g. parent teacher associations).

This wide community effort is complemented by targeted education for several community groups that play a key role in recovery:
• community housing owners and directors

- employers
- community leaders.

The community leaders are important; to change their attitudes is also likely to influence the wider community group.

The second area to be covered in the plan is the integration between providers of mental health services and other relevant agencies and organisations (e.g. welfare, education, primary healthcare, economic development, etc.).

For too long CMHS have tried to stand alone, apart from other networks. The CMHS should be working closely with primary care and other social services, and even participating in the community's economic development, since creating jobs is just as important as assisting users to develop work skills. Tackling the integration between agencies will support recovery, ensuring the relevance of services offered, simplifying the ways in which consumers can access the range of services they need and creating opportunities for consumers.

All of these efforts to help the community recover and take its place in the CMHS to support recovery will take time, and their impact should be evaluated over years rather than months.

Achieving recovery through partnerships
The third role for providers is in working in partnership with individual service users and their families to support the achievement of recovery.

Achieving recovery through partnerships requires two significant changes to the way providers work with people who use the service. The first change involves a shift away from 'looking after' to 'achieving recovery', and the second involves a shift away from 'doing to' to 'working with'.

People who use mental health services do so in order to recover from their problems. They do not expect to become dependent on the service to maintain their quality of life. Historically, however, first in the institutions and then in the community, providers have assumed responsibility for meeting the full spectrum of people's health, housing, work and social needs. Providers must therefore re-focus their efforts so that they now assist consumers to recover and live a meaningful life in the community of their choice. This will involve assisting service users to develop their own strengths, so that they can then participate in the full spectrum of community activities (e.g. work, social, religious and political activities) if they wish.

To achieve recovery, service users need a provider who will work in partnership with them, supporting them to identify what they need in order to recover, sharing decisions about the design of the recovery plan, and sharing the responsibility for implementing it. Both the provider and the service user need to track progress, agree changes and be accountable for outcomes. Learning to work in partnership with service users will be essential if providers are to contribute to recovery.

Many people have written about recovery for users over recent years, including Ron Coleman in the U.K., Mary O'Hagan in New Zealand, and Mary Ellen Copeland in the U.S. (Coleman, 1999; Copeland, 1998; O'Hagan, 2001). These authors give us useful guidance about the way in which the mental health service provider can best support recovery.

Community Recovery Plan Components

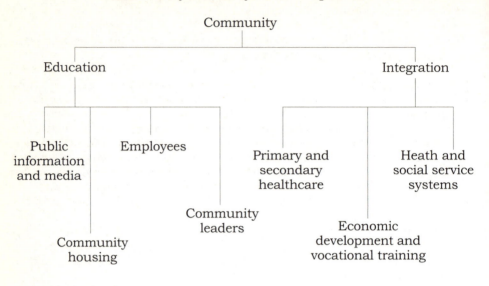

There are many different ways in which providers can adopt a recovery approach. Critical elements include:

- a belief in recovery
- an ability to work in partnership
- focusing on strengths
- supporting self determination and individual responsibility
- recognising the need for purpose and meaning
- building skills to access community networks and resources.

In the interests of supporting recovery, providers will also need to assist families and friends to recover from their own experiences and misconceptions and to therefore more fully support their family member's recovery.

Historically, when a member of the family[3] has become disturbed, families have often been left on their own and struggle to cope with a range of confusing emotions, including guilt, frustration, shame and helplessness. They seldom received good information about the distress, origins, treatments or likely course. As a result, they often have little resilience to offer the kind of empathic support that users need.

If the service user is to recover, then family members have the potential to play a major role in contributing to that recovery.

In order to play their part, families themselves need some supports to recover from their experiences. A provider can offer the opportunity for families to deal with their experiences, and can help to build their knowledge and ability to support recovery.

---

[3] In this context, family is taken to mean the people who are most important to the service user: family includes supportive friends including other service users, *de facto* partners and others.

One approach is to structure a family recovery plan using three strategies. First, build the family's knowledge about mental health problems so they better understand what is happening to their family member and so they can help other families. Second, help family members in a renewal process by dealing within their own emotional and psychological needs. Third, help families to divert their sense of responsibilities, so that they focus on helping the provider build the capacity within the community for their family members to be accepted and for users to receive adequate governmental support.

Providers can use the assistance of families to build a better environment for users who are re-entering community life. Families can assist in this plan by building strong alliances with user groups, providers and funders, and by becoming active in advocating within the general community about mental health issues. In some areas, well informed families have proven particularly effective in targeting misinformation in the media.

Being accountable to the wider CMHS

The final portion of a new community framework is to assure that whatever services the CMHS delivers are clinically effective and financially efficient. One way to achieve this is through an accountability plan. This accountability plan has four major comments:
- designing and measuring a value-based system;
- looking at benchmarks for clinical practice;
- measuring outcomes both those that measure effectiveness and those that promote efficient usage of resources;
- a strong measurement of user and family satisfaction, especially to understand users view of the effectiveness of their own recovery plan.

Funding for recovery

Money talks

Funders of health services have a vital role to play in creating a recovery focused CMHS, in addition to their contribution to designing the CMHS and building community capacity. Their role includes not only the provision of sufficient resource for the CMHS to function effectively, but also applying that resource in a way that allows flexibility to meet individual needs, creates incentives that align with recovery and ensures accountability back to the consumer, family, community and the source of the funding.

Adequate funds are necessary to offer the options and wide ranges of assistance that users need in order for them and their families to achieve recovery. A system of care that is inadequately funded will not be able to help users recover and may fuel community fear and stigmatisation.

Examples of this can be found in many parts of the world where de-institutionalisation was implemented as a way of saving money rather than improving recovery. In these places, as users were discharged from hospitals the developing community services were inadequately resourced. Resultant incidents within the community only served to confirm unfounded fears about community safety and to trigger the formation of groups who lobbied to re-introduce institutional care.

Even where resourcing is adequate, recovery can be impeded by inflexibility in funding mechanisms. Early in this chapter, we described a tendency for funders to develop a 'silo' based approach to funding, and this is one of the factors that impedes the delivery of integrated, recovery oriented services.

Governments or insurers spending money on healthcare want their funders to be able to account for the funds spent. Clearly what would be most meaningful would be to know how many people, with what illnesses or problems, achieved what outcomes from the array of services they used. It would also be useful to know what services they used to achieve these outcomes, so that more funding could be available for things that seem to work well.

Unfortunately, most funders do not have access to this information. Debates about what outcomes should be measured, and the complexity of some outcome measures has prevented funders from learning the most important things about services: do they work?

As a result, funders have focused on specifying types of service and quantities of service to be delivered, and tightly defining who is eligible for each service. This is what we mean by 'silo' based funding. Funds are not associated with a person who uses the service, to be used to ensure they can access a mix of services to meet their needs. Funds are linked only to the services provided. Each time a service is not available, there is a cry for a new 'silo' to fill the gap. Providers cannot take the risk of providing new services to meet emerging local needs (or better services to meet existing needs), as in doing so they may find themselves with a service for which there is no funding.

Silo based funding is often associated with financial incentives. An example is this: if funders reward providers on numbers of certified high need users, providers will find and certify users with the category that pays the most. This provides an outcome for society in that it influences the providers to respond to those users who need more services. Yet it also provides a strong incentive to keep users certified rather than to support them to achieve recovery.

This presents a major ethical dilemma: should finance drive the CMHS or should a recovery focus drive the CMHS? If we are to promote the concept of recovery, the CMHS funders must align financial incentives with recovery outcomes.

In summary, three things need to happen if funding is to support recovery. The first is that funders must be able to access information about the people who use the CMHS, their needs and the outcomes they are achieving. The second is that funders need to allow the CMHS the flexibility to provide the mix of services that is most likely to achieve the outcomes desired by an individual service user. Finally, the funders must find ways to align incentives with the achievement of outcomes.

Conclusion

The original idea behind community care was based on transferring institutional services into the community. Key staff at central locations created the designs for the community services.

The institutional style services are no longer the focus as service users seek support to live in a real community and to make that community a safe place for them.

The old style of central control has emerged from the institutional community into the real community. For recovery to be possible, the CMHS needs to evolve to embrace the wider community, family and service users, collaboratively designed for relevance in the local community and to achieve the outcomes that consumers seek.

The providers must no longer see themselves as the centre of the system, handling all aspects of care for users and meeting all consumer needs. They must now see themselves as facilitators who bring together users, families and the community in the interests of expediting the users' recovery and establishment of a full life the community of their choice.

In the new era, each and every person in the community will see himself or herself as responsible for each neighbour who needs help.

References

California Alliance for the Mentally Ill (1993) Integrated Service Agency *'The Journal'* *(California Alliance for the Mentally Ill),* Vol 4 (2)

Coleman, R. (1999) *Recovery; An Alien Concept?* Gloucester: Handsell

Copeland, M. (1998) *The Depression Workbook.* New Harbinger Publications.

Lineman, M (1993) *Skills Training Manual for Treating Borderline Personality Disorder.* New York: The Guilford Press.

O'Hagan, M. (2001) *Realising Recovery through the Education of Mental Health Workers; Recovery-based competencies and resources for New Zealand.* Wellington: New Zealand Mental Health Commission.

CHAPTER 16

Developing a survivor discourse to replace the 'psychopathology' of breakdown and crisis

JAN WALLCRAFT AND JOHN MICHAELSON

THIS CHAPTER IS ABOUT the creation of a self advocacy discourse which provides a clear alternative to the biomedical model of mental illness. The authors have claimed elsewhere (Michaelson and Wallcraft, 1997) that the biomedical model is in a paradigm crisis. Wallcraft (1996) argues that psychiatric survivors and allies are challenging the dominant medical model of mental illness and that survivor initiatives and mutual support are showing the way forward in alternatives to psychiatric acute wards for people in crisis.

Kuhn (1970) says that a failing scientific paradigm becomes unable to provide satisfactory answers to current problems and faces ever greater challenges from within the discipline. These signs are present. Growing numbers of psychiatrists and psychologists are outspoken in their criticism of the failings of the mainstream model of psychiatry. The setting up of a Critical Psychiatry Network (Double, 2000), and the recent report from the British Psychological Society's Division of Clinical Psychology (2000) are evidence of this. Critics focus on the central role of classification systems for diagnosis, genetic and biochemical research and medication. Psychiatrists Bracken and Thomas have defined their concept of 'post-psychiatry' in a series of articles, and state:

> For 150 years, psychiatry has fanned the flames of public hope and expectation, holding out promises of 'cure' and treatment for an ever-wider range of complex human and social problems. But these promises have failed to materialize . . . We believe that psychiatry should start a 'decolonization', a phased withdrawal from the domains it has laid claim to, including psychosis, depression and PTSD, by admitting the limited nature of its knowledge. (Bracken and Thomas, 2000a)

Boyle (1996; 1999; 2000) a clinical psychologist, criticises diagnosis, which she argues is currently central to psychiatry:

> Critical analysis of the diagnostic system and of particular categories such as schizophrenia, depression or personality disorder, shows that

their claimed resemblance to scientific or medical systems or concepts is a myth.

There is now widespread acceptance that psychiatric diagnostic categories do not refer to physical disease entities. They are theoretical constructs about the meanings of observed behaviour, subject to being modified and refined, and only as good as their predictive value and practical usefulness. The British Psychological Society expresses a view of diagnosis similar to that of Boyle:

> *Psychiatric diagnoses are labels which describe certain types of behaviour; they do not tell us anything about the nature or causes of the experiences . . . The diagnostic approach has not been as useful as has been hoped.* (The British Psychological Society, 2000: p. 16)

The report argues that diagnosis has not proved to be reliable in predicting outcome nor to reflect the reality of the way in which people's psychological problems are naturally grouped:

> *cluster analysis . . . has shown that the majority of psychiatric patients would not be assigned to any recognisable diagnostic group.* (British Psychological Society, 2000: p. 17)

The report suggests a continuum between mental health and illness and the normality of abnormal experiences. It recommends formulations of each person's specific problems, to help the person make sense of their experiences, while exploring complex causes (psychological and physical), so that treatment strategies are designed to suit each individual.

Whatever the outcome of the struggle within the science of psychiatry, it would seem that the post-war consensus, that biomedical psychiatry would eventually identify the causes of mental illness and find cures, has broken down.

Discursive practice and action

The above debates are among scientists and practitioners. The Kuhnian argument about paradigmatic change in science does not include the lay perspective. To include a greater diversity of voices, it is helpful to take a Foucauldian approach (Foucault, 1971; 1972), and talk about discourse, which is a wider notion than that of the scientific paradigm. Foucault uses the concept of discourse to describe how ideas about reality are conceptualised, recorded in texts and built upon until they take on an apparently concrete form. Discourse is the means by which knowledge is created and transmitted (Foucault, 1972). Foucault saw discourse as systematically shaping and acting upon the phenomena described. A medical discourse such as that of psychopathology (or mental illness), is made effective through a set of scientific, medical, social, educational and legal institutions and practices, which Foucault terms discursive practices. These in turn shape the lives of those identified as mentally ill. A discourse may originate in one person's writings, but as the ideas are taken up, it becomes a collective enterprise. Discourses arise at particular historic and cultural moments, but once established, their origins are often forgotten, and the entity created is assumed to have a real existence.

Such a discursive entity is mental illness, which is assumed self-evident because of the existence of people whose behaviour is different from the consensus view of normality. Once the people so described begin to find a voice for themselves, this consensual discourse can be challenged. Challenges to psychiatric discourse are not new, and can be dated back as early as 1620 (Campbell, 1996), but it was only recently that the increasing numbers of psychiatric patients and former patients living in the community began to find a collective voice strong enough to begin to create an alternative discourse. Many studied for academic qualifications specifically in order to make their own discourse more credible in a society which values academic learning (see Lindow, this volume).

During the past twenty years, the self advocacy discourse has begun to generate its own discursive practices through survivor-led services. It is now possible to discern a clear alternative discourse relating to the phenomena of severe distress, non-rational behaviour and beliefs.

We have chosen to concentrate here on the process of initial crisis and treatment, i.e. the moment when a person first comes into contact with formal psychiatric services. We refer to the process analysed in Goffman's (1961) classic study, wherein he described the making of a psychiatric patient through the depersonalising degradation rituals within the institution. Research by Barham and Hayward (1991) updates Goffman's work by showing the long-term effects that psychiatric admission and diagnosis have on people's lives. As one person put it:

> . . . *you wake up every morning and you think, 'Oh God, I'm a schizophrenic!'. If the doctor hadn't told me, I'd just have woken up and thought, 'Well, I'm just going through some sort of illness and I'll probably get over it'. But once you get diagnosed you start thinking all sorts from different corners about the illness and it just gets worse and worse.* (p.20)

The above quote demonstrates the potentially damaging results of naming the disease, a central feature of the discourse of mental illness. Though many patients find psychiatric intervention in crisis helpful and are reassured by diagnosis, many others have described their initial contact with psychiatric services as extremely damaging, and often regard this as having set them on a career as a mental patient (Chamberlin, 1988; Lindow, 1990; O'Hagan, 1996; Pembroke, 1994; Shimrat, 1997). The failure of medical staff to listen to the patient's own view of what is happening, and the imposition of an alien (to the person in crisis) discourse is often seen as the root of this changed identity:

> *Typically, on admission to a psychiatric ward, you are interviewed by a doctor. Many people expect this to be an opportunity to tell all that is troubling them to an expert who will help. But much of the interview is wholly baffling. 'Count backwards from 100 in sevens'. 'Do you believe your thoughts are being controlled?' There appears to be no space to say on your own terms and in your own words, just what are the difficulties*

that have reduced you to this situation. (Rose, Campbell and Neeter, 1993: pp. 320–21)

According to Lindow (1996) much of the negative outcome which is usually attributed to the progression of a mental illness is in fact iatrogenic (i.e. attributable to medical treatment):

> . . . *we know that the deterioration in the past was due to institutionalisation; that the deterioration in the present is due to damage from long-term use and abuse (by doctors) of powerful psychoactive drugs, and to social exclusion.* (Lindow, 1996: p. 187)

The hope that the biomedical discourse can be challenged and altered by the collective creation of a self advocacy discourse, offering greater hope of recovery and reducing iatrogenic damage and social rejection, is perhaps the underlying motivation for much of the activity of the self advocacy movement.

Challenging disempowerment, asserting citizen rights

The first step towards establishing a self advocacy discourse was to reclaim rights which had been denied to mental patients, by drawing up charters. Rogers and Pilgrim (1991) have described this aspect of what they term the 'MHUM' (Mental Health User Movement):

> *[the MHUM] has attempted to replace the notion of an atomised 'mentally ill' patient with a collectivised lay conception of empowered individuals making social and political demands of the state, statutory services and mental health professionals. It pre-empts the possibility of each individual actor being marginalised and pathologised by medical practices, thus preventing the deligitimation of demands made by users, which the health sector wishes to evade. As a collective, the MHUM has found a way of transcending the 'irrational' reputation of the mental patient.* (Rogers and Pilgrim, 1991: p. 146)

One of the authors (JW) was involved in the creation of two such national charters. The first was in 1987 at the Survivors Speak Out conference, attended by representatives of most of the existing self advocacy groups. The second was developed between 1992–94 and was commissioned by the Department of Health (Mental Health Task Force User Group, 1994). This reflects the increasing acceptance of self advocacy as a legitimate constituency for consultation by the government.

The creation of the second charter was a conscious attempt to build self advocacy consensus on a number of key issues, such as the right to self-definition, respectful treatment, choice, advocacy, involvement, and alternatives to medication. It is impossible to estimate whether any concrete results were achieved in terms of rights and improved services by the Charter, but a number of Trusts subsequently worked with local self advocacy forums to create local charters, and it was a major influence on the Department of Health's Mental Health Patients' Charter (Department of Health, 1996).

The self advocacy movement is currently challenging biomedical discourse and creating new discourses and practices through a number of other forms of action. These include:

- The redefinition of an episode of severe 'mental illness' as a breakdown, which is a less stigmatising term, or a crisis, which is seen as having a more positive connotation (Campbell, 1991).
- Recounting life histories, as a way to understand the complex origins of breakdown and crisis (Chamberlin, 1988; Campbell, 1989; Susko, 1991; Read and Reynolds, 1996; Shimrat, 1997).
- Developing self-assessment schedules of needs and wants (Leader, 1995).
- Developing self-management techniques for specific problems, including self-harm, hearing voices and periods of excessive 'highs' and 'lows'. (Manic Depression Fellowship, 1995; Coleman and Smith, 1997; National Self-Harm Network, 1998).
- Setting up alternatives to hospital, in the form of survivor-led crisis and self-help projects (Lindow, 1994; Spreizer, 1995; Read, 2000; Wallcraft, 1996).
- Designing and carrying out user-led research (Wallcraft 1998; Mental Health Foundation, 2000) (also see Lindow, this volume).
- Enabling service users to become trainers and designing training for mental health workers to be carried out by service users (Read and Wallcraft, 1992; Graley, Nettle and Wallcraft, 1994; Hastings and Crepaz-Keay, 1995).

Discourse depends to a large extent upon language, and as Table 1 below shows, self advocacy discourse provides alternative concepts to describe a number of the phenomena of crisis and breakdown, and proposes different courses of action from those advocated in biomedical discourse.

These various aspects of self advocacy discourse, taken together, provide a complete re-assessment of the meaning of the phenomena taken as a starting point by the discourse of mental illness. Self advocacy narratives of personal experience show that apparently meaningless behaviour has meaning to the person concerned. That meaning can be shared with others who will listen without judging. O'Hagan provides an example of this in a 'cut and paste' of excerpts from her journal and from her hospital file during an episode of mental distress:

> *Is attending the dining room with firm encouragement and eating small meals. Remains very withdrawn but occasionally gives vent to an incongruous sustained laugh — although says she isn't happy. Rx Chlorpromazine BD & Nocte as appears to be preoccupied with thoughts – hopefully medication will break the chain.*

> Last night they came to me
> with Chlorpromazine
> I refused it.
> I am afraid medication will dull my mind
> and the meanings in there will escape forever.

> *Refusing medication. States she hasn't been taking it because it doesn't do her any good. Not persuaded by explanations or reassurance....*

Every morning the night nurses
pull off my blankets
They are rough.
I can't fight back
Even their softest touches bruise me
A nurse said to me
'Face the world'
But I am facing the pain inside me.
I cannot face both ways at once.

Mary is not to hide away in her bed. She is to be encouraged to get up for breakfast and engage in ward activities. (O'Hagan, 1996)

Susko (1994) makes a plea for a narrative rather than a caseness approach to the treatment of people in crisis. He argues that in late 19th century medicine, the practice of allowing narrative meaning to emerge was lost when:

Clinical practice became increasingly obsessed with comparing 'measurable signs' to 'standardised norms' (Susko, 1994: p. 88)

Other societies, he argues, have not always had such a restricted view of the purpose of medicine: 'Suffering had meaning and served as an opportunity for cure and spiritual advancement' (Susko, 1994: p. 89).

Self advocacy networks have been powerful means of creating new discourses based on finding meaning in experience. The Hearing Voices Network has challenged the assumption that hearing voices is a prime symptom of schizophrenia by creating groups for voice hearers to identify meaning and share coping strategies. The work of the Self-Harm Network and the Bristol Crisis Service has been widely recognised and was recently featured in a leading nursing journal (*Nursing Times*, 1998). The Manic Depression Fellowship is currently running courses in self-management for their members. All of these organisations provide speakers and trainers who are influencing working practices in psychiatry. Bassett (2000) sees evidence that service user involvement in the training of approved social workers and mental health officers is moving from the sidestream to the mainstream and influencing the thinking of workers about all aspects of their practice.

Until recently, the creation of alternative residential crisis services by self advocates has proven difficult, and in many cases self advocacy groups had to work with and through voluntary or statutory organisations in order to be taken seriously by funders. One of the authors of this chapter (JW) was a participant observer for a year on an Advisory Group helping to develop a women's crisis house in Islington, North London. The project was managed by a Mental Health Trust, but with considerable self advocacy input. She interviewed key stakeholders about the origins of the project. It was clear that it had been set up in response to local pressure from service users for an alternative:

My understanding is that the local authority was trying to kind of respond to articulated users views, I mean, what a lot of service users are saying is, you know, 'we want somewhere to go in crisis, we don't want to be

admitted into hospital, we want something before we get to that stage.'
(Service Manager, NHS Trust)

The relationship between self advocate members of the Advisory Group and representatives of the Trust was tense. The self advocates had been involved in a bid to develop a user-run crisis project that was rejected for funding in favour of the Trust bid. They joined the project in the hope of persuading the Trust to create a genuine non-medical alternative to hospital.

Disagreement focussed on the role of psychiatric expertise. The Trust proposed to appoint a sessional psychiatrist. The self advocates and other voluntary sector representatives opposed this. They questioned what a psychiatrist could offer which could not be better provided by a therapist. They argued that the presence of a psychiatrist would deter potential users with bad experiences of psychiatry, and that staff would defer to psychiatric status. The Trust insisted on appointing a psychiatrist. However, during the year after opening the psychiatric input was quietly dropped.

Self advocacy members argued for women not to be excluded from admission on the grounds of assumptions made about them because of past violent behaviour or a tendency to self-harm, as they argued that this behaviour may have been provoked by oppressive psychiatric services. The mission statement, policies, procedures and job descriptions were drafted by the Advisory Group and adopted with little change. Self advocates were part of the staff recruitment process.

One of the mental health professionals who had backed the project hoped that the demonstrable success of the project would lead the way to radical change. She declared her belief that the project was of national importance:

If it works, and I think it will, it could be beginning of unpicking psychiatric hospitals; the problem is the need to prove the service is good or better, and cheaper. (Health Authority executive)

By the end of its first year 160 women had stayed at the house. The majority would otherwise have been admitted to hospital. Many more had received advice, support, and information. Women with young children were able to keep their children with them if they chose. Complementary therapies were provided. Feedback from service users was mainly positive; many said they had learned something new from staying there. The staff had experienced no violence from residents. The overall use of medication was low, and was being used to alleviate specific symptoms rather than to keep residents subdued. Self advocacy members of the Advisory Group were attending monthly House Meetings, and were able to meet with residents without staff being present, to hear their views.

The following year Wakelin (1998) reported that the house felt peaceful and not institutional. Staff and residents ate together. Residents told Wakelin that they felt their control was not taken away from them as they had experienced in hospital. In comparison with hospital they valued the greater amount of time staff spent with them, explaining things to them and helping with their practical problems. They appreciated the greater range of activities (including support groups, art therapy and complementary therapies). They referred time and again to a feeling of safety, and liked being with other women in a small, women-only space. The women that Wakelin spoke to had felt unsafe in hospital, and had been harassed or abused by men there.

Although this project was not a user-led service, it did go some way towards demonstrating that a service modelled on self advocacy discourse could be successful in meeting the needs of its users.

The Mental Health Foundation's current Crisis Programme has funded and supported seven user-led crisis projects, and the outcomes of these are currently being evaluated (see Mental Health Foundation website).

The above actions, and many others, are clearly influencing professional thinking and practice. A special feature on self-harm in the *Nursing Times* in 1998 indicated the extent to which many professionals are now taking user perspectives seriously and working with self advocacy organisations (Pacitti, 1998; Murray, 1998; Harrison, 1998). However, so long as the discourse of mental illness retains its economic, legal and political power, in particular the power to impose treatment via the Mental Health Act, reforms will be limited in their impact on the fundamental powerlessness of mental health service recipients to determine their own fate.

Reorienting policy towards a self advocacy discourse

For real change to occur, there needs to be a widespread understanding that the discourse of mental illness does not describe any fixed reality and should no longer be given a privileged position in the shaping of laws and institutions. It is the creation of a particular era in history (see Newnes, 1999) and has become increasingly inappropriate and oppressive in the more democratic and liberated society of the 21st century. Information can be shared more quickly and easily, and people are no longer willing to accept 'expert' opinion without question. Personal experience and viewpoint is now much more widely regarded as valid material for qualitative scientific research than when the radical psychiatrist R.D. Laing made his pleas for the validation of experience (Laing, 1967; 1982).

Self advocates who have begun to try to articulate the new self advocacy paradigm, or discourse as we have termed it here, have continually referred to the validity of experience as a starting point for reorienting mental health law, medical and social services to the real wants and needs of people in crisis. Craine (1998) has argued for a new discourse which:

> *views people who experience mental health challenges in a 'holistic' way, as rounded, complex human beings whose problems cannot be reduced to manifestations of an organic disease process.* (Craine, 1998: p. 12)

Craine also argues that the self advocacy discourse is a social model, i.e. that mental health service users are not disabled so much by physical and emotional conditions as by the response of society to their differences. Plumb (1999) seeks to replace the model of 'mental illness' with one whose key features are:

> *self-knowledge, self-advocacy, self-empowerment, and self-determination, within a context of mutual support and collective action.* (Plumb, 1999: p. 459)

She argues specifically against treatment without consent, which she says is a 'violation of body and self . . . a trauma that we have to deal with along with the other traumas of our lives that have landed us in the psychiatric system in the first place' (Plumb, 1999: p. 463). Instead, she argues, there should be a right to:

> *Non-medical sanctuary and support without drug treatment for a person during, and following, a crisis where consent to medical treatments is not given.* (Plumb, 1999: p. 463)

The right to refuse treatment is, along with the validity of experience, a central tenet of many recent articulations of self advocacy discourse. The current reshaping of the Mental Health Act presents an opportunity for change, though at present a change in this direction seems increasingly unlikely (see Beresford and Croft, this volume).

It may be that the fundamental changes in law and service provision that self advocates are seeking will only happen once popular notions of mental illness belonging to the discourse of psychopathology formulated in the 19th century have been transformed by the social action of the self advocacy movement and its allies. One important way forward could be through good quality and well-funded research in which 'mental illness' is treated as an unproven hypothesis. Popper (1987) argues that a hypothesis is only valid so long as it cannot be proven otherwise. Scientific research should seek to establish the best solutions for people in crisis rather than continuing to work within a set of medical assumptions about the existence of 'diseases' with no physical pathology. We would argue that the biomedical model of crisis services has rarely been put to the test against alternatives such as those described here, taking into full account user perspectives, long-term results and long-term cost effectiveness.

Such research would take account of self advocacy discourse in order to give due weight to the meaning and value of the experience of madness as potentially positive and transformative, the importance of social factors, the complex nature of crisis, and the importance of individual choice and natural healing. It is likely that research would be more often qualitative than is usual at present. It would involve people who had been through crisis as co-researchers and hypothesis-generators not just as research subjects (see Lindow, this volume, for further thoughts on this issue).

Encouraging personal narrative both as a means of healing and of research should have a far higher priority. The information gained by listening to people's life stories could form the basis for mental health training programmes, for service planning, and for public education programmes which enable people to recognise and cope better with the onset of their own crises and those of others.

Beyond science, there is a continuing need for political action to extend the rights and responsibilities of normal citizenship to people diagnosed as mentally ill, and replace a model of combating stigma with one of non-discriminatory practice (see Campbell, this volume). Bracken and Thomas (2000b) argue that challenging stigma without revising our assumptions about mental illness cannot be effective. So long as the medical model continues to perpetuate the links between schizophrenia, danger and irresponsibility, people diagnosed mentally ill will continue to be socially excluded. Sayce, a former Policy Director of MIND, argues that a non-discriminatory position is one which recognises that mental disorder *per se* does not invalidate judgement:

> *Mental health problems do not obliterate judgement. They can make thinking so difficult that society may decide it should intervene to ensure safety — often for very short time periods....and often in ways that can be resolved through advance planning when the person is well, through advocacy or simple creative thinking: for example, problem solving with someone within their own frame of reference, rather than resorting to force.* (Sayce, 2000: pp. 94–5)

It is the central argument of this article that self advocacy has posed a challenge to the prevailing discourse of 'mental illness', inspiring and validating the arguments of critical professionals such as Boyle, Bracken and Thomas. Without a vibrant self advocacy movement, the efforts of radical professionals on behalf of service users could not achieve widespread change. The self advocacy movement working with its allies is capable of creating a shift in both the scientific and the common sense view of mental health problems, in which personal life history, self-assessment of needs and self-management of problems are central, and services offered are geared to supporting community self-help networks.

Together, the self advocacy movement and its professional allies can create a new discourse through research and political action that can underpin future services. Such a vision inspired the authors to create the SPIRAL model (Systematic Prevention, Intervention, Recovery and Learning) for the Mental Health Foundation (see the Mental Health Foundation website). This model extends the current self advocacy discourse on crisis and breakdown to take in ideas of community action to prevent crises occurring, and to help recovery, self-management and re-integration after a crisis period is over. An integral learning loop, pursued through methods such as action learning, collaborative conversation, user-led research and evaluation, and IT based interactive dissemination, would bring the results of this programme back to the communities and stimulate new ideas and developments. The aim is to replace community fear of an entity called 'mental illness' which can only be defined and treated by a specialised branch of the medical profession, with a human phenomenon infinitely complex yet comprehensible for which the whole community is responsible. Knowledge and action can exclude or include. Survivor led research and services are creating the basis for inclusive and empowering services that could become the norm in the future. Allies in the statutory and voluntary sectors can help this process by using survivor discourse as a basis for research and development projects.

Table 1: A comparison of the discourses of mental illness and self advocacy in relation to crisis, breakdown and treatment

Phenomenon	Explanation or solution from discourse of mental illness	Explanation or solution from self advocacy discourse
Behaviour that appears to be out of control and possibly dangerous	Mental illness, biochemical imbalance, resulting in psychiatric emergency.	Usually caused by factors such as early trauma, life events, realisation of problems in the world, spiritual crisis, lack of sleep, poor nutrition or excesses of drugs/alcohol.
Hearing or seeing things that others don't hear or see	Delusional systems as a first rank symptom of schizophrenia, a disease with genetic and biochemical causes.	Possible explanations: heightened awareness, connection with other realities, early trauma; can be positive and can be self-managed.
Experiencing periods of being unusually 'high' or depressed	Manic depression: a disabling disease caused by malfunctioning biochemistry, requiring long term medication.	Possible explanations: deep apprehension, desperate need to change things, powerlessness and hopelessness; can be self-managed, with medication as one option among others.
Intentional self-injury	A sign that the person has become a danger to him- or herself; need for close supervision and control in hospital.	Usually an expression of deep distress; requires sensitive treatment that does not remove personal control.
System for making sense of the above behaviours and symptoms	Psychiatric diagnosis, e.g. DSM IV and risk assessment.	Listening to people telling their own stories, techniques of self-assessment.
Suitable location of help for a person exhibiting any of the above	Acute wards or community mental health centres.	Crisis houses, crisis drop-ins, informal community support networks.
Source of information and knowledge about these phenomena	Genetic and biochemical research, psychiatric textbooks and journals, DSM IV diagnostic manual.	Asking the person in crisis, self advocacy publications, survivor-led research and training.

References

Barham, P. and Hayward, P. (Eds.) (1991) *Relocating Madness: From the mental patient to the person.* London: Tavistock Routledge

Bassett, T. (2000) Sidestream to Mainstream. *Openmind, 105,*18

Boyle, M. (1996) Schizophrenia: the fallacy of diagnosis. *Changes, 14 (1),* 5–13

Boyle, M. (1999) Diagnosis. In: C.Newnes, G. Holmes and C.Dunn (eds.) *This is Madness: A critical look at psychiatry and the future of mental health services* (pp.75–90). Ross-on-Wye: PCCS Books

Boyle, M. (2000) Diagnose This. *Openmind, 101,* 8

Bracken, P. and Thomas, P. (2000a) Prison wardens or mental health professionals? *Openmind, 101,* 20

Bracken, P. and Thomas, P. (2000b) Stigma or discrimination? *Openmind 105,* 20

The British Psychological Society, Division of Clinical Psychology (2000) *Recent advances in understanding mental illness and psychotic experiences.* Leiocester: BPS

Campbell, P. (1989) Peter Campbell's Story. In: A. Brackx (ed.) *Mental Health Care in Crisis.* London: Pluto Press

Campbell, P. (1991) In Times of Crisis. *Openmind, 52,*15

Campbell, P. (1996) The history of the user movement in the United Kingdom. *Mental Health Matters: A reader.* Basingstoke: Macmillan/The Open University.

Chamberlin, J. (1988) *On Our Own.* London: MIND

Coleman, R. and Smith M. (1997) *Working with Voices!!: Victim to Victor.* Runcorn: Handsell Publications.

Craine, S. (1998) *Shrink Resistant: The survivor mOovement and the survivor Perspective.* US Network Working Papers 3. (unpublished paper)

Department of Health (1996) *Mental Health Services: The Patient's Charter.* London: H.M.S.O.

Double, D (2000) Critical Psychiatry. *CPD Bulletin Psychiatry, 2,* 33–36

Foucault, M. (1971) *Madness and Civilisation.* London: Routledge

Foucault, M. (1972) *Archaeology of Knowledge.* London: Routledge

Goffman, E. (1961) *Asylums: Essays on the social situation of mental patients and other inmates.* New York: Anchor Books

Graley, R., Nettle, M. and Wallcraft, J. (1994) *Building on Experience.* NHS Executive.

Harrison, A. (1998) A harmful procedure. In: *Nursing Times* (1998) Self-Harm. 94 (27) July 8, 36–39

Hastings, M. and Crepaz-Keay, D. (1995) *The Survivors' Guide to Training Approved Social Workers.* London: Central Council for Education and Training in Social Work

Kuhn, S. (1970) *The Structure of Scientific Revolutions.* Chicago: Chicago University Press

Laing, R.D. (1967) *The Politics of Experience and The Bird of Paradise.* Harmondsworth: Penguin

Laing, R.D. (1982) *The Voice of Experience.* London: Penguin

Leader, A. (1995) *Direct Power: A resource pack for people who want to develop their own care plans and support networks.* Brighton: Pavilion Publishing

Lindow, V. (1990) Participation and Power. *Openmind, 44,* 10.

Lindow, V. (1994) *Self-Help Alternatives to Mental Health Services.* London: Mind Publications

Lindow, V. (1996) What We Want from Community Psychiatric Nurses. In J. Read and J. Reynolds (eds.) *Speaking Our Minds.* Milton Keynes: Open University

Manic Depression Fellowship (1995) *Inside Out: A guide to self-management of manic depression.* (booklet)

Mental Health Foundation (2000) Strategies for Living Report.

Mental Health Foundation website http://www.mentalhealth.org.uk

Mental Health Task Force User Group (1994) *Guidelines for Local Charters for Users of Mental Health Services.* Department of Health, NHS Executive (unpublished report)

Michaelson, J. and Wallcraft, J. (1997) Alternatives to the biomedical model of mental health crisis. *Breakthrough, 1* (3), 31–49

Murray, I. (1998) At the cutting edge. In: *Nursing Times (*1998) Self-Harm. 94 (27) July 8, 36–39

National Self-Harm Network (1998) *The Hurt Yourself Less Workbook.* London: National Self-Harm Network

Newnes, C. (1999) Histories of Psychiatry. In: C. Newnes, G. Holmes and C.Dunn (eds.) *This is Madness: A critical look at psychiatry and the future of mental health services.* Ross: PCCS Books

O'Hagan, M. (1996) Two Accounts of Mental Distress. In J. Read and J. Reynolds (eds.) (1996) *Speaking Our Minds.* Basingstoke: Macmillan Press

Pacitti, R. (1998) Damage Limitation. In: *Nursing Times* (1998) Self-Harm. 94 (27) July 8, 36-39

Pembroke, L. (ed.) (1994) *Self-Harm: Perspectives from personal experience.* London: Survivors Speak Out.

Plumb, A.E. (1999) New mental health legislation: a lifesaver? Changing paradigm and practice. *Social Work Education, 18* (4), 459-478

Popper, K. (1987) *The Logic of Scientific Discovery.* London: Hutchinson.

Read J. (2000) More than a Crisis House *CrisisPoint 11.* London: The Mental Health Foundation

Read, J. and Reynolds, J. (eds.) (1996) *Speaking Our Minds.* Basingstoke: Macmillan Press

Read, J. and Wallcraft, J. (1992) From Anger to Action Training Pack. London: Mental Health Media Council.

Rogers, A. and Pilgrim, D. (1991) 'Pulling down churches': accounting for the British Mental Health Users' Movement. *Sociology of Health and Illness 13* (2),129-133

Rose, D., Campbell, P. and Neeter, A. (1993) Community Care: Users' Perspectives. In: M. Weller and M. Muijen (eds.) *Dimensions of Community Mental Health Care.* London: W.B. Saunders.

Sayce, L. (2000) *From Psychiatric Patient to Citizen.* New York: St. Martin's Press.

Shimrat, I. (1997) *Call Me Crazy: Stories from the mad movement.* Vancouver: Press Gang Publishers

Spreizer, I. (1995) Recovery at home. In: J. Read and J. Reynolds (eds.) *Speaking Our Minds.* Basingstoke: Macmillan Press

Susko, M. A. (ed.) (1991) *Cry of the Invisible.* Baltimore: Harrison Edward Livingstone

Susko, M. (1994) Caseness and Narrative: Contrasting Approaches to People who are psychiatrically labeled. *Journal of Mind and Behavior. Challenging the Therapeutic State, 15* (1), 87–112

Wakelin, D. (1998) Being There. *Crisis Point,* Mental Health Foundation 5, 6-7

Wallcraft, J. (1996) Some models of asylum and help in times of crisis. In D. Tomlinson and J. Carrier (eds.) *Asylum in the Community* (pp.186-206), London: Routledge

Wallcraft, J. (1998) Survivor-led research in human services: challenging the dominant medical model. In: S. Baldwin S. (ed.) *Needs Assessment and Community Care* (pp.186–208). Oxford: Butterworth Heinemann

CONTRIBUTORS

Steve Baldwin was Professor of Psychology and Director of the CACTUS clinic at University of Teesside, UK. He was a clinical psychologist and film-maker until his tragic death in the Selby train crash in February 2001.

Peter Beresford works with the Open Services Project, is a long-term user of mental health services, active in the psychiatric system survivors movement and Professor of Social Policy at Brunel University.

Peter Breggin, M.D., is Director, International Centre for the Study of Psychiatry and Psychology, Bethesda, Maryland, USA.

Olive Bucknall is an ex-user and survivor of the mental health services and a founder member of the Patients' Council in the local psychiatric hospital for over nine years. Through these experiences and those of her son she holds very strong views regarding the use of ECT, and would like to see its abolition. She is a member of ECT Anonymous and Survivors Speak Out. Because of the immense power within the psychiatric stsyem she supports Independent Advocacy. She is also a strong supporter of alternative health routes for mental health other than psychiatry.

Peter Campbell is a mental health system survivor. He is a founder member of Survivors Speak Out and Survivors' Poetry and has been involved in action to change the mental health system since the early 1980s. He has been working as a freelance writer and trainer for more than ten years and has contributed chapters to a number of publications on mental health issues. His third collection of poems is in preparation.

Suzy Croft works with Open Services Project and is a social worker at St John's Hospice, London. She is a member of the editorial collective of *Critical Social Policy*.

Sara Cureton is a service user representative and provides mental health services in a voluntary capacity. She represents individuals who have experienced eating distress in her locality as well as general mental health service users. She has received training in psychotherapy and counselling, CBT, CAT, Swedish body massage and reflexology.

Duncan Double is Consultant Psychiatrist, Norfolk Mental Health Care NHS Trust and Honorary Senior Lecturer, School of Health Policy and Practice,

University of East Anglia. He is website editor of the Critical Psychiatry Network (http://www.criticalpsychiatry.co.uk/)

Cailzie Dunn is a clinical psychologist working in a Community Mental Health Team in Shrewsbury, in Shropshire. She has interests in working with voices, and in finding alternatives to Psychiatry.

Susan Hallwright is a fellow of the Royal Australian College of Psychiatrists and has a Masters degree in Business Administration. As manager of mental health services, she led her team in purchasing innovative services including flexible crisis respite and community support work, and in developing new approaches to purchasing, incuding involving consumers in making funding decisions. Sue is recognised internationally for her purchasing expertise, knowledge of quality improvement and information systems capabilities. She currently works in both the United States and New Zealand providing advice to organisations that plan, fund and deliver mental health services.

David Healy is the Director of the North Wales Department of Psychological Medicine. He is a former secretary for the British Association for Psychopharmacology. He has written over 100 articles and chapters as well as ten books including the reference history of antidepressants, *The Antidepressant Era*, Harvard University Press, 1997. A forthcoming history of the antipsychotics is in press.

Guy Holmes, like Kurt Vonnegut, thinks we are what we pretend to be, so we must be careful what we pretend to be. One of the things he pretends to be is a clinical psychologist working in a CMHT in Telford. He has published articles on service users' views of psychiatric services, patients' councils, medication, the medicalisation of human distress and male victims of sexual abuse.

Biza Stenfert Kroese is a clinical psychologist who has worked with people with learning disabilities since she qualified in 1984. She was, until recently head of psychology services for adults with learning disabilities in Dudley Priority Health NHS Trust. She now works for Shropshire's Community Mental Health Services NHS Trust. She is also a senior lecturer in clinical psychology at the University of Birmingham and is the psychology specialist advisor for the British Institute for Learning Disabilities (BILD).

Peter Lehmann is a survivor of the psychitric system, author and publisher.

Vivien J Lewis is a photographer, smallholder and consultant clinical psychologist specialising in women's mental health and eating distress. She is concerned about oppression in all forms, but in particular the ongoing oppression of women world-wide. She has a special interest in creativity and alternative ways of living.

Vivien Lindow is a survivor of the psychiatric system who is interested in the psychiatric survivors' liberation movement in all its forms including the provision of survivor-run projects of many kinds. She works as a freelance researcher, trainer and consultant on mental health issues. She is author of 'Self Help Alternatives to Mental Health Services' (MIND).

John Michaelson works at Middlesex University. He currently lectures in Digital Audio Technology. He was formerly course head of the degree in Science, Technology and Society. His background is in Operational Research, and he is interested in modelling and systems approaches to decision making. He has written on chaos and complexity theories and their relation to mental health. He is also a musician and composer.

Craig Newnes is a dad and gardener. He is Psychological Therapies Director in Shropshire's Community and Mental Health Services NHS Trust and editor of *Clinical Psychology* and *The Journal of Critical Psychology, Counselling and Psychotherapy.*

Mark Rapley lives in Fremantle, Western Australia, with Susan, Tom and Seymour the dog. When he is not obsessively tidying the house he teaches (critical) psychology at Murdoch University and tries to persuade colleagues and students that doing discourse analysis is, actually, 'real' research.

Pete Sanders worked for over 25 years as a counsellor, he founded BACP Accredited counsellor training courses in Wigan and Manchester and supervised counsellors for many years. He has written several books and articles on counselling and still dabbles at the fringes with odd contributions here and there. He now spends most of his time concentrating on creating a strong library of person-centred literature through PCCS Books.

Fran Silvestri received a Masters degree in Business Administration. Affiliated with Monadnock Family Services since 1973, he was Chief Executive Officer from 1998 to 1999 and now works part-time in project development. A long-time advocate for mental health consumers, he has consistently promoted the development of innovative service delivery and support models for long term consumers of mental health services. He developed the Wyman Way Cooperative, an independent, nonprofit corporation run by consumers for 15 years. A founding member and Board officer of Behavior Health Network, an alternative managed care network, he currently works internationally building alliances between providers and consumers.

Keith Tudor is a qualified social worker, a qualified and registered psychotherapist, and an experienced supervisor, trainer and consultant. He has over twenty years' experience in the fields of mental health and mental illness, including as an approved social worker (ASW) ('approved' under the 1983 Mental Health Act). He has also designed and run a CCETSW approved training course for ASWs. He has an independent practice as a therapist in Sheffield, where he is also director of Temenos and its person-centred psychotherapy and counselling and post-graduate training courses. He is the author of a number of articles and of four books: *Mental Health Promotion* (Routledge, 1996), *Group Counselling* (Sage, 1999), *Transactional Analysis Approaches to Brief Therapy* (Sage, 2001) and (with Tony Merry) *Dictionary of Person-Centred Psychology* (Whurr, 2001). He is the editor of a forthcoming series on *Advancing Theory in Therapy* (to be published by Routledge). He is particularly interested in promoting the integrity of the person-centred approach and in the cultural and poltical context of therapy.

Jan Wallcraft is a mental health system survivor and mental health researcher who currently works for the Mental Health Foundation for whom she wrote the publication 'Healing Minds' — a report on complementary therapies in mental health. She was the first co-ordinator of the Mindlink network at MIND. Her key research and personal interests in mental health include ECT and alternatives to conventional treatments.

NAME INDEX

Agency for Health Care Policy and Research 25, 32
Aman, M. 74, 79
American Psychiatric Association 29, 32, 51, 57
Anderson, R. 106, 110, 112
Andreasen, N. 29, 32
Antaki, C. 36, 38, 43
Arnold, L.E. 49, 57
Arscott, K. 5, 9, 129, 133
AWWT 137, 145
Ayd, F. 64, 66
Baastrup, P.C. 27, 32
Baker , J.P. 27, 32
Baldwin, S. 3, 37, 43, 106, 107, 112
Barham, P. 94, 101, 179, 188
Barker, P. 108, 112
Bassett, T. 182, 188
Bates, Y. 151, 152, 158
Beasley, C. 60, 66
Beasley, C.M. 64, 66
Beecher, H.K. 65, 66
Bender, L. 111, 112
Bender, M. 5, 9
Beresford, P. 3, 4, 18, 21, 144, 185
Biermann-Ratjen, E-M. 154, 158
Bird, L. 19, 21
Black Health Workers and Patients Group 148, 158
Blashfield, R.K. 28, 32
BMA & RSPG 74, 79
BMA Board of Science and Education 115
Boardman. A. 63, 66
Bock, C. 86
Bogle, I. 116
Bohart, A.C. 154, 158
Bond, A.J. 60, 67
Booth, H. 8, 9
Boseley, S. 64, 67
Bowden, C. L. 27, 32
Bowes, A. 141, 143, 145
Boyle, M. 7, 9, 29, 32, 37, 43, 72, 79, 177, 186
BPS 124, 178
BPS Division of Clinical Psychology 177

Bracken, P. 177, 185, 186
Branford, D. 74, 79
Breggin, P. 3, 5, 6, 48, 49, 50, 52, 53, 54, 57, 106, 107, 110, 112, 151, 158
Brindle, D. 17
British Medical Association, 124
and Royal Pharmaceuticical Soc. of GB 79
British Psychological Society, 124, 178
Div. of Clinical Psychology 177
Brooks, G.W. 84, 90
Bulhan, H.A. 155, 158
Burman, E. 43
Cade, J. 26, 27, 32
California Alliance for the Mentally Ill, 166, 175
Campbell, Jane 136, 137, 145
Campbell, Jean 138, 144, 145
Campbell, K. 138, 145
Campbell, P. 101, 135, 145, 181, 185, 188
Caplin, R. 119, 121
Cattell 75
Chadwick, P. 132, 133
Chalmers, I. 25, 32
Chamberlin, J. 179, 181, 188
Charcot 24
Charlwood, P. 139, 145
Charney, D.S. 24, 32
Chouinard, G. 82, 90
Chua, S.E. 29, 32
Church, K. 143, 145
Clark, M.J. 24, 32
Cocks, G. 155, 158
Coleman, R. 86, 90, 130, 132, 133, 171, 175, 181
Common Agenda 18, 21
Concise Oxford Dictionary 117, 124
Cooper, D. 31, 32
Copeland, M. 171, 175
Coppock, V. 138, 145

Cornwell, J. 61, 67
Crabbe, H. 74, 79
Craine, S. 95, 101, 184, 188
Creaney, W. 60, 67
Critical Psychiatry Network 31, 32, 177
Cummins, R. A. 36, 37, 43
Dace, E. 138, 145
Daniels 61, 67
Dasgupta, K. 60, 67
Davey, B. 87, 90
Day, M. 25, 32
Deegan, P.E. 136, 145
Degkwitz, R. 84, 90
DeGrandpre, R. J. 106, 112
Department of Health 14, 20, 21, 95, 101, 112, 180
Double, D. B. 4, 5, 9, 23, 26, 32, 177
Drake, R.E. 61, 67
Dunn, S. 22
Edwards, D. 43, 45
Eichenwald, K. 64, 67
Eisenberg , L. 30, 32
Ekblom, B 83, 90
Engelman, E. 24, 32
English National Board 98, 101
Etherington, J. 74, 79
Even, C. 26, 32
Fairclough, N. 43, 45
Farrell, B.A. 31, 32
Faulkner, A. 137, 138, 140, 141, 144,145
Fava, M. 62, 67
Feighner, J.P. 28, 32
Felce, D. 43, 46
Fernando, S. 138, 145
Fischer, C.T. 154, 158
Fleming, I. 74, 79
Food & Drug Administration 65, 67
Forsyth, R. 4, 9
Foucault, M. 178, 188
France, A. 157, 158
Franklin, A. 141, 145
Fraser, W. 73, 80
Freud, S. 4, 24, 33
Furst, M. 100, 102
Galton 75

Gardner, W.I. 80
Garrett, T. 121, 124
Gijswijt-Hofstra, M. 31, 33
Gilbert, P.L. 82, 90
Glantz, S.A. 65, 67
Goelner, B. 85
Goffman, E. 179, 188
Gosden, R. 106, 112
Gourevitch, R. 2, 9
Graley, R. 181, 188
Gull, W.W. 115, 116, 118, 124
Gunzburg, H.C. 76, 80
Hagnell, O. 63, 67
Halbreich, U 82, 90
Hanley, B. 139, 145
Hansard 153
Harries, U. 143, 146
Harrison, A. 184, 188
Harrison, D. 138, 146
Haslam, J. 24, 25, 33
Hastings, M. 181, 188
Heal, L.W. 37, 43
Healy, D. 3, 4, 25, 60ff. 74, 80
Heiligenstein, J. 60, 61, 67
Heslop, K.E. 64, 67
Heuyer, P.G. 111, 112
Hillman, J. 3, 9
Hoehn-Saric, R. 64, 67
Hoelling, I. 89, 90
Holland, R. 150, 158
Holland, S. 124
Holmes, G. 1, 3, 152, 158
Holtzman, N. A. 28, 33
hooks, b. 137, 138, 146
Hoover , C. 60, 67
Hopkins, N. 43, 45
House, R. 151, 158
Houtkoop-Steenstra, H. 43, 45
Hughes, C. 38, 43
Hulme, P. 132, 133, 154, 156
Isaac, R.J. 5, 9
Jefferson, J.W. 27, 33
Jenkinson, P. 129, 133
Jenner, P. 23, 82, 90
Jensen, K.B. 88, 91
Jesperson 86
Jick, S. 62, 63, 67
Johnstone, L. 6, 9, 29, 33,
    131, 132, 133
Jones, A. 122, 125
Jones, Y. 105, 112
Jorm, A.F. 5, 9
Jowell, T. 18, 116
Kaasa, S. 37, 44
Kallmann, F.J. 28, 33
Kasper, S. 62, 68
Kearney, A. 151, 158

Kelly, C. 63, 68
Kempker, K. 81, 90, 91
Kierkegaard, S. 156
Kiernan, C. 74, 80
King, M. 152, 158
King, R. 60, 61, 66, 68,
Kirsch, I. 26, 33
Kline, N.S. 27, 33
Kuhn, S. 177, 188
Kutchins, H. 7, 9, 72, 80,
    107, 112
Laing, R.D. 28, 31, 33, 130,
    134, 184
Lambert, N.M. 51, 57
Lane, R.M. 62, 68
Lasegue , E.C. 115, 116
Laskowski, E. 88
Leader, A. 181, 188
Lehmann, P. 3, 5, 75, 82,
    85, 86, 91
Lehtinen, V. 81, 91
Leon, A.C. 62, 68
Lewis, V. J. 3, 116, 125
Lilly, Eli 60 – 64, 68
Lindner, U. 85
Lindow, V. 3, 4, 89, 91, 97,
    138, 146, 179, 180,
    181, 188
Lineman, M. 167 175
Lipinski, J.F. 61, 68
Lovett, H. 76, 80
MacSween, M. 125
Madness Group, The 138, 146
Malson, H. 125
Manic Depression Fellowship,
    The 181, 188
Mann, J.J. 60, 68
Marshall, E. 47, 57
Masand, P. 60, 68
Masson, J.M. 24, 33, 120,
    124, 125, 152, 159
Maudsley, H. 25, 33
McCubbin, M. 107, 112
McGuffin, P. 28, 33
McHoul, A. 44, 45
Medicines' Control Agency,
    The 65, 68
Medusa 124
Melega, W.P. 50, 57
Mental Health Foundation
    181, 189
Mental Health Task Force
    User Group 180, 189
Meyer, A. 30, 33, 87
Meyer, C. 87
Michaelson, J.177,189
MIND 16, 22, 100

MIND South East 18, 22
MIND/BBC 18, 22
Moher, D. 25, 33
Moldin, S.O. 28, 33
Monahan, J. 142, 146
Moncrieff, J. 27, 33
Monitoring Team, The 140,
    146
Moore, M. 139, 141, 146
Morris, J. 25, 33, 137, 146
Moss , S. 73, 80
Mowbray, R. 151, 159
MTA Cooperative Group 57
Muijen, M. 139, 146
Murray, I. 184, 189
Nakielny, J. 60, 61, 64, 68
Nasrallah, H. 50, 57
National Early Years
    Network, The 108
National Self-Harm Network
    181, 189
Neuberger, J. 143, 146
Newnes, C. 1, 8, 9, 44, 75, 77,
    80, 130, 159, 184, 189
NICE 2, 7, 54, 110,112
Nicholls, V. 138, 146
NIMH 53, 110, 112
NSPCC 108
Nurnberger, J.I. 24, 25, 33
Nursing Times 182
Ochsenknecht, A. 84, 91
O'Brien, J. 129
O'Hagan, M. 175, 179, 181,
    182, 189
Pacitti, R. 184
Parker, U. 87
Patel, N. 148, 159
Pearson 75
Pembroke, L. 146, 179, 189
Pembroke, L. R. 119, 123, 125
Perkins, R. 96, 102, 146
Perkins, R.E. 135, 144, 146
Perry, J. 36, 37, 44
Peters, U.H. 82
Pfizer 66, 68
Pilgrim, D. 75, 80, 121, 125,
    127, 133
Pinka, A. 105, 112
Plewes, J.M. 64, 68
Plumb, A.E. 184,185,189
Popper, C. 53, 57, 185, 189
Potter, J. 44, 45
Powell, M. 12, 16, 22
Power, A.C. 60, 68
Priest , R.G. 26, 33
Prouty, G.F. 154, 159
Quitkin, F.M. 26, 33

Rapley, M. 3, 35, 39, 44, 78
Rath, N. 87
Read, J. 181, 189
Redig, E. 87
Reuter, T-R. 86
Revicki, D. A. 37, 44
Reynolds , G.P. 29, 34
Richters, J.E. 53, 57
Rieff, P. 24, 34
Robertson, G. 152, 159
Rogers, A. 180, 189
Rogers, C.R. 147, 150, 152, 153, 154, 156, 159
Rogers, S.C. 25, 34
Rose, D. 189
Rose, N. 35, 44, 75, 80, 180
Rosenbaum, J.F. 63, 68
Rothman, D. 64, 68
Rothschild, A.J. 60, 68
Royal College of Psychiatrists 74, 80
Samuels, A. 151, 159
Sanders, P. 2, 9, 147, 159
Sands, A. 157, 159
Sassoon, M. 138, 146
Sayce, L. 16, 22, 99, 102, 138, 146, 186, 189
Schalock, R.L.   36, 37, 38, 44
Schneider, C. 153, 159
Schou, M. 27, 34
Schulte, J.P. 61, 68
Shapiro, A.K. 25, 34
Shelley, R. 119, 120, 125
Shimrat, I. 179, 189
Shlien, J. 153, 154, 159
Silvestri , F. 167, 169
Slade, P. 121
SNMAC 98
Spearman 75
Spece, R. 104, 112
Spreizer, I. 181, 189
Stamatiadis, R. 157, 159
Standing Nursing and Mid-wifery Advisory Committee, The 102
Stecklow, S. 64, 68
Stein, D.B. 107, 112
Steiner, C. 151, 153, 155, 157, 159
Stenfert Kroese, B. 3, 73, 74, 75, 80
Strategies for Living 137, 146
Straw, J. 153
Sturmey, P. 73, 80
Susko, M. 181, 182, 189
Swales, J.M. 37, 44, 45

Swales, T.P. 44
Swanson, J.M. 49, 52, 53, 58
Szasz, T.   29, 31, 34, 104, 113, 150, 159
Tansey, E.M. 27, 34
Tantum, D. 31, 34
Taylor, P. 17, 22, 38
Taylor, S.J. 38, 44
Teicher, M.H. 60, 62, 69
Thase, M. 25, 34
Thatcher, M. 11, 13
Thomas, P. 20, 22
Thompson, J.W. 111, 113
Thomson, R. 26, 34
Thorne, B. 151, 159
Todd, S. 35, 44
Tollefson, G. 60, 63, 69
Treacher, A. 136
Tsuang, M.T. 28, 34
Tudor, K. 147, 153, 154, 155, 157, 159
Ungerstedt, U. 82, 91
Valentis, M. 124, 125
Van Putten, T. 60, 69
Van Werde, D. 154,159
Wakelin, D. 183, 189
Wallace, M. 17, 95, 102
Wallcraft, J. 2, 3, 130, 137, 141, 144, 146, 177, 181
Warner, M.S. 154, 160
Warshaw , M.G. 62, 69
Wehde, U. 89, 91
Williams, J. 150, 160
Wilson, M. 29, 34
Wintour, P. 14, 22
Wirshing, W.C. 60, 69
Woggon, B. 82, 91
Wolfensberger, W.   37, 45, 72, 77, 80
Wollstonecraft, M. 115, 116, 117, 125
World Health Organisation 29, 34
        /European Commission 90,91
Yalom, I. 155, 160
Young, J.M. 66, 69
Zavaroni, L. 119
Zito, J.M. 47, 58

SUBJECT INDEX

absent-survivor research 140
abuse/ive 1, 106, 132
         therapist 121
academic performance 52, 53
acupuncture 88
Adderall 47
ADHD 7, 47, 106, 107, 110
         diagnosis 47
         -like behaviour 52
adoption studies 27
ADRs 49, 50, 59, 74, 81, 111
         behaviourally suppressive
         49
advanced directives 89
adverse drug reactions (see ADRs)
advocacy 1, 77, 88, 177
         schemes 78
advocate 5, 78
akathisia 60, 61, 66
alcohol 6, 164, 187
alienation 153, 155
alternative medicine 88
Alzheimer's disease 164
amitriptyline 120
amphetamines (see stimulants)
anger management 79
anorexia nervosa 115
anti-psychiatry 31
anti-psychotic medication 5, 74
antidepressants 59, 84
         and suicide 62
         efficacy of 25
appetites 117
Ashworth inquiry 5
Ashworth Special Hospital 6
assent bias 108
Attention Deficit Hyperactivity-Disorder (see
         ADHD)
authority figures 104
BACP 2
beauty 117
behaviour therapy 71, 120
behavioural family therapy 2, 132
         toxicity 59
benefits 133
         system 18
Berlin Runaway-House 89
Bill of Rights 103
biochemical imbalance 48
         solutions 16
biological factors 116

psychiatry 23, 47, 59, 72, 81,
         103, 127, 177
blurred vision 74
body dissatisfaction 116
         size 116
         talk 117
brain
         function 29, 50
         size and development 53
Bristol Crisis Service 182
British Association for Counselling and
         Psychotherapy (see BACP)
British Medical Association 115
California Alliance for the Mentally Ill 166
capitalism 149
carbamazepine 84
care
         in the community 16, 95, 161
         management 14
         package 14
         plans 14, 95
Care Programme Approach 14,
         131
carers 127
         groups 131
categorising people 2
challenging behaviour 74
child abuse 107
childhood sexual abuse 116, 138
Children Act 108
children's rights 104
citizen rights 93, 98, 180
civil human rights 96, 103, 107
         legislation 101
client-centred therapy 147, 154
clinical governance 2
clinical trials (see RCTs)
CMHS 161
coercion/ive 11, 105
         treatments 104, 105, 106, 137
cognitive therapists 149
         toxicity 49
         -behaviour therapy 152
         -behavioural approach 7
collaborative conversation 156
communitarianism 13
community
         capacity building 169
         care 16, 17
         philosophy 162
         housing 171

community leaders 171
community mental health 161
    recovery focused 168
    system role 167
    teams 14
compliance 95, 137
    therapy 2, 144
compulsion/complusory treatment 15, 18, 89
compulsory sterilisation, 28
computer technology 149
ComQol-ID 38
congruence 154
consent 104, 106
    form 109
    implied 108
    informed 1, 72, 76, 78 103, 104,
        108, 109
    exceptions to 109
    presumed 108
    procedures, breach of 111
    unequivocal 108
    with minors 108, 111
control agendas 94, 105
convulsions 83
core conditions 154
critical psychiatry 23
Critical Psychiatry Network 177
cult of the expert 152
cultural
    construction of beauty 117
    context of competition 117
cure 155
damage caused by neuroleptic use 74, 81
dangerousness 15, 16, 95, 130, 153
de-institutionalisation 162
Declaration of Helsinki 105
delirium 83
dementia 74
dependency 153
depression 47, 59, 154
Dexedrine 47
diagnosis 7, 28, 72, 130, 147, 152, 154, 162
diagnostic
    labels 153
    system 177
Dialectic Behavioural Therapy (DBT) 167
disability benefits 19
Disability
    Discrimination Act 20, 96
    Living Allowance 133
    Rights Commission 97
discrimination 18, 93
    black and minority 18
discursive practice 178
disempowerment 180
distress 18
dopamine 50

hypothesis of schizophrenia 29
drug company
    propaganda 5
    sponsorship 9
drug/s 5, 25, 47, 59, 74, 81, 103, 128, 164
    administration of 103
    adverse reactions (see ADR)
    coming off 81
    effects on academic
        performance 53
    side-effects (see ADRs)
    treatment of children 47
DSM 28, 107, 187
eating disorders distress 115
Electric shock/ECT 5, 18, 105, 107, 111,
    120, 128
    efficacy of 128
Eli Lilly 60
emotional flatness 64
empathic understanding 154
employers 171
enetic factors 116
English National Board 98
epidemiological studies 62
equality of opportunity 79
ethical
    and personal issues 142
    committees 64, 142
ethnic minority communities 16, 18, 103,
    138
ethnocentric theories 148
ethnocentric theories 148
eugenics 3, 28, 75, 155
European Network of (ex-)Users and
    Survivors 81
evidence 3, 17, 136
    -based practice 2, 138
    -based research 152
exclusion 19, 101
experts 149, 162
exploitation 104
extreme emotional and behavioural effects
    49
family 116, 172
    members 132
fatal consequences 82
female in our society 123
    shape and form 117
forensic psychiatric services 138
Foucauldian approach 178
frustration 172
funders 161
gender 5, 135
General Medical Council 110
genes in schizophrenia 28
genetic factors in eating disorders 116
    predispositions 116
    transmission 27

genital mutilation 107
genocide 75
genuineness 154
government
       mental health policy 12
       social policy 12
GP led primary care 7
Greater London Action on Disability 99
group therapy 155
guilt 172
haloperidol 83
harm prevention 105
health fascism 111
Hearing Voices Network 182
helplessness 172
holistic 184
homeopathic
       decontamination 87
       medicine 88
hospital
       alternative to 181, 183
human condition 4
       genome 28
       rights 103, 107
Human Rights Act 20, 96
humanistic psychology 158
hydrotherapy 105
hyperactive behaviour 110
hyperactivity 51
hypersensitivity-symptoms 83
ideology 150, 151
immoral control 121
impulsivity 51
inattention 51
incarceration 118
individual programme planning 104
information revolution 7
inheritance 28
institutionalised 71
instrumental reasoning 103
insulin coma 128
       therapy 105
intelligence test 75
internal agitation 74
Internet 1, 7, 137
involuntary treatment 89
irreversible brain dysfunction 50
Jack Straw 153
joined-up thinking 13
kindness 79
Kuhnian argument 178
Labour 12, 18
Largactil 120
lawsuits 109
learning disabilities 35, 71
leeches 105
legal themes 107

Leponex 83
liberationists 103
life histories 181
Lilly 66
lip service research 140
Lithium 26, 84, 154
       efficacy of 26
       manic patients 27
lobotomy 5
locus of evaluation 153
long-stay hospitals 71
love 79
Lustral 59
Madness Group, The 137
magic recipe 84
managed care 165
managerialism 7
Manic Depression Fellowship 138, 182
mass media 17, 100, 101, 115, 116, 150
       exploitation 100
measuring 35, 75
medical
       experimentation 71, 109
       model 23, 71, 99, 132, 148, 150,
          177
       negligence/malpractice 110
medication (see drugs)
Medicines Control Agency 65
mental health
       education 98
       nurses 8
       policy 11, 16, 17, 20
       services, future of 7, 77, 161
Mental Health Act 1, 153, 185
Mental Health Foundation 100, 186
Mental Health User Movement 180
Mentality 97
methamphetamine 50
research methods
       and procedures 140
       of collecting data 141
methylphenidate 47, 49, 106, 110, 111
middle-class values 151
mime 77
MIND 97, 100
Mindlink 98
misuse 107
modernisation 13
monitoring 130
mutilation of females 117
myths 170
Napsbury Hospital 93
National Early Years Network 108
National Institute for Clinical Excellence
    (see NICE)
National Institute of Mental Health 53
National Self-Harm Network 138

National Service Framework, The 2, 14, 129
     Standard One 93, 97
     Standard Six 131
natural healing 88
naturopathic remedies 87
nausea 74
Nazi concentration camps 105
Nazis 75
needs-led services 104
neglect 106, 107
neuroleptics 5, 18, 81
     withdrawal from 5, 83
     risks of 74, 82
neuropathology of mental illness 29
neurosurgery 106
neurotransmitter dysfunction 29
New Labour and mental health 13
NHS and Community Care Act 1990 94
NICE 2, 54, 110, 111
Nipolept 83
norepinephrine 50
Novartis 54
NSPCC 108
nuclear family values 104
Nuremburg Code 105
nurses 8, 11
nutrition 88
obsessive-compulsive ADRs 49
occupational health 147
olfactory hallucinations 83
opportunity
     lack of 150
oppression 104, 115, 117, 145, 148
organisational change 7
partnership/s 13, 98, 168
     research 140
patients' council 6
peer-groups 150
PeopleWhoNet 137
person of tomorrow 156
person-as-biological-system 149
person-centred approach 147, 154, 158
personal narrative 185
personality disorder/s 8, 14, 148, 153, 157, 164
Philadelphia Association 130
pharmaceutical industry (see drug company)
phobic avoidance 116
physical therapies 152
pindown 110
placebo 26
political and social control 104
politics 147
post traumatic stress disorder 164
potassium levels 116
poverty 5, 19, 150

power relationships
     in therapy 152
     in training 152
Primary Care Groups 14
problems
     with practitioners 150
     with psychology 75
     with (the) system 151
     with theories 148
protection/ists 103, 104
provider organisations 161
Prozac (see SSRIs)
Psy-complex 6, 36
psychiatric
     hospitals 11, 17, 71, 93, 128
     provision for children and teenagers 107
     training 5, 23, 30
     wills 89
psychiatrist/s 149, 151
psychiatry
     biological bias in 24
psycho-technology 149
psychoanalysis 148
psychological
     approaches in psychiatry 24
     tests 35, 76
psychosis/es 83, 154
psychosocial interventions 48
Psychotherapists and Counsellors for Social Respon 151
psychotherapy 1, 3, 147
psychotropic medication (see drugs)
public
     (and service user) safety 15, 95
     education 97, 101
     enquiries 111
punishment 107
QOL 36, 37
     measurement 39
quality of life (see QOL)
quick fix 165
race/racism 5, 45, 148
radical
     psychiatry 158
     psychology 147
Radical Therapist Collective 157
Randomised clinical trials (see RCTs)
RCTs 5, 25
     and legal jeopardy 63
rebound 51
     -effects 82
     symptoms 83
Reboxetine 65
recovery-oriented systems 162, 166
redefinition 181
relatives 127, 172

religious groups 104
reorienting policy 184
research 135, 181
       partnerships 139
       payment of informants 143
Research Support Network 140
respect 79
restraint by chemical or physical means
      150
rhetoric of organic psychiatry 6
rights 96, 103
       -based client services 104
       of children 106
       of women 116, 123
risk
       and dangerousness 95
       assessment 2
Risperidal 83
Rispolin 83
Ritalin (see stimulants)
role-play 77
Roxiam 83
Sainsbury Centre for Mental Health 139
St John's wort 87
SANE 4, 17, 95
schizophrenia 1, 128, 1878
seizures 74
selective serotonin reuptake inhibitors (see
      SSRIs)
self
       -advocacy discourse 177
       -assessment schedules 181
       -determined withdrawal 82
       -Harm Network 182
       -management 76
            techniques 181
       -starvation 117, 119
Serdolect 83
serial abuse of children and teenagers in
      adult care 111
serotonin 50, 59
Seroxat (see SSRIs)
Sertraline (see SSRIs)
service user involvement in social work 99
service user/survivor
       activists 18, 97, 99, 101
       as educators 98, 130, 181
       movement 81, 94, 97, 101, 161,
           177
       organisations 18, 97
       research 135
       - run services 8, 89, 161
severe and enduring mental illness 2
sexual abuse 120, 121
shame 172
shooting the messenger 6
side effects (see ADRs)

silo 164
Sisters of the Yam 138
social
       adjustment 155
       behaviour control 111
       construction of intellectual
           disability 35
       control 2, 105, 106, 107
       exclusion 13, 19
       inclusion 19, 93, 94, 99
       inequalities 157
       politics of New Labour 13
       role valorisation 72, 77
       withdrawal ADRs 49
sociocultural factors 116
speaking out 5
specialist service for eating distress 122
spin 12
spiritual practice 88
SSRIs 59
stakeholder/s 169
       groups 161
stigma 1, 35, 43, 95, 100, 130, 138, 185
stimulant/s 7, 47, 106, 107, 110
Strategies for Living 137
suicidal tendencies 83
suicide 59
surgery 150
survivor (see service-user/survivor)
Survivors Speak Out 5, 9, 98, 119, 180
systemic family therapy 132
tabloid press 16, 17
tardive dyskinesia 74
teenagers 103
thalidomide 109
therapists-in-training 151
therapy training courses 150
theories, problems with 148
Third Reich 155
third way 13
time-out 71
torture 107
toxic effects 53
training of psychiatrists 23
treatment/s 18, 105, 154
       involuntary 89
trouble-maker 6
Tuskagee Syphillis Study 109
twin studies 27
U.S. Food and Drug Administration 47
unconditional positive regard 154
unemployment 19
unfinished adults 103
United Kingdom Advocacy Network 98
user
       monitoring scheme 139
       movement 93, 157

user, contd . . .
       -focused research 140
       -led agenda 7
       -led research 140, 181
       -run crisis project 183
       /survivor-movement 88
valerian 87
Village in Los Angeles 166
voices 132
welfare to work 18, 19
whistle-blowers 5
withdrawal 82
Wokingham MIND Crisis House 129
woman's mental state 116
work opportunities 101
zeitgeist 149
zinc deficiency 116
zombie effect 49, 50
Zyprexa 83